*To Diana
with best wishes*

AS I WANDERED THROUGH THE MARKETS OF THE WORLD

Grisell Beauchamp

Grisell Beauchamp

MINERVA PRESS
LONDON
ATLANTA MONTREUX SYDNEY

AS I WANDERED THROUGH
THE MARKETS OF THE WORLD
Copyright © Grisell Beauchamp 1998

All Rights Reserved

No part of this book may be reproduced in any form
by photocopying or by any electronic or mechanical means,
including information storage or retrieval systems,
without permission in writing from both the copyright
owner and the publisher of this book.

ISBN 0 75410 125 8

First Published 1998 by
MINERVA PRESS
195 Knightsbridge
London SW7 1RE

2nd Impression 1998

Printed in Great Britain for Minerva Press

AS I WANDERED THROUGH THE MARKETS OF THE WORLD[†]

[†] Rabindranath Tagore

For my nephew/godson for whom I wrote this book, in thanks for his unfailing interest in my activities – and to his wife Yumi; to my husband Geoffrey Beauchamp for his tolerance with all my scribblings; also Eirene Crook for persuading me to send this book to a publisher; last but not least, Anne Merriman in thanks for her patient correcting and typing of this book.

About the Author

Born in Malaya in 1916, I was brought up in Edinburgh, my father's home town. I sang with the Royal Carl Rosa Opera Company throughout the war, and then became a make-up artist for the BBC. Later I moved to Bristol and established the BBC's make-up departments there and in Cardiff.

Since retiring I have continued my travels.

Contents

One	Earliest Travels 30th July 1916	9
Two	Germany 1939	11
Three	Touring with the Royal Carl Rosa Opera Company 1939–1945	28
Four	Greece 29th September – 1st October 1965	41
Five	Portugal January 1966, 1967, 1968 and later with my husband, Geoffrey Beauchamp, 1980s	59
Six	Spain January 1967, 1968, 1969, 1970 and then with Geoffrey in the early 1980s	75
Seven	Morocco Casablanca, January 1969	107
Eight	Ceuta 1968	127

Nine	Germany 1960s	129
Ten	Germany 5th April 1986	136
Eleven	Austria and Germany	
	8th May 1986	141
	16th June 1986	144
	21st June 1986	154
Twelve	Turkey	
	Early spring, 1970s and 1980s	157
	1975	163
	1980s	164
Thirteen	Yugoslavia 1970s and 1980s	176
Fourteen	Lantau	
	Lantau Island, February 1975	201
Fifteen	Far East Tour	
	Heathrow, 10th November 1977	212
	Thailand, 22nd November 1977	262
	Hong Kong, 28th November 1977	282
	Macau, 6th December 1977	293
	Hong Kong, 9th December 1977	301
	Taiwan, 18th December 1977	304
	Hong Kong, 22nd December 1977	314

Chapter One

Earliest Travels

30th July, 1916

I took an unconscionable time on my first journey – nine months – during which I stupidly forgot where I had come from. I arrived in Malacca in the Malay States on the 30th July, 1916.

My mother was very ill after I was born, so her 'beautiful slim baby' (her words, not mine) was farmed out with friends who had kindly offered to house me until she was better. These friends were very nervous about this, not having children themselves, and a new-born baby at that. The result was that they overfed me, so much so that when my mother saw me again she gasped, saying, 'Where is my beautiful child?' However, she decided to keep me.

After a short while, three months to be exact, I was on the move again. In 1916 the First World War was in full spate but my father, who was older, had been told that because of his heart trouble it was imperative for him to return at once to Britain.

My father, John Burn Lindsay, tea and then rubber planter, and my mother, Winifred (known to all as Winkie), immediately booked berths on a steamer which was to leave from Malacca for Britain. We arrived well on time, but the ship had sailed early. Luck was with us and another, also going to Britain, was already in dock. This they took, but with the great decision whether to join their original one at

Singapore or to stay where they were. Eventually they decided to stay. My amah was also with them, sleeping outside their cabin door all the way to Britain – or, as it transpired, France – with a ceramic brick for a pillow, the recognised way for a Chinese servant woman.

My mother was very worried about torpedoes and bombs with such a small daughter to guard. However, they became friends with a King's Messenger, also on board, who had a pet monkey, for whom he had made a lifejacket of canvas and cork. One day he presented my parents with this lifebelt, saying that their tiny daughter was more important than his monkey – a generous act. I still have this small lifejacket.

Later on in the journey we arrived at the more dangerous war zone. My mother told me that they had passed the wreckage of the steamer we should have been on, and that amongst the drifting debris was a baby's wicker sleeping basket.

We had to disembark in France, staying the night in Paris where there was a Zeppelin raid in progress. In spite of all of this we arrived in Britain safe and well. However, unknown to me, I had not yet had my fill of torpedoes, for several years later John, my young brother, and I were sitting on a beach at Gullane, a lovely seaside spot outside Edinburgh, where we now lived. Our rather strict nanny was sitting on the beach watching us play by the water's edge. Later she called us to come back to her, as we had to return to the hotel for lunch. My brother obeyed the call, but I loitered. A second call from Nanny was enough. I complied, fearing retribution. Just in time, for a few minutes later a warship practising in the Firth of Forth released a torpedo which misfired. It landed exactly on the spot I had just left and, although it was only a non-lethal one, the speed and weight of it would have killed me.

Chapter Two

Germany

1939

Danzig – dead or buried? The unworldly settlement 'peace in our time' progressed towards an, as yet, unknown war.

My singing teacher, Mona Benson, thought it would be a good thing if, during the summer holidays, I went to Germany to further my German speaking. In those days I was being engaged to give quite a lot of Lieder recitals, which required a good accent and a feel for the language.

My teacher had sung for several seasons with the Glyndebourne Opera Company in Sussex, and there had met a charming young German girl called Munte Braunfels. They had become good friends over the years, as Munte came each year to Glyndebourne to help look after the children of Herbert Reid, the famous poet and critic, and his wife, who played in the orchestra. Mona thought that it would be advantageous if I could go and stay for the summer months with the Braunfels, absorbing and learning good German.

This was duly managed, with some trepidation on the part of my parents. It had been such a short time since all the Hitler troubles had worried the western world.

Munte's father was a famous musician, a composer and conductor of note, as well as having been the head of the Conservatoire in Cologne until the Nazis had discovered that his grandmother had some Jewish blood. He had been stripped of his job, his passport and any security. He and his family had gone south to live in the tiny village of Süssenmühler on the Bodensee (Lake Constance).

I duly set off, a very young and green person, overly naïve, having had a sheltered childhood, never having travelled abroad apart from being brought back from Malaysia many years before. How young we were, living-wise, in those days.

It was about the beginning of July so the weather was good. I had all my instructions in my handbag on how to get there safely, and so I set off.

Eventually the Ostend train came trumpeting and steaming, like an asthmatic elephant, into the dim colourless station of Cologne. Figures, furtive in the dim impersonal sombre light of 2.0 a.m., chilled the heart. A porter examined my ticket, tried to communicate, his hands working in translation to a language he did not know, and I, answering in questioning words 'Ueberlingen? Ueberlingen?' with the piteous cry of a lost cat in record-sticking monotony, tried with my small amount of German to sort out the confusion of my train.

A German, of dubious youth and undistinguished in his suiting, with a small (though then unrecognisable) Gestapo badge in his lapel, asked in English if he could help. Again I repeated that I wanted to get to the town of Ueberlingen; with that he said he would come with me. The porter watched with Germanic silence while the battle raged, me declining the offer, he insisting, until eventually beaten he told the porter which train I needed, and vanished.

I boarded the now discovered night train. The compartments were shrouded in mystery; a dim ceiling light, which struck a chilling gloom in the fetid atmosphere, greeted me. The porter followed with my bags. On hearing the throb of the heavy engine starting up again, he thrust me through the dirty heavy brown curtain which covered the door and windows, threw my luggage on the rack, grabbed his tip and ran for the exit door, just as the train shuddered and screeched into motion.

With lonely relief I sat down. At last I had got rid of the rather frightening stranger who had offered to travel with me.

The train rattled on. I put my cases more safely on to the rack, and settled on the further seat where I could look out of an uncovered window at the moon-painted scenery peeling away at my side, feeling far too overwrought for sleep.

Suddenly the curtain over the door silently moved, the foggy figure of a man entered and sat down beside me. Deep in thought and tired, I did not look properly in his direction until he spoke. My heart leapt; it was the disturbing 'Cologne' man. I recognised the smooth impersonal voice as he started to question me – did I really think that I could get rid of him so easily? I tried to look cool, calm and very adult as he pressed on with his, 'Where was I going? Why was Britain trying to start a war with Germany? Why did Chamberlain incite you all to hate us, while preparing for war?' Questions, questions, on and on and on, like the rhythmic inescapability of the wheels. I mumbled replies; this sudden attack had unnerved me. In my youthful naïveté I thought my answers could plunge Britain into an unwanted war.

He became quiet for a while. I feigned sleep, soon to be prodded awake. He was telling me again that he was coming all the way to Ueberlingen to see whom I was going to visit.

We were passing the Rhine, its cold silvery surface mystic in the moonlight, its castles – Grimm's fairy tales come true. The man started again: 'Wouldn't I like to be walking on the banks of the Rhine on a romantic moonlight night like this, with my boyfriend? Had I a boyfriend? What did he do?' Again on and on until eventually he stopped. I again leant back and shut my eyes, every nerve in my body tense, my breath uneven; the silence vibrated with unspoken thoughts. After a very long time he quietly got up and left. I suppose he realised that I was so clueless I must be harmless. I also suppose he got off at the next stop. I never saw him again, but I had had to suffer his questioning for about two hours.

Later on I was to learn that the badge he wore was a Gestapo one, and that he was one of the many who interrogated unaccountable visitors arriving in their country at that time.

I eventually arrived at Ueberlingen, to be met by friends of the Braunfels, who were allowed much more movement, not being Jewish, and was taken to Süssenmühler. The Braunfels themselves were not allowed to travel into the town itself – not even to their village.

What marvellous people they were. As I have already said, he was a famous composer and conductor. She, I understood, had been engaged to Furtwängler before she changed her mind and married Braunfels, a delightful gracious woman, tall and slender, who had in the good old days held famous salons, where the intellectuals of Europe used to gather.

They had five children, all grown up, three boys and two girls. The eldest son was a fine pianist, like his father, so the Nazis broke all his fingers and sent him to work on the Siegfried Line; no Jewish blood must be successful. The second son had escaped into Italy, where he lived, occasionally managing to steal back for a few days to see his parents. The youngest son was a very simple delightful person, who wanted to become a priest. Years later I learnt that he had been put into the army, sent to Russia and was never heard of again.

The daughters fared better, I understand. One, whom I never met as she lived elsewhere, was married, producing a baby while I was there. Munte had to go and help her at that time. Then there was Munte herself, who ran the house. She was extraordinarily kind to me, as were all her family.

Where they lived outside the village was a beautiful spot. Their delightful bungalow, on the slopes of one of the hills leading down to the Bodensee, was covered with pink blossomed trees. The sound of the cicadas and bees filled the warm fragrant air. These trees gave shade from the deep blue sky and hot sun and framed the view down to the sapphire blue water of the lake.

I had a lovely sunny bedroom, fairly sparsely furnished, but enough for the clothes I had brought; a chair and table for my books and writing materials; and, best of all, a small bookcase, which Munte had kindly stacked with English books.

I ate with the family, just the four of us. The eating was questionable. I, and only I, was allowed a small pat (about an inch square) of so-called butter a week as I was a visitor to Germany! But the whole time I was there, about two and a half months, we lived on pancake soup; pancake with lettuce (main course) and pancake with fruit; no meat or fish, eggs probably twice a week and very little cheese, and of course ersatz coffee!

Every evening, sitting on the balcony, looking at the stars glinting on the water beneath us, we would listen to Herr Braunfels' playing, how beautiful, with no other sound except the occasional drumming of thunder and the brilliant lightning playing around the mountains which ringed the lake. He was a wonderful pianist, as Bruno Walter wrote in his autobiography:

The most interesting production of my Munich period took place in the year 1920. It was Walter Braunfels' *Die Vögel*. Those who were privileged to hear Karl Erb's song of man's yearning and Maria Ivogün's comforting voice of the nightingale from the tree top, and those who were cheered by the grotesque scenes and moved by the romantic ones, will surely remember with gratitude the poetic and ingenious transformation of Aristophanes' comedy into an opera. The composer was the son of the translator of Spanish dramas, Ludwig Braunfels, and the son-in-law of the sculptor Adolf Hildebrand. He was guided in his artistic creations by two fundamental impulses: a dramatic repletion and an intense religious feeling, both of which were occasionally expressed interestingly and strikingly in his music. In addition to the Munich performance of *Die Vögel*, I produced the same composer's exceptionally fine and heartfelt *Te Deum* at the Odeon with the Teachers' Singing Society of Munich and, on a later occasion, with the Vienna Philharmonic Chorus in the Konzerthaus of that city, his clever orchestral variations on a theme by Berlioz in Berlin, Leipzig, and New York. Braunfels, the director of the Cologne College of Music, was an excellent pianist as well as a thorough connoisseur of church music. When the Nazis forced him to relinquish his Cologne position in 1933, he retired with his family to a small village on Lake Constance. There, in the quiet imposed on him by fate, he wrote an opera based on Grillparzer's *The Dream – A Life*, which I accepted for performance when I was at the head of the Vienna Opera but was no longer able to produce. Thereafter, I met Braunfels several times at the Winterthur home of Werner Reinhart, a Swiss lover of the arts. The composer, yearning for human companionship, frequently made the two-hour trip from his quiet village for the sake of a friendly interchange of thoughts. He became immersed more and more in Catholic thinking and feeling. At our last meeting, he played for me parts of an opera based upon a religious play by the poet Paul Claudel.'[1]

I went to the village the first day, to send a card to my parents saying I had arrived safely. Herr Braunfels said he would be able to take me halfway there only, as they were not allowed to go very far from the house. He explained to me how to get to their village, then he returned home.

I went to a shop to buy them a pot of jam, as I had noticed they had none, only to be told, 'Who do you think you are? You cannot buy jam, there is a war on.' Guns before butter. Of course the war had not yet started, but the German people had had to live with this food shortage long before the war began.

It all seemed so peaceful away from the terrible drama of the cities, of which at that time I had heard nothing, yet even all around us we would hear of country people against the régime, having accidents – so called – carts slipping down cliffs on badly made up roads and much else. No one could prove or dared to prove this was deliberate sabotage done in retaliation; the Gestapo always found a way of arranging these incidents, or even more frequently it was a wife or child of the informant against Hitler's tyranny, the innocent families that were the victims – a tragic pernicious situation. No wonder many would not revolt.

One day the Braunfels told me that they had some musical friends who were also Jews and therefore banished

---

[1] Bruno Walter, *Themes and Variations*, Hamish Hamilton, 1947.

from any town, who so wanted to meet 'this young English singer'.

They, like many others, could not buy sugar or butter except by secret barter with non-Jewish friends. This they had done, so that when I came to see them they could offer me tea and their famous *Torte*.

We had a marvellous afternoon singing the old *Minnesänger*'s songs. The *Minnesänger* were aristocratic German poet musicians of the twelfth to fourteenth centuries; they wrote and sang these courtly love songs. What charming, cultured people my hosts were.

They then provided me with a gorgeous tea, an enormous *Torte* of gooseberries and cream in its delicious casing. I was incredibly touched by such generosity.

They then, as did the Braunfels, questioned me about the state of Britain, saying how grateful they were to Chamberlain, their hero, on whom they had been depending to save Germany from any more take-overs of countries and war – in hindsight how tragic. These conversations always had to take place in a field or some large empty open place, because of the massive bugging system there was in houses, shops and anywhere it was feasible to have it.

Every Sunday my hosts went over the hills to church. They were ardent Catholics and such a thing was not permitted. Every Sunday they said to me, 'If we do not come back, you will have to make your own way home to England as quickly as possible.' They would have been imprisoned for their faith, and possibly I might have been taken in retaliation.

He was extremely kind to me, a student, as well as the rest of the family. Each evening he brought me an opera score, put on the radio and told me to sit, listen and learn. What a joy – so many operas I had never even heard of. In Germany there were operas on the radio every evening –

there was no television in those days. He would later discuss the music with me.

He would also often call me to come for a walk with him in the forest, a magical place with a whispering silence, then he would talk to me, to improve my vocabulary and accent. The rest of the family also did this, except Munte, who was always wanting to talk about so many interesting things that I could not have coped with in their language.

I slept well in my lovely light room. The only sound in my cool bedroom was the staccato sound of birds waking to the dawn light. The early morning sun sprayed the room as I slept, simulating death so deep was my reposed sleep.

Suddenly, like an unkempt mob, two members of the local Gestapo threw open my heavy oak door, breaking the finely wrought iron handle as they came. Their faces were of the faceless unhinged fraternity that patrolled the country, the mock great, their raw edge of cruelty unleashed and uncontrolled.

I awoke to the noise, lying ignored, an inanimate object, like part of the unimpeding bric-à-brac. I had by now learnt never to question this kind of goings on. It was not worth it, for so small a reason, risking interrogation at their headquarters.

The men, with robot-like gestures, threw all the contents from the cupboard and drawers on to the red-tiled shining floor, slamming and breaking as they worked like demented ants, then, nothing being found that could cause a stain on their *blessed* Führer's name, they left the room. Still speechless, they stampeded up the polished uneven wooden staircase, to contaminate the other rooms with their odious presence.

I looked long at my tangled lifeless mass of property on the floor, so reduced it looked unnecessary and futile in a country where priorities were ground down to survival. I, being British on this July morning of 1939, could only guess at the soul-tortured lives of my Jewish-ancestored hosts. He, his music rent from him, forbidden to compose or perform, the world's freedom removed by the savage confiscation of passports; an existence that forced them to live in seclusion, with these perpetual 'accidental' fatal accidents around, and the brave spirits who rebelled to point a warning to those that remained in a hope that, however useless, it might gradually undermine the régime.

In those days we knew nothing of the terrible camps, the sweeping away of every Jewish element – the brains of so many intellectuals being squandered by the gas chambers and oh so much more.

By that time I had learnt to keep quiet and not bandy words with them, as it would only mean that I could be detained in the police station. They were arrogant, cruel men who would not brook any interference.

The German people had had to put up with this kind of treatment, little food and no rights for so many years, carefully subjected, gradually, carefully and cunningly – oh so cunningly – from the time soon after the First World War. From great poverty the 'miracle' man Hitler had organised them into wealth, giving them plenty of food and jobs and much else, getting these grateful people to join his clubs, societies and groups to assist the recovery; until one day, much later on, they found that they were given arms, cards of identification and rules, and in fact that they were completely in Hitler's sway, so that if anyone complained they would retaliate by killing a member of their family or a close friend. It had begun to be a terror-ridden country ruled by reprisals and torture.

The young at school were indoctrinated before they could think for themselves, betraying what their families did, in a zeal to help their country.

Everywhere were the criminals who revelled in causing pain and the feeling of lording over others.

During my time there, the Braunfels' second son, who lived in Italy, managed to slide into Germany unknown to the authorities – a charming, good looking young man of, I suppose, about twenty-three. He used to take me out locally, as he did not want to get involved with the town. His great love was the poems of Shelley, which he read to me in both German and English. I remember too one hot sunny Sunday afternoon, when all the villagers were having their sabbatical snooze, he rushed me round the houses, me riding a very precarious pillion, with the bike thundering and shaking on the uneven small roads; however, no one stopped us. He came twice when I was there. We became good friends, with promises on his part to see me again when the crisis was over. Of course, like so many promises, war intervened.

The Braunfels could only have me for part of my time in Germany as their married daughter and her family were coming to stay. It had been arranged that I would go and stay with another family, the Jaegerhübers, in Ueberlingen itself – a woman who was British, from Glasgow, and her two German children. Her German husband had died several years earlier.

It was interesting living quite a different life. She had a bungalow on the edge of the town, new, bright and clean. Such a nice person, as were her two daughters, about nine and five. Both were indoctrinated at school to report anyone who said anything against their great Saviour – note capital S – Hitler.

I slept in the sitting/dining room on a very comfortable couch. The only thing was that one was always starving, so in the late evenings when I went to bed I could smell the tantalising pong of the *stinkkäse* (a cheese with a particularly horrible smell) which was kept on the sideboard. Oh how hard it was not to take a nibble, which would of course have meant that next day someone would have had to go without. Our daily share was only a nibble.

During my stay there I was able to do a lot of sightseeing. Before that I used to go for long walks in the countryside, with the peasants still happily giving me *'Grüss Gott'* as I went by.

This was a most beautiful medieval town, with its splendid baroque churches, town hall – the *Rathaus*, such a gorgeous name – and many of the buildings, the fascinating narrow streets and a lovely museum. As the Nazis could not stop them, there was also a multitudinous array of the most splendid coloured flowers.

I was always wondering how well I was getting on with my studying and speaking in German. Then one day Frau Jaegerhüber said she would come on later, meeting me in the museum. I had a chat with the woman in charge of the postcards, bought some and went upstairs to see the fascinating objects being displayed. Later Frau Jaegerhüber arrived downstairs, asking the woman if the English girl was still there. The woman replied that no English girl had been in today; the only person was a young German girl. I *must* have been improving!

During my stay I was told that the wife of a rich industrialist, who was staying at the Bircher Benner Clinic (Bircher Benner was the inventor of muesli) was coming to stay with us on her way back to Berlin. She duly arrived. I found her very highly strung and distressed. They were apparently having trouble with the Nazis, so much so that her husband had had to go into the Clinic and she was trying, rather unsuccessfully, to cope, not knowing what would happen in the long run.

During the evening meal she started ranting on about Hitler. Almost before she said a word Frau Jaegerhüber grabbed the youngest child and rushed her from the room, locked her into her bedroom upstairs, then rushed back again, saying that the child would report all that was said at school the next day, and that not only the woman herself but all of us would be taken to the police station, from whence who knows what might have happened. Luckily her elder daughter was old enough to know of the danger, so would never repeat the conversation.

After a while the woman calmed down, having said the most terrible things about the régime. She was almost insane with worry.

Later on in the evening, she, Frau Jaegerhüber and myself went for a walk in the pretty suburbs where we lived. It was a beautiful, balmy moonlit night, but suddenly, as before, the woman started shouting at the top of her voice about how wicked Goebbels was. We tried desperately to stop her, pulling her as fast as we could away from the houses, which were mercifully back from the road with front gardens. As we went, terrified we would rouse someone in the police force or such like, she suddenly stopped; only a blessed silence remained. From then until she left the next day she was her normal self.

One evening I was taken to a magical concert in the castle on the island of Meersburg. The castle, its grey feet paddling beneath the star-shadowed water of the Bodensee, looked as if the straying winds of the seventeenth century had cemented it into an eerie bastion of time, locking it into a secret untouched world... superb.

Inside the large octagonal stone room – by reflection seemingly transformed into a cool green watery cell – a strange underwater balloon, the quartet played, their shadows caricatured into jerking puppets by the flickering candlelight on the walls. They were dressed in the clothes of the eighteenth century, so fitting for a purely Mozartian evening.

The violins fretted the lacy music with its maze-like pattern of glorious sound, the cello and viola breaking into this column of melody. The silent listeners were transported, the sound was so intense, sending them into uncharted lands where music, colour and love are the norm. At the finish, amid waves of applause, they trooped into the night.

We walked down to the harbour to find our ferry boat. It was too early, the place was empty. Only the shlap, shlap of the tiny waves, as they gently castigated the tethered fishing boats and the flickering reflections of the water as the spasmodic moon caught their blue and red hulls were alive.

We walked into the tiny village to find a drink. Above us and behind the needle-pointed Renaissance rocks, warm still from the earlier sun, huddled the humped houses. A small apothecary's shop, with its little bull's-eye glass windows, distorted the bright light that glared from inside. An elderly long-haired chemist pounded with his pestle and mortar some a concoction made from the contents of some of his myriad dark-blue and green ribbed bottles. They stood, row upon row, gold-lettered, on the dusty dark shelves, held there as if they were too tired to speak, yet struggled, like one with a speech impediment, to communicate. The framing of the dark night round the window threw the brightly lit interior into a five-dimensional experience. The periods of men were mixed by the pestle of the ages, so that time was no more an accredited commodity.

We found our ferry boat and steamed back to normality.

My parents kept sending me letters to return home. The code they had decided on was that I had to come home if war seemed near. They could not write that so they said that I as to come home for a very special family wedding.

At last I obeyed them; things were getting fairly bad. I told Frau Jaegerhüber I was leaving, then went back to the Braunfels to wish them goodbye and best wishes. This was on a Wednesday. He looked at me solemnly and said wryly, but with a twinkle, 'At least I am glad that the war will not start until Friday!'

On bidding Frau Jaegerhüber goodbye she took me outside and asked if I could possibly arrange for her to bring some schoolchildren to Britain as a sightseeing trip – in other words, they wanted to escape. This I could not do, as it was just a few days before war started and no one could arrange anything.

She kept up with me for years, after surviving with great hardship. The girls had grown up, one falling in love with a French soldier, which was forbidden. Later they did marry, but she became schizophrenic and had eventually to be put in a home. After the war the younger one had gone to America. A year later her letters suddenly stopped and, although her mother wrote several times to her address she received no reply. Tragically she had committed suicide in New York's Central Park; her mother found out that later on.

The journey home was not very pleasant. I boarded a train that would take me right through to Ostend. No one seemed to be on it except me, certainly no one in the coaches near mine. The journey was very long and tedious, filling me with many uneasy fears as to whether one would ever reach Belgium. There was no food or drink aboard. I can't remember now whether I had anything with me. Eventually we did reach the border. It was very dark outside. A huge German customs officer came into my compartment and started haranguing me about my luggage and anything he could think of. Luckily by then I was reasonably fluent in German and started arguing back. All ended well – he stamped out of the coach looking very angry. When the Belgian officials came on to the train they both spoke English and were very civil, although it was obvious that they too were under great strain.

We eventually reached the docks at Ostend. Everything seemed in chaos, no one to ask anything, searchlights playing continuously across the sky, and noise everywhere. It was about three o'clock in the morning.

I was lucky and eventually found the ship for Dover. It was fairly packed, so many, like me, making a quick exit from what seemed by now chaos. I managed to get a seat on a long hard bench; no cover from the night cold, but at least safe.

I only had one more thing to worry about. I realised that in my hasty departure from Germany I had only a few coins of either German or English money. This was fairly desperate, as my cousin who lived in London had told me she would be away when I returned. My home was Edinburgh! What on earth was I to do? I began quietly to laugh: I had escaped war only to be penniless in a fairly crime-ridden London. So what?

On arriving at Dover and London, I thought I would ring my cousin in the hope that she just might be there. God was on my side. She had not gone as the impending war news was so bad. She sent a car to meet me. What bliss.

Before leaving for Scotland I rang my singing teacher, who was staying with friends (in fact the ones for whom Munte had worked) near Penn in Buckinghamshire to thank her for all her help in getting me to Germany in the first place.

They asked me to come up for the night on my way north as they all wanted to much to hear how the Braunfels were managing.

I arrived at Penn and got a taxi to their house. On the way there the driver started insulting the Germans. I forgot I wasn't in Germany and shouted, *'Nein, nein!'* Then, recollecting myself, I apologised and explained that I had just arrived back and how it was unsafe to say a single word against the régime.

I arrived at a lovely house where Mona Benson was staying. She was visiting the vary famous poet, critic and professor, Herbert Reid, who, as I said, knew Munte Braunfels at Glyndebourne. Mrs Reid was a violinist in the orchestra there. I was, and still am, a great admirer of his work, so was thrilled at the idea of meeting him. But fate was not so good this time – he was in London. Still it was good to meet his family and my teacher.

The house was extraordinary inside. In the basement the walls were covered with lurid existentialist fresco paintings – not to my untutored taste. As they only rented the house they could not do anything about them. Luckily they amused the Reids.

Then on to my home in Edinburgh, a little bloody but unbowed.

Chapter Three

Touring with the Royal Carl Rosa Opera Company

1939–1945

I rushed back from Southern Germany with only days to spare before the War burst upon us in September 1939. Things were grim.

I put in to join the WRNS – much the nicest uniform! They responded that there was a waiting list and would let me know when and where. The time went by and I learnt to touch-type.

I also helped in a big forces canteen for overseas troops in Princes Street, Edinburgh, serving breakfasts from 6 a.m. onwards to thousands of troops and getting offers of the equivalent number of assorted types of dates!

Still a student, I was in my fourth year training to be a classical singer with the representative of the famous Webber Douglas School of Singing and Drama in Edinburgh, Mona Benson, herself a very well known singer and teacher.

While I was still waiting for my call-up to join the WRNS, both the Royal Carl Rosa Opera Company and the Sadlers Wells Opera Company came to Edinburgh. My teacher suggested that I audition for both companies. I got into both but both lots said that, as I only looked about fifteen years old (I was twenty-two), I would be too young for parts yet but that they would like me in the chorus. In hindsight this was a bad move, but I was delighted and chose the Carl Rosa. They then gave me a long list of opera chorus (contralto) parts to learn in a short space of time. This I did, working nearly night and day.

I had to travel to Sheffield to do this final test, arriving late one morning, two days after a tremendous air raid on the city.

I asked a porter at the station where the theatre was; he gave me an odd look and said he thought it was still standing but that most of the other buildings around it were flat.

I found my way there amidst chaos and, true enough, the theatre was intact. The only place for me to do my test was in the tiled gentlemen's lavatory, where the large Bösendorfer piano was standing in solitary state. I happened to be born with a big voice so the result was loud but successful.

Life in a touring company was a revelation: a large orchestra, a large chorus, electricians, wardrobe, office staff and, of course, a fleet of principal singers, all arriving either weekly or fortnightly in a town, with everyone requiring digs.

If not already booked in somewhere, what hope had one? These nostalgic places sadly do not exist any more, or few of them anyway.

We could not afford hotels on our three pounds a week salary; mercifully, at least the principals could, which eased the situation slightly. There was never enough accommodation and, on occasions, the police helped out by giving us a cell for the night, or one of us would commandeer 'Mimi's bed' in the scene dock.

When we went to London I stayed in great comfort with an elderly cousin, who had a very large house in Cheyne Walk, Chelsea.

However, the first time we came to London with the Company her house was shut and all the servants on holiday. We arrived at Kings Cross Station about six o'clock with three of us young girls without digs.

It was a Sunday evening, an air raid was in progress and there was snow on the ground. What a prospect!

A policeman came up to us and wanted to know why we were *loitering about* (his words). As we told him, the All Clear siren went and he said he would find us somewhere for the night. We followed him across two short streets, not the most salubrious part of the town. He then stopped and knocked at the door of a crummy-looking house. The door opened slightly and an old face peered out. He said to her that she must take us in for the night and, with that, she thrust a scrawny-looking arm round an almost closed door and demanded the rent.

Thanking the policeman for his help, we went into a dark musty hallway and then up to a small room on the top floor. By the time we entered the room she was gone and we discovered that there was no bulb in the light socket. Two of us crept carefully down the creaking, worn carpeted staircase to the kitchen where we asked for a bulb. She beckoned to a burly young sailor and told him to go up and put the bulb in for us.

Unfortunately he thought he was wanted for a more entertaining pastime. However, three against one prevailed.

We then went out to Lyons Corner House in Piccadilly for supper. While waiting for our meal to be brought, the head waiter came across to us for a chat, as he said we all looked so miserable. On hearing our plight, he offered us jobs as waitresses, saying that that would be better than touring round Britain during the war. We declined gracefully but were given our meal 'on the house'.

Life was like a Greek drama, the comic and tragic masks swiftly turning, causing life to be a pool of twisting emotions, but thankfully getting better and better as one coped with wartime life on tour.

Working was pure magic, although hard. We rehearsed every morning except matinée days, having done our own personal practice at about nine o'clock in some studio in town and then raced to the theatre for the company rehearsals. Our conductors were marvellous coaches and our producers excellent. The music filled one's being – Mozart, Puccini, Verdi, Donizetti and many others. The music, the sets and costumes filled the world with the most exquisite colour and sound. We were always learning new operas, as well as polishing up the old ones. One became a large travelling family as the years went by so one was never completely alone.

Digs became easier. If someone you knew was called up and you were a friend, they would give you the name of their digs in several towns, if particularly good, and five minutes later would find you writing off to see if they could accommodate you.

You travelled with a huge basketwork skip into which went, every Friday night, your clothes, books, scores and all the everyday things of life. You had already been to the station and paid them to collect your skip on the Saturday morning, which you would not see again until Monday morning in the next town. As hand luggage, you carried your washing bag, extra shoes, a book and, most important, a portable radio. Portable in those days meant that you could actually carry it or *just* carry it, lugging this monster as well as a heavy weekend bag.

Some of our journeys were about eight hours long and you arrived tired and sleepy. The men immediately joined a 'club' where they could get a drink, as in Wales and Scotland you could not get a drink in a pub on a Sunday evening.

The women unpacked, making their new 'combined' (bedsitter) home for a week or fortnight. We stayed a fortnight in the large cities, such as Liverpool, London, Edinburgh, etc. One immediately put out one's radio – having asked permission from your landlady (some charged you, some said 'no' and some were happy for you to use it whenever you liked) – then out came your books, tapestry work, and flower vase, the flowers to be bought next day when the shops opened. The photos and ornaments, and even a cushion, made a non-stop tour (five years in my case) seem as if you had a home to go to.

I always toured with a lovely Dog of Fo, which I had bought when I was about ten years old in a junk shop in Chelsea, for the large price of two shillings and sixpence. I also had a very pretty vase that I had bought in Southern Germany *just* before war was declared. My books were about places and musicians, as well as several of poetry. We could get novels from the local public libraries, which helped the carrying load. It was amazing how quickly a place could look like home, in spite of the décor. I find I still do this when arriving in a hotel bedroom.

The rest of the evening one could relax, not a frequent commodity other days of the week, and later on your landlady would bring you in a large supper, later on being about eleven o'clock, our usual time for eating after a show. Many of us had a light breakfast, a tiny lunch and then enjoyed our full meal during the late evening. If you feel full, you cannot sing well, as it affects your breathing and slows the brain.

If one were a fortnight in a city one achieved a blessed Sunday free. Then you could go sightseeing to National Trust-type buildings, old churches, or anywhere of interest – but, best of all, you could see friends or relations who lived fairly nearby. One could either go for the day or for a meal or stay with them, going late on Saturday evening, until either Monday morning, in time for rehearsals at ten o'clock, or late on Sunday night. What a change! Lovely décor, lovely furniture and the bonus of friends' smiling faces.

We either had to cater for ourselves – the landlady cooked what you had bought – or it was 'full board', where you gave her your travelling ration book and she bought your food as well; the latter was more satisfactory for, although we had these travelling ration books, the shops were often so low in goods you could not get your one egg a week or many other things. The port towns were the best; like Liverpool, where the man in the shop said, 'I bet you don't always get what you are entitled to?' and he would slip an extra bit of bacon and an extra egg and more... life was good then!

Our stage clothes were given to us but we had to supply all our own theatrical make-up (also in short supply) and jewellery – Woolworth's best usually.

When I did a part that needed a wedding ring, I blushingly and hesitantly walked up to the ring counter of Woolworth's. It took several goes before I had the courage to ask for one and then tried them on for size. As she packed it up, I kept looking around in case anyone I knew was watching; even the shop assistant's face remained blank. What a change nowadays.

One time I was rushing down the corridor of the theatre as we had had our call. I was in my *Faust* dress, tight bodice and very, very full skirt, when I met our conductor, a well known musician, also on his way to the stage. He was becoming more than friendly to me, with no response in return. As I rushed past him, he caught me to him in a tight embrace. I was trying to push him off when the door of the principal baritone's dressing room opened. That was it. He was a friend of mine and was furious at what he saw. He knocked the conductor aside but, in doing so, the heavy skirt of my dress was partially ripped from the bodice. Panic, the final bell rang for the curtain to go up, the men raced down to the orchestral pit and the stage. I could not go with my dress all torn, so I rushed to the wardrobe, pleading that I had caught my dress on a door handle. They quickly pinned it up and I raced down to the stage with the opening music in my ears – late. Luckily for me the stage manager did not see me slip on to the stage late, as he was busy cueing the lighting at the time, otherwise there would have been hell to pay.

There was a universal ruling that, if a raid took place during a show, the theatre management was, by law, obliged to let the audience know so that they could leave if they wished. As we sang we could hear the siren and anti-aircraft flak and, of course, any bombs that were being dropped, but no one stopped. The stage has to be high so that the scenery can be hung, so there is only one roof; the auditorium has more than one layer of ceiling, so the sounds outside are fairly muted.

The Golders Green theatre, where we were on this particular evening, had a long spade-like board, with 'WARNING' written on it in large red letters. By putting this out at the side of the stage you could warn the audience without disturbing the action on the stage. This particular evening we were doing *Butterfly* and were well into the first act, where Pinkerton, the tenor, was about to seduce Butterfly, the soprano. She thought that she was legitimately married to him and that all was well – oh, the deception of men! The lights were romantically dimmed and he drew her to the bed; they were singing the longest, most beautiful duet of the whole opera. As he leant to lower her on to the bed, from the opposite side of the stage appeared the warning spade with its notice. The audience collapsed with laughter. The singers, who could not see it, were alarmed. What had they done: forgotten to put on a garment used for modesty, or what? They had to finish the scene but, when the curtain came down, they were up in a trice finding out the cause for the mirth; even they had to laugh.

One of the members of the chorus was so frightened when the siren went that she panicked so, if any of us heard sounds of trouble in the distance, we all started singing in our large dressing room and she thought we were practising and joined in; we kept this up all the way down the stairs and on to the stage. Life was never dull.

When a new opera was about to be mounted we had to go to the theatrical costumiers and wig firms for fittings. They were mainly dotted around Shaftesbury Avenue in London. It used to be fun seeing what you would be given. A new production of *Traviata* was being rehearsed and for that the dresses were truly glamorous. A young artist came and, for one whole pound, did a pastel sketch for anyone who wanted it. Like most of the others, I had one done for my mother. My dress was a turquoise blue silk with a white lace bertha and trimmings, off the shoulder, and worn with a beautiful little hat with feathers. These dresses meant that we could never sunbathe; can you imagine a lady of that period looking anything but pale and delicate! We had clusters of ringlets to pin to our drawn-back hair, under the hat. We also had fans of that period. These we had to buy for ourselves, beautiful painted ones and very delicate. Luckily the junk shops were full of fans at that time and very cheap, as we were still on three pounds a week. We needed several fans, Japanese ones for *Butterfly*, others for *Tales of Hoffman* and many more. What marvellous collections we had, and all for a few shillings. Now they are collectors' items.

Transporting them was the worst thing; they were so delicate, even someone knocking into one could break them. I had a most beautiful one from my mother, small, with ivory staves, creamy lace and delicate ivory coloured ribbon. Many of the cast collected them and had quite a valuable accumulation of them by the end of the war. There was great competition in this and great jealousy when someone found an unusual or extra attractive one. Now, of course, there is a fan society and people collect in earnest, spending large sums of money buying them; they are harder to find and have to be really searched for.

Funnily enough I was in both the first and last raid on Britain. The first was in Edinburgh where no sirens went but the Spitfires, which were always practising, came roaring out and, mercifully, stopped the Germans before there was any damage done to the Forth Bridge and the ferries that were crossing to and from Fife at the time.

The last raid was on lovely Hull, the city so devastated by bombing; the beautiful light stone buildings, the fascinating statue of the poet, Andrew Marvell, a native, and I always remember the little street near the docks with the enchanting name of 'The Land of Green Ginger'!

This particular raid was in the early morning. It was sunny and peaceful when, suddenly, I awoke to hear the heavy drone of low enemy planes coming closer and closer. I was in a small modern house in a row, where the sound became deafening as the anti-aircraft guns started. The planes were trying to spray the open windows with gunfire. I covered my unprotected head in my bed. A miracle had happened: the anti-aircraft guns had chased them off. Certainly near me no houses were hit in our row; elsewhere there was chaos.

Food was a great topic of any conversation. As I said before, we so often could not get our full rations and even full rations, although healthy enough, were not a feast.

I wrote a weekly letter to my mother, who kept them all. When she died, several years later, they were returned to me. I opened them thinking, well there must be *something* of interest here; after all it had been a momentous part of one's existence. I started. How awful, they seemed to be mainly about food and clothing coupons and highlights about obtaining anything unusual, like when I chased a barrow of bananas round the back streets of Nottingham. I had been buying them when the lookout man spied a policeman in the distance; without a word the barrow man grabbed the long handles of the barrow and started running. We too all ran for our lives but kept with him. The story ends well. I got my two bananas, a real black market illegality, but I am afraid to say that I was delighted.

When one presented one's ration book at a shop, one was so often told that all their supply of eggs, bacon, butter, etc. had gone to their regular customers and that they had been given no extras.

One marvellous digs in Liverpool – note, a port town – turned out to be run by a lovely Irish/Liverpudlian, whose husband worked on the ferries going back and forth from Southern Ireland. Of course they could buy hams, eggs, butter and all rationed commodities with no coupons. Luckily for me, the wife took a liking to me and said that I must eat with the family as the dining room was rather full! There were several of us in these digs. The fat of the land lay before me at mealtimes and never a word said to the others – what bliss.

All coupons were difficult to manage on, clothes coupons among the worst. There were no nylon clothes, so we had heavy lisle stockings and underclothes, which also took ages to dry after being washed in our large dressing rooms. Digs did not usually permit the washing of clothes or ironing. In winter, particularly, we dressed and made up under lines of dripping clothes, a real Chinese laundry.

At one of the digs in Herne Hill (we were playing in the park, in a glorified bandstand, part of the war effort) I landed up with a bit of luck. There were four young army officers also billeted there. One was very shy, as I was myself, but he wanted me to be his friend. He eventually plucked up enough courage to ask me if I would go swimming in the public baths next morning about 6 a.m. and, for that, he would give me his yearly supply of clothing coupons, sixty in all – he was about to be sent abroad.

He was a nice lad but I was not interested, so that was that. A week or two later a letter arrived from him, from the usual 'unknown destination'; he had enclosed the coupons and a poem he had written to me (a very good poem, actually). This occurred quite often during the next year, but then I received one where he proposed marriage to me and an outline of what I was to do! He would marry me on his first leave; then I would have one more year in the Carl Rosa before going to Leeds, his home town, where we would settle, he joining me when the war finished. He had it all worked out. As they say now, *it was not my scene*. He kept on trying for several years, still enclosing his poems for me, then all stopped. I never knew what had happened to him; whether he had met someone else (I do hope so) or the sad alternative in wartime, that he had been killed.

This park bandstand where we were working was bombed flat one evening two days after we left it; such was one's luck – or not.

The huge, beautiful house where I stayed with my cousin when in London was in Cheyne Walk, Chelsea; it overlooked the road where there were trees and beyond the Thames glinting through them. One day a very old aunt of my mother's was staying there; we were about to have tea in the drawing room when Aunt Blanche leapt up saying, 'Oh, darlings, do look at the most beautiful sunset.' We all went over to look at it and burst out laughing. What she had seen with her ninety year old eyes was a Hovis sign on the Battersea side of the river! The working Thames, a liquid highway with all its crafts crowding the water, was fascinating to watch.

This cousin had offered her house to the government to use as they wished, as there were only herself, some servants and us visiting relations to use it. They asked her to turn it into a hostel for junior officers, using the large rooms as dormitories, she kept a ground floor room as a bedsitting room, even installing a sitz bath for herself. Everyone used the huge dining room, run by her cook and butler and a few other helps.

The one time I went there, I was late in arriving. We were working south of the river which meant, as there had been a raid, that the tubes could not cross until the All Clear. When I arrived it was about midnight. My cousin said that all the beds were being used that night but that I could sleep on an old camp bed in the billiard room. At about four o'clock, when, for no reason, except I suspect age, the legs of the bed collapsed under me, I awoke thinking that the house had been bombed. I was half under the billiard table, its huge legs blocking my view. My heart raced but I noticed that the rest of the house was silent, so I was thankful for small mercies.

This house had at one time belonged to a retired Archbishop, who evidently suffered from the cold, for every room and corridor was filled with old fashioned central heaters. He had also made a sanctuary of one small room, which was partially retained and where, if all else were full, I was given a 'holy' bedroom. A small bed had been put in against what at one time had been an altar – a far cry from many of my digs.

The only time we were allowed to miss a performance was if we were very unwell and had quite a high temperature. However, one day I arrived at the Winter Garden Theatre in London for a matinée and was clocking in when a voice behind me called my name. It was a very handsome tall Marine whom I knew, in full dress uniform, one of the best in all the services, so bound to impress people. He asked me to spend the afternoon with him, as he was being sent overseas. I was about to say that I could not when the chorus mistress, an elderly woman, entered, heard what he said, winked at him and said, 'Yes, she is not at all well but both of you go quickly.'

What a marvellous afternoon we had; first to the theatre, then tea at Gunters. All worth the deception. As he had to travel that evening, I recovered (!) and did the evening show.

I would not have changed my life then, in spite of the scarcities, digs, air raids and most of all the bombs that you could hear cutting out seemingly above you, while you waited breathlessly for annihilation or crippling, the latter being much the worse.

There was the comradeship, the glorious music, the chance to see beautiful parts of Britain and a job that was what one was trained for (once I was in the Carl Rosa, I was not allowed to move into the WRNS or anywhere else). In every town you went to, the public queued to get seats. In fact, in some towns you would see, for example, miners come off night shift, queue for the matinée; then come out halfway through the performance, so as to queue for the evening show.

I was lucky beyond words.

Chapter Four

Greece

29th September – 1st October 1965

And so I set off on my journey of sheer delight.

I have now been to Greece roughly twenty times, but its magic never leaves me. Greece is the land of my heart. The first time I went there was in 1965, not so long after their dreadful civil war.

I had read the myths and history of this country since I was quite small, small enough to try to make a family tree of the Greek Gods! With of course no avail as at one moment a god had a wife, the next, and shortly, she seemed to be his sister! Being strictly brought up in Presbyterian-oriented Scotland, this did not seem to tally with the mores of the father, mother and children syndrome.

A friend of mine, Ruth Lovell, who produced the news on the West of England TV daily slot 'Points West', came with me. We had been on holidays before together, and found that we enjoyed doing and seeing the same type of things.

This year we went in the autumn. I had not had enough money to go abroad since my 1939 trip to Germany, which my parents paid for, so I was even more excited about the event, and much more so when we both decided on Athens as our destination.

At that time there was a £50 limit on the money you could take abroad. The result was that, after buying one's ticket and paying for the hotel (half board), there was only about £20 left to spend on excursions, lunch, etc., which even in those days was very difficult to manage on.

We landed one late afternoon at Glyfada airport. I got off the plane to be engulfed in joy and anticipation. The air was heavy with the scent of herbs and pine, the low line of grey hills surrounding the north of the city was washed in the atmospheric light of the retiring sun. Their colour made them look like grey elephants, whose faded skins glowed in the light, the runnels of their skins fissured by the rains.

The airport bus drove us to our destination, the hotel in Omonia Square, a most uninteresting spot – could this be my dream Athens? In the middle of this large square was a fountain, its water spraying multicoloured diamond drops on the sun's rays.

Later on in our visit we were having a late dinner when suddenly we heard a tremendous noise, which gradually became rather alarming in intensity. We could hear the march of many feet, accompanied by the reiterated chant of 'Papandreou, Papandreou'. I never like to miss anything unusual, so I left my table and made for a balcony that was overlooking the square and was mercifully one floor up. It was dusk. Parading round and round the square were hundreds of students carrying banners and torches – the source of the chanting. The atmosphere was uneasy. As I watched, our waiter from the dining room came over to me. He spoke little English, but managed to ask, with a puzzled look, if I liked riots? I told him that I did not, but that I was curious to know what was happening. With that he laughed, but also warned me that if I went out in the evenings I would be safe as long as I kept away from the University and its surrounding small streets. He also added with a smile that if I liked to see unusual things he would take me to the big Wine Festival being held in a large park in the outskirts of Athens every evening. I smilingly refused. Other evenings when we went out we could hear the hum of dissent in the distance, and so we kept well away from the troubled area.

I was longing to see the Acropolis, and especially the Parthenon, but could not get up enough courage to go. The reason was that, from photos I had seen, it had become the most fascinating place imaginable. I could not bear to be disappointed – coward that I was. So on our first day we got out and about Athens itself – this was now my Greece.

The outskirts of the city were intriguing. The fascinating deep acrid colour of colourlessness, olive trees knotted and gnarled in the dusty parched orange earth, looking like old men in silent contemplation of... nothing, guarding them at variable points, tall dark remote cypresses, unbending, uncommunicating and aristocratic.

The churches, small, huddled and dustily arched, were dressed overall inside, like junk shops honouring God; lamps; silver-framed icons, kissed by the reverent to a holy uneven smoothness; knickknacks of distinguishable value, sacrificed in devotion and love by their believing owners. Sausage-like ruddy slates cover the small cosy domes of the arched roofs of these aged Byzantine churches, while on their ceilings the mosaics glow in their primary and gold colours, vivid and arresting.

The Pantokrator and his ever faithful followers sit in their secure bed of gold tessarae; the most marvellous being the overpowering face of the Pantokrator in the beautiful monastery at Daphni, which is in a very prosaic suburb of Athens. It is said to be the most splendid painting of God in the world – this solemn, slightly stern face, with his magnetic eyes holding one, someone you could always rely on. You really have to lie on the floor to get the full overwhelming impact. As one famous historian said, 'It is lonely in its greatness and sacred austerity.' I do not think one could ever forget this deeply moving face. Coming out of the door you look over the cloisters, now a mass of flowers and herbs. The custodian joined me, a woman of middle age, dressed in the usual widow's black, her black scarf showing little of her fair hair. In Greek, she explained that she always gathered herbs here for her salads and stews. It is amazing how much one can understand by sign language, smiles and even frowns; neither of us spoke the other's language. I took a sprig of rosemary, which is growing in my garden in Bristol, along with a sprig I brought from the Saadan Tombs in Morocco and another from Jerusalem.

Each church that one sees has so much of its own identity, although built to the same designs. One we saw was surrounded by lemon trees, their bitter lemons hanging brilliant near-globes of yellow. Yellow and so bitter, it seemed as if Judas must have hanged himself on such a tree, his gall-like blood dripping from this suicide tree, in an agony of unassuaged repentance, but I believe it was the *Judas Tree*, which of course has in spring beautiful tiny clusters of tight pink and white buds, bursting out of the hard bark, its leaves following, a pale smear of green.

We could just manage on our money by skipping a midday meal and coffees but, as the heat was so intense, over 100°F, we bought the occasional *orange pressé*. In this way we were able to afford a guided trip to Delphi.

This trip took us up through Arachova, perched on its mountainside (the Parnassus Range) and also earlier to the famous monastery of Osios Lukas. We started early, being picked up from our hotel at about seven o'clock.

The Greek guides are superb, known to be among the best in the world. Their strenuous training shows – university for several years and learning at least three languages perfectly, as well as learning the complete history of Greece, myths, flora, fauna, archaeology and much else.

They then have to live for several years in the country of their language choices.

The journey was a joy, the air was balmy, the hot sun had not yet risen too far and the countryside intriguing. Having left the suburbs, it was, one felt, as the early Greeks must have seen it in their days, far from the *maddening crowd*.

The first place we stopped at was the monastery of Osios Lukas, situated high in the mountains, near the crossroads where Oedipus killed his father, one of Greece's tragic stories. The monastery is so silent, hot blue sky framing the buildings. There is the occasional flap of a bird's wing and trees everywhere, while looking around mass after mass of huge rugged mountains spread in the unending distance.

The monastery has two churches, side by side. The first and larger one is amazing. Open the door and instantaneously one is almost blinded by the glinting light thrown by the hundreds of gold tesseraed backgrounds of these near perfect coloured mosaic pictures of the holy realm, and especially again by the Pantokrator (the Holy Christ), a magnificent presence gazing down from the lofty dome, and again some of the most splendid mosaics in Greece. God is surrounded by his apostles. The faces of the saints and followers are unique, their expressions alive, their garb deliciously ornate and personal to each one. The whole interior of the church is like a magnificently jewelled casket; the pleasure of scrutinising it is endless.

We then proceeded to Delphi, the 'navel of the earth', one of the most famous oracles anywhere. The renowned of all ages came here to consult the Pythian Priestess. I have never met anyone (and I have met many who have been there) say anything but how much the place had affected them – a magic spot, overwhelming, even to the most sceptical of beings.

It lies on a hill rising 2,000 feet above the Corinth Canal, backed by the great Mount Parnassus Range, one of the homes of the gods, and hemmed in on one side by the Phidriades (the Shining Ones), a steep fissured rock which paddles in the famous Castalian spring. The setting is a glory to the mind, beyond one's everyday comprehension. Its light, colours, shape, almost stun reality out of the ordered existence of things. It seems to confuse the centuries, diminishing and crossing their defused lengths.

Here, as you probably know, is one of the great, if not the greatest, oracles of the world, where throughout the ages princes, kings, philosophers and all else came for advice and help. The help given by the Pythian Priestess could be taken more than one way, a useful attribute.

The journey for all must have been arduous, through the mountain range, on uneven tracks, in all weathers. After going into a trance, and also having seen that she had received money from the supplicants (plus, often, a sacrificial goat), the Priestess pronounced, sometimes in hexameters, the oracle's utterances. Aeschylus has written in his play *The Eumenides* that the Pythian Priestess said, 'Now on the seat of prophesy I take my place; heaven grant that this day's service far surpass in blessings all former days. Let any Greek enquirer here, as custom is, cast lots for precedence, and come as Phoebus guides my lips, so I pronounce the truth.'

Delphi has been partially destroyed by earthquakes several times, also by a fire in 548 BC, after which gifts and money from all over the known world were sent to rebuild it. So much is underground that much still mercifully remains.

This too is a most moving place. You pass through the ruins of temples, an *agora*, treasure houses, and much more, standing in their silent history, to the accompaniment of bees searching for pollen for their honey making, small lizards sunbathing on the broken capitals and columns. Your ascent continues, eventually arriving at the theatre with its stupendous view, small flowers nestling in the crevices, worn over the ages by the continual drumming of sandalled feet and winter's storms. Ultimately you arrive at the stadium, which crowns the site; the walk alone must have given the competitors plenty of training, especially as there is almost no shade the whole way.

Making your journey back to the main road, the steep slope of the mountainside tries the muscles of the legs. What city dwellers so many of us have become.

On reaching the bottom, you cross the road to another sloping site. Its small path leads to the Tholos of Athena Pronaea, to me, the most beautiful part of all. This small temple is situated with a wonderful backdrop. Behind you are the overhanging Phidriades and the oracle site, reaching what seems the deep blue heavens, then around one are millions of many coloured wild flowers and small trees (Greece has more varieties of wild flowers than any other country). There is utter silence; so many people never cross to see this delicate place, least of all the tours.

At the front the land takes a sudden deep plunge down to the sea, where far below the small ships, fishing boats and ferries rock like miniature toys in their torpor. It also leads down to the town of Itea. Leading down also to it is the unusual sight of thousands upon thousands of olive trees, massed together until they reach the coast. This view is known as the *river of olive trees*.

On another visit to Delphi years later, while holidaying with my artist friend, Euphen Alexander, and my sister, we stayed the night in a hotel, mainly to see the fabled sunset and sunrise, which from this point painted the sea, the olive trees, the mountains as well as the sky, with a surrealistic array of purple, pinks and orange, as if the whole world had suddenly become a place of mainly primary colours.

We again thought that we would explore more of Athens. What a mixture of brash modern buildings, mixed with tantalising glimpses of long gone days. More and more old parts have now been found in the city, as I discovered during my later visits.

The churches, as I have said, are enthralling. One could walk along a busy street of shops when suddenly one would see beyond the bustling people and cars, and as always noise, a rather toadstool-like squat old Orthodox church, hunched right in the middle of this very busy street, looking as if it had grown there. No one has ever interfered with these obstacles. The traffic has to take a narrowed road round either side of them. These are the very old Byzantine-type churches, very holy still and revered, many of course still in use – a delight to the eye. Their old tiered roofs and rounded slates and also their round cosy domes are so fitting to their shapes.

In one of these particular churches a wedding was in progress. A guest came out as we were passing. On seeing us and that we were not Greeks, he asked us to join the wedding. We were already going elsewhere, so said that we wished we could, but not today. We were very pleased to be asked, but time was flying and we still had so much to see. However, on a later visit I did see a wedding in the Cathedral.

The Cathedral itself is a huge modern monstrosity but, as if sheltering under its wing, was the most delightful old, small church, which indeed had been the cathedral until the new one was built, hundreds of years later.

I sat and looked at it with joy. It was set in a small sunken square of flowery garden. Traffic roared around it, people – dozens of them – rushed around the shops, talking as usual. I then went down the few steps and entered the dim interior. As always, there were black-dressed women kissing the icons and crossing themselves. The candles smoked, the incense was pungent, but what a happy reverence! The custodian of the church was plucking away the candles before they were a quarter burnt – still the prayers had had time to rise to the heavens and all therein! Outside on its walls were inserted beautiful blocks of even more ancient stone, with carvings of the zodiac and much else. These were usually brought from old churches not now in use, having been ruined by weather. The city is full of these delightful historic churches, a history in themselves.

The Agora is a great intriguing sprawl of a place (Greek and Roman entirely, none of your modern rubbish!), except for the very well built American Museum, done to the plans of an old arcaded building. One could take months to explore it properly, wandering amid statues, many with, as usual, heads or other extremities missing, capitals lying amid a welter of wild flowers and shrubs, their lost columns sometimes found in the deep undergrowth of an unexplored area. How careless. All the paths and crevices are filled with wild flowers including, in season, the very dark red small poppies of Greece.

Taking one of the many paths that lead up the hill, one reaches the Temple of the mighty Hephaistos. The walk is a pleasure, the hot sun brings out the scent of the many shrubs, herbs and olive trees, while against the distant skyline of blue sky stands proudly the Acropolis, strangely moving in its glory. We still had not been up there; this was ridiculous. I set my mind and decided to go.

We took ourselves there the following day, my heart racing. It had for so long been my pinnacle of perfection. Through the great portico, made of giant building stones, I went – then stopped in wonder. Perfection it was, is and always will be, standing silent and lonely against the intense blue sky. Even with the crowds milling around its feet it is untouched. Its presence, the atmosphere of the past and its sheer simplicity fills one with awe. The great simplicity was done by genius, outclassing any other work of art. It is unexplainable. In those days one was privileged to be able to wander about this roofless interior; sadly now no one is allowed to do so, owing to the pollution gnawing at its fabric. Still, many years later and after many visits to this incredible building, if I am worried, upset or unwell I clear my mind and quietly visualise this stately, silent, immaculate monument to Athena, and all is well; its joy and tranquillity takes over.

We thought that we would take a ferry to the island of Mykonos, in the Cyclades, a journey of about six hours. The ship was packed and Piraeus was dense with steamers, yachts, people and the inevitable ferries. Many Greeks were on their way home to the sanity of their peaceful islands. There was hardly a seat to be found on the ferry for, as with all Greek ferries, it was also filled with livestock – hens screeching, even a goat or two – let alone all the produce and farming machinery and to them, joy of joys, brightly coloured plastic pails, buckets, bowls and all else. The live part of the stock was tied to sacks of grain, their very vocal annoyance equally annoying to us visitors, but what a feeling of life! The only place we could find to sit was on the hard benches round the body of the ship. There was no food, we had brought no sandwiches and drink was non-existent. The others had brought their own garlicky bread, soaked in olive oil. It smelt rancid in the heat, the loos stank to high heaven and were certainly not cleaned very often. Well, it was an experience.

Once we got going, the inky blue-black sea was crystal clear. The famous Aegean rocked one into a dozy haze. We passed many islands, some of which we stopped at, but most we passed. They looked like treasure islands, the wash from our ship and the gentle tide massaging their shores. The ship itself was trailing beautiful white foam and viridian-green waves in its wake. I fell asleep in the intense heat, only to be wakened by a mass of people leaning over me, shouting excitedly, '*Delfini, delfini.*' It was a long drawn-out chant of delight. I struggled round to see what was causing all the excitement. To my delight, a school of dolphins, shining and smooth, was leaping in and out of the water with great elegant movements, their flirting eyes brightly watching and laughing with us. They were playing games in an ecstasy of delight, which in turn filled us with joy; even the Greeks themselves, who are so used to them, respond to their charisma.

Eventually we arrived in the uncertain, unpredictable waters round Mykonos, to be engulfed in a storm, the great empty echoing chords of the wind shuddering the body of every traveller into a turmoil of unattainable excitement and fear. How many times does one's ship become caught in the mighty waves of the Levant?

By this time we were dying to find a lavatory on land, to get something to eat and buy our return tickets to Athens. After a long struggle, in sign language, we found what seemed to be the only public 'toilet' in the whole of this small harbour town. What bliss, except that it was one of the ones that you had to straddle on two china footpieces – no more, except to say the smell was nearly as bad as on the ship, but at least there was plenty of air. The next thing was to join a queue at the ticket office to get returns to Athens that same day, or rather evening. We had been told when buying our tickets in Athens that you could not get returns. Gradually the patient queue ahead diminished. We were now the proud possessors of a means of return. We now had about three-quarters of an hour to 'see' Mykonos so, grabbing a couple of *tyroppites* (lovely hot filo pastry parcels, filled with delicious feta cheese), we munched our way around the harbour shops and, looked at the beautifully proportioned crescent bay and the white painted churches;

it is said that there is one for every inhabitant on the island – oh so many churches – and the low hills which seemed to have a cluster of windmills on the harbour end and then on the jetty itself is the tiny white church of Paraportiani. It is a great landmark for visitors. There is always a mixed blessing at the dock, a pelican to greet one on arrival. As it tried to bite me my welcome was not so cordial.

We arrived back in Piraeus very late, it must have been midnight. Ruth suggested that we find a small taverna that a friend in Britain had recommended. It was very cheap and very good, she had been told. We wandered round the back streets of the port, occasionally meeting, in the dim light, a man who would look askance at us. Safety got the better of us. It was getting very late, so we caught the tube back to Omonia Square. The rioters were no doubt in bed by now, but the tavernas were crowded with bright lights and laughter.

There was so much to be seen. The next morning we took a bus along the coast to see the Temple of Poseidon at Sounion, the most beautiful of small temples, standing on a headland, a point of interest for every ship to see. We looked up at its columns, standing delicate and upright against the sky, and facing of course the Aegean Sea. At sunset, if you stand beside it, you can see through its centre the enormous orange ball of the sun sink gradually into oblivion under the waves, having scattered its rays right over the water on its way – a stupendous sight, bringing holidaymakers and professional photographers there in their dozens. They all look like black, but upright, ants against the brilliant sky. Sadly the columns are covered with graffiti, although one is of interest historically for Byron signed his name on one of them.

After the sun had set everyone made for their cars, and we went to our bus stop for the trip back to Athens. Time went by, no bus. By now it was very dark, so we went to the café to find out what time the next bus was due. To our surprise they were closing. Having asked about the bus, we were told that the last one had gone an hour before. But being truly Greek he said he would ring for a taxi to take us back to Levadia, the nearest town, where he said we should be able to get a bus to Athens. He rang; the taxi driver told him that the last bus would be leaving shortly, but that he would race out to Sounion to collect us, and rush us back, hopefully in time to get the bus. In about a quarter of an hour the taxi hurtled in, we were more or less thrown into it, and he set off at a mighty pace. We, in what seemed ages, arrived in the town square, our bus was moving out into the middle of the road. Our driver leapt out of his vehicle, waving his arms at the bus and then stood in front of it, so that it could not leave. We were scrambling out after him, he literally shoved us on to it, as we were trying to pay him, he grinned, waved his hands in goodbye and would not take a penny – or rather *drachma*. The last we heard of him he was shouting, '*Kali nichte, kali nichte*' (goodnight).

One note about Levadia. It was an ancient site, where the ancient Greeks mined for silver, a very important place in those days.

The taxi driver was, and is, typical of Greeks. This is a land of extravagant sincere gestures. One is always being given things – drinks, meals, a flower or a melon from a man passing you in the street. Such natural gallantry and kindness. Then they pass on. You even find this in tavernas. Your bill is sometimes very low, or nothing, and nothing is expected in return. In fact they would be mortified if you offered them anything in return.

One time on a later visit I was sitting on a wall with my artist friend Euphen, having walked right up Mount Hymettus (of honey fame) and then down again. We were exhausted in the heat. It was Easter Day and all was well. Up the hill came a woman of about forty-five, with her grown-up daughter who spoke English. They stopped and chatted, then as they moved off I said, *'Christos anesti,'* which means 'Happy Easter', or more correctly 'Christ is risen'). With that they swung back, saying to me, 'Are you Orthodox?' Saying 'No,' I explained that I knew that that was their Easter greeting. With that she said that she and her mother would be back in a few minutes, would we wait, and they would take us to their house for an Easter drink. We agreed and, on their return, took us to the bus, paid our fare, then on arriving in the middle of Athens took us off the bus. We walked quite a bit, then the girl turned to me laughingly and said, 'Don't worry, we live in the best part of Athens!' I must have been looking bewildered.

Eventually we arrived at a street which was obviously in the best part of Athens and entered a beautiful building, which had been her grandmother's house and where they now had a sumptuous flat. There they gave us a delicious Greek Easter meal, including hard-boiled eggs, their shells dyed a deep red, which were ours to keep. When we were leaving they said we must always come and see them. I used to get a Christmas card every year, then one Christmas the daughter wrote to say that she had married an American professor and that they lived in New York. Then she added, 'We have a spare room and do hope you will come and visit us.' Sadly I never have.

Even the very poor ask you into their houses. You can see that they could hardly feed themselves, yet with a welcoming smile, they greet you in sign language and give you a small glass of wine and a spoonful of jam, their symbolic gesture. Should you offer them any payment they wave it away, feeling very hurt. Still today the same thing happens. Quite recently I left my handbag behind on a bench. Several hours later I went back and there it was. It is the only country I know where this could happen.

At this time in Athens, so close to the finish of the civil war, all sites were open, no charges, no railings to keep one out. Also, once away from the very main roads, you found you were walking on earthy rubble.

The flea market at Monasteraki in the old Turkish part of Athens is a wonderful way to spend an hour or so on a Sunday. Goods were spread out all over old mats, or anything at hand, the goods for sale scattered on them in no definite order, junk, useful items and, as always, a chance to find a good antique treasure. For the first time in my life I bartered and may say enjoyed it; so did he. There are also open-fronted shops lining the lanes. There I bought, to my delight, a small original pottery head of a man on a little black plinth. I understand that the farmers still turn them up with their hoes. I only know that it is ancient Greek and I got it for £2. Then in another shop further down the market I saw a smallish Byzantine icon, rather disfigured on one corner but otherwise intact. This I bought for £3. During the purchase of both objects I had to fill in a form, which was in three parts, like three tickets. When I paid the man told me that one part had to be sent to the Archaeological Museum, the second he kept and the third was mine. Greece liked to know where any of its treasures were going, so I know that both of them are genuine. I was so thrilled to be the owner of two such exciting objects.

There was an unusual heat wave in progress, a few days before October, that year. It was 98°F, so one became fairly tired moving around.

That year also there was a great international exhibition of sculpture, a fascinating exhibition. It had more than a hundred and fifty sculptures, scattered amid the trees and shrubs of the hill of the Muses. They had come from sixty-one European museums or private collections to the first of a series of biennials as part of the Athens Summer Festival. A marvellous spot, as it looked over to the Acropolis. It had works by Picasso, Dali, Henry Moore, Hepworth, Renoir and many others.

We had our evening meals in the Plaka, often sitting at a table and chair on some of the wide steps that lead up eventually to the Acropolis Hill. It was still quite cheap and very unspoiled. This is the oldest part of Athens, apart from antiques, dating from the time Byron was there; in fact the old Turkish part of the city. What charm it has, with its tinkling bouzouki music, also a relic from the Turks and, joy of joys, the elevating glimpses of the Acropolis, high above the trees, the dark velvety sky enfolding it. It looked rather like great ships moving majestically across the sky. What a back-drop. The moon and stars like silver designs mingling and interweaving in the dense dark.

Living was so extraordinarily cheap in Greece at that time for us Britons that we managed to see more than we ever thought we could have. This also included going to the old Roman theatre, the Herodus Atticus, which is situated under the Acropolis. Sitting there one was transported. Looking up, you see just above you the great ancient citadel and temple of ancient Greece, which has weathered so much: gunfire of the Turks, a fire and now pollution, the one that has the tragic signs of finishing it off for ever. You could see from your seat the great portal and the Temple of Nike and behind the magic Parthenon. It was hard to believe that it was real, lit up against the darkening evening sky. One sat on the stone seats, although a cushion was provided if wanted, enclosed in the three-quarter circle of stone and hearing every word from the orchestra (the stage). We saw *Plutus* by Aristophanes; it was being performed by some of the most famous actors in Greece. We decided to come out at the interval, as we knew no Greek. It was a very amusing play, as Aristophanes' comedies are; we were highly entertained by their antics. When it came to the interval we decided to stay and watch the rest of the play. We sat on and on, only to realise that most people had gone home. Laughingly we did so too.

On the way we stopped off at a very famous patisserie, by Syntagma Square. It is called *Floka*, and very expensive, so we thought we would indulge only in one small delicious cake and a cup of Greek coffee. It was interesting to watch the rich and famous relaxing. We sat at a table on the pavement in the warm summer night. Luckily in Europe one can sit forever with just the one small coffee or drink.

The houses in Athens after the cessation of the hideous civil war – friend killing friend – are for the most part in a state of disrepair. All over, the ironwork is twisted into serpentine shapes, these having been the often massive gates which guarded their no man's land courtyards, leading to monster houses, with their orange and lemon treed gardens.

The fields outside the city have vineyards. The leaves of the vine look like taut green silk, shuttering the sky and sliding their bat-like shapes in the breeze, often tracing tendrils clinging to the broken walls of ruined houses, the leaves secreting beneath their shade the royal-purple velvet textured globes – the grapes, pyramids hanging in worship to their pagan mysteries, the juice deliciously honeyed. One could imagine the priests in their temples dropping the precious fruit into the waiting mouths of their votive maidens – and forbidden pleasure – spilling the sensuous golden liquid on to the sun-warmed marble to their gods, in the name of Dionysos.

We occasionally went and sat by the sea, sitting under the grey-green dusty spikes of the tamarind trees. Looking up through them it seemed as if they brushed the burning blue sky.

Our time was up in this exotic land, our government's allowance well – and I mean well – and truly spent. What a feast of sights.

We left next day, with me silently swearing to myself that I would return soon.

I have been to Greece about twenty times, and now with my husband Geoffrey, who like me adores Greece. I still think that God must have thought to give the world a taste of heaven when he invented Greece.

Chapter Five

Portugal

January 1966, 1967, 1968 and later with my husband, Geoffrey Beauchamp, 1980s

My friend Ruth Lovell asked me if I would like to go with her to Spain via Portugal; she was taking her car and sailing from Southampton. With pleasure I said yes.

We sailed on the Normandy Ferries, which did their winter trips not to Normandy but to Lisbon, a cheap way for us to get to Spain, where Ruth had Spanish friends whom she wanted to see again after a break of several years. So we were to sail to Lisbon and go on from there. I wanted to go to Spain very much, especially the south, as I was, and still am, fascinated by Moorish architecture.

We set sail from Southampton one early evening at the end of December, a whole month away from work, in the sun – bliss! The ship was twenty minutes late in leaving. I joked to Ruth about losing twenty minutes of our time in Portugal. We were spending three nights in Lisbon before driving on into Spain. We had a good dinner aboard, discussing all we might visit on our arrival.

During the night we reached the Bay of Biscay. The ship lunged and shuddered; one could hardly keep in one's bunk. The sound of the ferocious wind howling round us sounded like a horror movie or a pack of tormented monsters incessantly clamouring for human flesh, the waves fighting each other for supremacy. In the morning we got up and with difficulty dressed. We opened our door on to the deck and tried to go outside. Immediately we were soaked to the skin by the enormous waves which seemingly engulfed the whole vessel.

I retreated back to my bunk, not because I felt seasick but because I could not keep my feet and seemed to be gasping for air that was unadulterated by sea water. Ruth managed to struggle to the dining room, only to be met with broken crockery all over the floor, but she was served with some tepid coffee at one of the tables, which luckily were nailed to the floor. There was only one other passenger there as well as herself; even the stewards were hard pressed to keep their feet. It was a lost day. The only person working full tilt was the doctor doling out seasick pills and plastering broken bones.

I have always had a phobia about water, ever since, as a child, a cousin/godmother decided to teach me to swim when on holiday with them at Littlehampton. She took me into the water and let me sink. I can still remember struggling for breath. She eventually hauled me out. I was too young to understand what was going on. To this day I cannot swim. I am sure that my godmother had no intention of despatching an unwanted godchild. She was in fact the most loving and generous one to me all her life.

What bliss when we eventually arrived in calm waters and eventually were steaming up (on New Year's Day) the broad beautiful Tagus (Tejo) River in the warm sun and, believe it or not, piped in by an imported Scottish piper playing on the bridge of the ship. The welcome was most appreciated and seemed to relax the storm-worn passengers, who were watching the familiar sights reassuringly appearing: the elegant Salazar Bridge, delicate yet tough, arching the cool blue sky; the enormous figure of Christ dominating the uneven skyline on the further shore, while close by, on our side, we passed the white, new-as-new looking Henry the Navigator, still scanning the marine traffic of the world as if to say how easy it all is in this day and age; then, to me, the most beautiful of all, the small beautiful snub-nosed Torre de Balem (Belém Tower) with its background of the immensely large and immensely carved Jeronimo's Monastery (Mosteiro dos Jeronimos). Still the ship went on eating up the busy waves, passing close to the shore where we could see buildings of every period decorating the varying levels of ground which make up this hilly city.

Then at last, standing on the busy quay, one could smell and feel the personality of Lisbon, teeming people with seemingly barbaric voices; the flower and fruit market drawing its colours over the dark barn-like building; people sitting in the sun drinking coffee or cognac on their way to work. They looked brooding and saturnine – an unsmiling race, who, we found, neither welcomed nor discouraged their visitors.

On landing we passed through Black Horse Square, centre of business and traffic, all compacted into this large but tight spot, before dispersing, like a delta, through the arched entrances to a warren of streets, many of which lead eventually to the magnificent stately wide Avenida Liberdade. This leads its long way up to the summit, which is crowned on the topmost stretch, like a rakish hat, with the enormous bronze statue of Pombal, Saviour of old Lisbon.

Funnily enough, each time we arrived in Lisbon or left it we had some trauma or another. The following year, Ruth developed a flu-type cold. Feeling terrible, she drove us to our hotel and went straight to bed, where she remained for many days. The only trouble was that we were due at our Spanish friends (by now they had become friends of mine as well) in several days. We knew we must let them know that we would be several days late in arriving. We also knew that José Luis, who was a great worrier where women on their own were concerned, would get into a terrible state if he knew that Ruth was ill. The result was that I said I would send them a telegram saying that we were detained and would be with them in about a week. All went well except that the Spanish for detained is *detano*, which implies that the police have got you in custody; this luckily I did not know. When we eventually arrived with Pepita and Jóse Luis, Pepita laughingly told us that Jóse Luis nearly went berserk with worry, but that she had gathered that we were all right and had managed to pacify him!

In Lisbon, our small pension was just off the elegant Avenida Liberdade, a charming place, white rooms with delightful Spanish furniture, the leather settee and chair with studs. The patroness was a young middle-aged woman, dressed from head to foot in black. Her hair, long and very black, was built up beautifully on to the top of her head.

There was so much to see in this very grand city, which is built in a ravine. The Avenida that I have mentioned already was built in the centre of it, while to the right and left are great inclines, on the left side filled with tiers of shops and on the right crowned by an ancient castle, fascinating very old small shops and houses, in twisting lanes, many cobbled. Back again on the left side and at the foot of the incline there is a monstrous open-worked iron elevator, also a funicular, both of which we sampled. One street was a Bond Street type. As we were coming down it one day, an African woman hurried past me, clasping a lovely child of about one and a half years. On reaching a smart doorway to one of the shops, she flung down a folded cardboard box, opened it, flung in the child and disappeared into the emporium. I managed to take a photo of the little round-eyed child, sitting quietly where she had left it; it seemed quite used to this kind of treatment.

There is so much to see here: museums, concerts and, what I loved most of all, the stately buildings, tiered high over the harbour and up the Avenida. Also high over the harbour, which it overlooks, is the Museu de Arte Antiga, which houses mainly fifteenth and sixteenth century paintings. When I arrived there I went straight to the early art, as it is always my favourite period. The great light gallery had on one side an almost wall-sized painting, which was in sections, two narrower ones first, then two large central panels, finishing up with another two narrower ones. I was struck dumb; it was magnificent. I learnt that it had been painted by the artist Nunco Gonçalves in the fifteenth century. The painting is called *Panéis de São Vincente*; it is of Saint Vincent receiving homage from all the people of Lisbon. The faces of every person – and there are many – are the most beautiful portraits; they come from every class, occupation and degree. I stood and drank in this irresistible scene and the time flew. I saw nothing else and on leaving enquired if there were any postcard reproductions of it. Mercifully there were. In fact, later on, in the good shops, I found there were reproductions of it on trays, mats and all else possible.

We found a fascinating tile shop when we were there, half hidden between two large shops at the top of the elevator, where you could buy tiles of any sort. Many years later when my husband Geoffrey and I were in Lisbon we went there, watching all the local people buying for their shops and houses or anything else. We bought several for our kitchen.

Much of the architecture is Manueline (the flamboyant, marine-influenced style of late Gothic architecture, developed in the reign of Manuel I, 1496–1521). The Mosteiro dos Jeronimos, 1502–1517, is a Manueline building with Spanish influences and, although it is considered the finest monastery in Lisbon, it does nothing to me. The cloisters I liked best are vaulted and almost over-embellished. It is a unique mixing of many architectural concepts, canopies, Renaissance decorated beautiful twisting divisions, within the arches. It is like a musical composition. The columns in the church itself are also fascinating: palm tree trunks extending up into branches, so unusual as to be almost amusing.

One evening we went to hear some *fado* being sung by one of the best singers in Lisbon. For the price of one drink we sat in the old stone-vaulted cellar of what was now a night club and listened to the deep slow melancholy strains of the singer. The low heavy legato songs seemed to bring the woes of the world to the listeners, so poignant and yet so heart-stirring. It was many an hour before one emerged from the web of sadness it wove through one's thoughts. It is said that it originated in the Congo and was brought to the Alfana – the old district round the castle. It is like Jewish and other oppressed peoples' music, full of lamentations, and brings the deeper parts of one's soul nearer to the surface. What a good thing for one every now and then, this dream of life.

There was so much to see, but we had to get on. We were going south to the Algarve, from where we were crossing into Spain.

We went through Setúbal, where we saw in the countryside men high on a slope quarrying white marble. We only knew what it was by the chunks that had fallen into a ditch below the side of the road. I 'do' geology as a hobby, so called to the men then mimed that I wanted, if they would permit, to take a piece of the marble with me. They laughed back, indicating that I was to take a large piece. For ever after I have had a large piece of white marble as a door stop.

We passed many groves of solid cork trees, looking like grotesque ballet dancers preserving their legs with thick woollen stockings up to the thighs. In reality, of course, these are deep brown barkless trunks from which the cork has been removed every few years, to sell for a meagre living.

We also went down a road at Monchique near the Algarve, which was like heaven. We drove under a long arch of flowering mimosa trees – the scent was overpowering – and looking up to the blue sky through the tiny powdery yellow balls it was magic. Praia de Rocha was also so beautiful: deep blue cold Atlantic sea, great rocks of deep orange-yellow and dark reddy-brown, some like arches on the beaches, all, then, completely unspoilt.

We had to cross the sea coast to the east, to get to Spain. At the small village of Ayamonte is the ferry, which held about three cars and wobbled over to Spain. It took about fifteen minutes.

I believe that the Algarve and around is now very different: many high-rise hotels and all that goes with them, also that the ferry has been moved a little up the coast and is bigger and better.

I have an odd affinity with Portugal. It is like having a conversation with a woman who is cold and unbending yet not actually hostile. In spite of that I have passed through the country three times and stayed with my husband at Estoril for three weeks, coming there by plane.

On the second visit I again came with Ruth Lovell, at the same time of the year, again on our way to Spain.

We explored the other part of the Lisbon area, going by train along the coast to Cascais, a delightful fishing village which I understand is now a great holiday area. The harbour is entirely covered with a pebble mosaic of huge waves in memory of the 1755 earthquake and tidal wave. It is odd walking on it; one feels one has to step over the black waves. You then put your feet down and find that it is completely flat. One year, when I came with Geoffrey, we found the whole of the pebbled esplanade covered with TV cameras from all over the world. Unbelievably, it was the annual strong man competition, extraordinary to watch. Among the events they have to pull a DAF truck for several feet. The place was also littered with onlookers. We took ourselves to a small café and had a delicious sardine (proper sized ones) lunch.

We also went to Sintra, beloved of Byron, who wrote in *Childe Harold* 'Cintra's glorious Eden'. One climbs the hill (it seems to be built entirely on hills) from the highly tiled station, then round a bend into what seems like a set of a romantic musical comedy. Facing one is the large sprawling Palácio Nacional. This building is unmistakable because of its two conical chimneys, which dominate the skyline. The building is very old, having been enlarged about 1385. Later, it was inhabited by the Moors; the battlements were added then. Later still, King Dom Emanuel and others made changes in the inevitable Manueline style. The building is now a museum.

You look across from this extravaganza to a hill, which brings to mind Milton's *bosomed high in tufted trees*, for there, tantalisingly half-hidden, seem to be two buildings of note, one high above the other. These are the great Palácio de Pena and the Castelo dos Mouros. I was not able to climb to them, owing to an arthritic hip. How unromantic. The square itself had a mixture of old and uninteresting shops of many kinds, one being a shop, rather expensive, selling pottery, jars and much else, with typical old designs painted on their fronts. I later succumbed to one of the jars; I now always use it in our bathroom.

We also went to an exhibition. The pictures were delightful – landscapes of many countries. We were introduced to the artist when he came in, a delightful man who later on kept shouting greetings to us when we met in the streets. He was youngish, and had had exhibitions all over the world. He also told us that his agent was negotiating a show in London for him, and *'please* come'. Very sadly we cannot now remember his name, and certainly could not afford one of his paintings.

We also went to Queluz Palácio, which was nearer to Lisbon. We had been told about it by one of our BBC announcers, who had found it by accident several years before and fell in love with it. He said that no one much seemed to know of this gem of a place.

We drove through the lovely countryside, full of blossom and fresh green herbage, then, on turning a corner, suddenly discovered ourselves in a large courtyard surrounded by Versailles-type buildings painted pink and fairly well looked after. The whole of Queluz made us think of a smaller version of Versailles. It is said to be the finest example of Rococo architecture in the country. We were thrilled especially as we found that we could go round it. We had been told that it also had one of the world's great restaurants and was accordingly expensive.

The interior of the Palace had very grand rooms. It is built in a half-square shape; then, leading from the huge French windows are the formal gardens. On the opposite side of the outer square were (or rather had been) the imposing stables and houses. Then at the curving side of the palace entrance was the great kitchen, now the restaurant.

It was amusing when several years later Geoffrey and I, without a car, went to look at Queluz. We walked down to the small town from the station (me, as usual, with difficulty because of my hip). It was a louring day and chilly, not surprising as it was November. We toured the Palace itself, I noting that many renovations had been done since my last visit several years before. Geoffrey was particularly interested in the paintings; many were portraits. Eventually the custodian came and said that he was sorry but we must leave as it was twelve o'clock and the place had to be completely closed during their two-hour lunch break. He ushered us to the front door and, like us, looked in horror at the downpour. We had no mac, no umbrellas and no car. He said that he was desperately sorry, but could not keep the door open for us to shelter, but that he would ring for a taxi. He tried in vain; with the rain everyone else was taking them in their rush for lunch. None were available. He again apologised and suggested that we go to the restaurant. We laughed sourly to ourselves – one of the most expensive ones in the world.

I could not walk uphill for long. However, we started off. We were soaked, no taxi, and little money as we had not cashed a traveller's cheque recently. We walked past the renowned restaurant and in desperation and on the spur of the moment we decided to risk going in and having a minimal meal. We walked back to its entrance and into its opulent hall, dripping water from every garment, hair and face. A very smart old-fashioned waitress in black (it must have been bombazine!) with a highly starched lacy apron and cap, came from the dining room and delicately, with outstretched fingers and distasteful looks, took our outer garments. Inside, through the grand glass door, we saw a horrified manager watching us.

We went to our respective 'powder rooms' dried our faces, rubbed and smoothed down our soaking hair and presented ourselves in the dining room. An underling waiter led us to a table, handing us each a huge imposing menu.

The dining room was a sight to be seen. Great stone walls hung with old glistening brass pots and pans, some of enormous size; thick carpet cushioned our very wet feet and each table glinted with beautiful glass and silver on a whiter-than-white damask surface. We looked at the menu. Already we were very hungry but we found the cheapest dish we could and also a salad between us. In that way we could just manage to pay for the meal. We ordered, the waiter asking suspiciously who the salad was for. I, being quicker with a lie than Geoffrey, said, 'Me.' The head waiter was still keeping a wary eye on us and when we asked for water instead of wine his disdain knew no bounds. As we waited for the meal we scanned the room. It was full of very smart city gentlemen, having huge business lunches. There was a reverent hush, except for the muted voices of the eaters. As we were eating our one and only course, Geoffrey suddenly laughed, saying, 'I had forgotten about our Barclaycards' – in those days these were a newish phenomenon – 'I will pay with that so we can have one of their luscious puddings and even coffee.' The head waiter was looking quite relaxed. He had evidently noted that we did not eat our peas on a knife, we seemed fairly civilised and, when he heard us ask for pudding and coffee, all seemed to be well. How we enjoyed our meal. When we were finished, the great boss himself came forward obsequiously with the bill. As arranged, Geoffrey gave him the card, thanking him in Portuguese, and smiled, saying that he only knew five words in the language. As we left he came up to us, asking us to come again and said goodbye in Portuguese, adding with a twinkle, 'And now you know six words in Portuguese!' Actually the meal, although expensive, was not as expensive as we had expected and so we saw one of the world's greatest restaurants and all because of a downpour of rain.

Getting back to earlier times: Ruth and I went to Estoril, where I found, in my usual geological searchings, fascinating stones lying on the beach. They were nearly the size of my clenched hand, completely coated with white crystals. I brought one home and have used it on my desk as a paperweight ever since. The crystals now look grey rather than white, but still beautiful. Many years later I told an archaeologist friend, Maggie Hyatt, about these stones as she was going to Estoril and wanted to find one like mine. When there she searched everywhere, but sadly they had swept the beach flat and added tons of sand over it.

Estoril, the former playground and home to many deposed royalties, still supports their large casino, but a royal head rarely, if ever, enters its portals. Estoril has a strange no man's land feel to it, full of forgotten intangible ghosts and memories. Palm trees line the sea front and the town's gardens, many very grand houses and estates mingling with the modern disease – huge high-rise hotels. Geoffrey and I stayed in one of these for three weeks, eating mainly at a tiny family restaurant at the end of a back street. It had first-class food. The proprietors – a plump young woman, her stick-thin husband and young son of about ten years – watched the TV nonstop. She served us our delicious meal, often large fresh sardines and all that went with them. The TV was in the darkened end of the large room and they watched avidly, but with no sign of amusement. The show was... 'Fawlty Towers'. There were subtitles, but every country has its own type of humour.

Another time that Ruth and I went to Portugal, and again on our way to Spain, we did not go via the Algarve but by a border town called Elvas, leading across to Badajoz, as we wanted to see the renowned city of Mérida with its ancient theatre. More of that later.

Elvas had a marvellous Aqueduto Amoreira near the entrance to the town, which was built in 1498, and also thirteenth century fortifications. The town was originally Moorish, right from the eighth century.

When in the south we also visited the most beautiful small town of Tavira, founded in 400 BC. It has many grand architectural buildings, two Roman bridges, churches of note, and still many oriental rooftops.

We also stayed a night at Faro, the capital of the south, an intriguing little place. We arrived latish, it was dark, we found all accommodation that we could afford full. We had with us this year an older friend, Diana Abrams, whose husband was head of all the public gardens in Bristol. Luckily she was very accommodating. We booked into a very sleazy-looking *zimmer* (rooms) of dubious standing in the harbour. The rooms were clean, the sheets white, but thick and roughly woven, the furniture old and slightly decrepit, but highly polished. To crown it all there was no bathroom or loo; you had to use the public one in the harbour square. What one does for adventure!

We had quite a lot of food in the boot of the car. Restaurants were conspicuous by their absence. This was, after all, January. We stood on this reasonably balmy evening round the bonnet of the car finishing up plenty of leftovers, biscuits, cheese, fruit and much else, washed down by the nectar of bottled orange juice. Last of all we spent a penny and went over to our *zimmer* and bed, a fairly lumpy one as far as mattresses and pillows went. Then, to the accompaniment of the very audible neighbouring rooms (interesting and revealing of lives as lived by others) I tried to sleep. One unexpected addition was that, although on the first floor, one could hear the sibilant confidences of people stopping to converse, more or less all night, or, as an alternative, the loud arguments of the eternal non-getters-on with others. Why my window particularly attracted them I will never know.

Come the morning at last, we were all out of our beds pronto, half-dressed and queuing for the only public lavatory seemingly for miles. We decided that when we were dressed completely we would pack our bags, except for our sponge bags, stack them into the car, then treat ourselves to an expensive breakfast at the nearby hotel, with a preface that we would use their sumptuous Ladies' Room as our own private bathroom. We then presented ourselves in the dining room fresh and spruce, ordering a most delicious breakfast of hot coffee, orange juice *pressé*, toast, butter and the lovely non-sweet jams that they serve on the Continent, also, as often in these parts, a slice of cake.

Faro itself, with its typical and unique chimneys seen all over the Algarve, was not an exciting place except around the harbour, small and old and still a working harbour. Small cobbled streets, old houses and churches, this part was well worth seeing.

We also saw, another time, Santarém, capital of the Ribatejo, which is known for bullfighting, horses, and the bulls themselves, both of which were happily grazing in their separate fields. This town is north of Lisbon, and celebrates bullfights many times a year, as well as supplying other places with the livestock for their fights. It has been known as such a place since the times of Julius Caesar; lovely old buildings still make up some of the town.

When we were returning to Lisbon from our visit to Spain we hit a great storm. Many trees were across the roads, the rain deluged and the storm *donnered* and *blitzened*, as the oratorio *St Matthew Passion* by Bach says – so much more satisfying to say than thunder and lightning! When we reached the Salazar Bridge the storm was so bad that cars were only allowed to cross it singly and according to weight. It was a nerve-racking drive. Ruth's heavy car was being slewed sideways the whole time. The structure of the bridge is very open, revealing only too clearly the huge waves tossing far beneath us, and the parapets at the sides exceedingly low. It took many hours for cars to wait and then attempt the crossing. However, eventually we reached the Lisbon side and made rather late for the port to get our ship home.

There was no sign of it. The queue of waiting cars was increasing with every moment. Funnily enough the man who was waiting in front of me was called Scrimgeour Wedderburn, and was a relation of several girls with whom I had been friends at school. He now lived in the Algarve, but was on his way to England for a holiday.

After a while the port authorities announced that the ship for which we were waiting was in danger, drifting without any power off Gibraltar, and that they had booked us all into hotels for the night, providing transport there and back. They said that they hoped that the ship would arrive intact later that night, so would we be at the port in the morning.

Ruth and I were taken to a very plush hotel in a part of Lisbon we hardly knew. So we were able to sightsee in that area, which had the large Gulbenkian Complex of museums, one being of modern art, and, as we found, a mixed blessing!

We arrived early next morning, but still no ship. We were told that we would sail in the early evening, as the ship was due with them fairly soon, but would need some repairs.

We set off again, after phoning our families about being late starting. This too, of course, was on the shipping firm.

We got back to the port fairly early, to see the ship staggering into port. They had managed to regain power just as the ship was close to the rocks. It was late at night when we eventually got away. There had been much more to do to it than they had at first thought. However, it was a joy eventually to sail under the Salazar Bridge with all its lights outlining it against the dark soft sky, our own ship dressed-over-all in celebration of its safe return.

In the days of 'live television' in the BBC, whenever a programme had to stop owing to troubles the announcers said, 'We are sorry, but it will soon be under control.' Well, we arrived in the Bay of Biscay when the engines stopped and the lights went out. Almost immediately, a voice over the tannoy said, 'We are so sorry, but it will soon be under control.' Ruth and I could do nothing but laugh – home from home.

There was very little food on board as all the fridges had been affected and again there was no hot water for drinks or heating, but this time mercifully it was soon all rectified and we progressed. Later on all the passengers who had done the whole disastrous journey were given certificates of merit, as a lasting memento.

It was good to be on terra firma again.

Chapter Six
Spain

January 1967, 1968, 1969, 1970 and then
with Geoffrey in the early 1980s

We arrived the first time in Spain at Ayamonte, from Portugal, making our way to Seville via Huelva, famous for its Rio Tinto Mines and the best and longest beach in Spain. This is the Costa de Lux, which is battered by the mighty Atlantic at this time of the year. Huelva has many connotations to Columbus, as we were soon to find out; everything was called Columbus!

The place in itself is not very interesting so we pressed on, passing through the most beautiful countryside; the great orange, yellow and ochre rocks glowing in the sunlight, especially when they had just been cut, which much of this road was, as the mammoth road building project had begun. When uncut, the rock has a soft grey colour; you can see this weathering on the mountains. These mountains were such a delight. Right up to their tree lines were almond trees in full blossom against the warm, deep blue sky. Below much of the earth was arid, large landscapes of nothing but an occasional silent farm, which always seemed to consist of a wall and a gate, then, at quite a distance beyond, a low large long farmhouse with outbuildings, peace enveloping the whole place.

The people one met were lovely and welcoming, shouting *Buenos dias* as we passed through their small villages, which themselves were heart-rending. What with a civil war, then the Second World War, and still ruled by a dictator, life had not much to give them: the poverty was abject. We only spent about a pound a day on food, accommodation plus petrol (admittedly our hotels were not sumptuous places) yet the people, in general, would always give one a drink and even something to eat, with no thought of payment in mind.

We pressed on to Seville, the weather gloriously warm. On reaching the outskirts of this city it was often hard to know which road to take. I found that many people discover this.

Unfortunately it was rush hour; there was traffic everywhere. We seemed to be going round in circles in this city of tall handsome buildings. Eventually we saw a *Guardia Civil* (policeman) on duty directing the traffic. Ruth said to me to go and ask him how we could get to the *Dom* (cathedral); our hotel, we understood, was near it. I leapt out of our static car-bound vehicle, shouting over the noise of traffic to him for directions to the cathedral; he turned with a smile and, abandoning his duties, took me down the road and further down another and pointed out the way. We then returned to the now chaotic scene of screaming drivers, hooting horns and general mêlée. I returned to Ruth, he to resume his duties, only hesitating as we passed him, to bow and smile in farewell. Ruth had been very worried as she saw me disappear into the distance with him. The *Guardia Civil* in those days were very vigilant, arresting anyone on the slightest pretext, real or imaginary. We had been warned to be careful if having to deal with them in any way. Even with his help, it took us another good half hour to find the cathedral.

Funnily enough, another time arriving in Seville we were again attempting to reach our hotel. We stopped in a suburb to look at our map, when an elderly small Spaniard on a bike came up to us, asking if he could help. Again on asking for the *Dom* he nodded and smiled, indicating to us to follow him; he sped off. Following him was hilarious, trying to keep up with a bike that could dart in and out of the traffic. Again it was the rush hour. However, we eventually arrived at the required spot, where he doffed his cap, grinned and sped away, our heartfelt thanks following him. One English soldier we met later on told us that he always hired a taxi to get into Seville, and followed it! What I do love about the Spaniards is their humour, smiles and openness. After Portugal it was heart-warming.

While Ruth tried to find a parking place, as before almost impossible, I went on with some of our baggage to the hotel. Just before turning into our road to my surprise I met the Head of the Bristol BBC. We both juddered to a halt, said, 'What are you doing here?' and then laughed. In fact, we were both on holiday.

I so remember the first visit. Our hotel was very inexpensive but delightful, in a narrow old street. The surprise was that when you walked into the arched hall you were confronted with a small strip of water and fountain – still the Arabs' ever continuing passion for water. Round this were low chairs, leather-seated and backed, studded with bright brass nails to the framework and swathed round the bottom of the seats with dark red and green fringing.

We had only two days here before going on to Ruth's friends in Cadiz, so we made for the *Dom* which turned out to be incredibly smelly, so much so that I spent very little time in it. But again on a later visit I went back there. The smell, thank goodness, had gone.

I leisurely explored this vast dark uninviting building. I found it oppressive and depressing. The lack of light does not help and, although it is said to be one of Spain's greatest achievements of the fifteenth century, and one of Spain's greatest museums, a treasure house – although still the religious centre – its worth was lost on me. In spite of all the pomp and glorification I did not get any sense of my God there; others obviously feel differently. In spite of saying this, there are some parts which fascinate me. One is one of the many entrances, called the Puerto dei Perdon, an exquisite *Mudejar* (Muslim living under Christian rule architecture) work, in addition to a *Almohad* (a fanatical sect in Morocco) doorway, which has the *cufic* painted writing from the Koran. Much of the carving is done out of larch wood, and how fabulous it is. These Muslim carpenters were of the highest quality; this is the same throughout southern Spain, the Moorish legacy. They were not allowed to copy anything living so this fascinating *al farje* (decorative geometric patterned woodwork) were on the windows, doors and ceilings, also on the stucco; no 'graven images used', as the Bible says.

To me the most fascinating part of all is the Giralda minaret, left from the great Mohad mosque of 1184. When the Sultan of that period, Yakub Yusef, died the work stopped, only being allowed to resume when his successor, Yakub Al-Mansur, sanctioned it. One can always tell when this happened, as the first part is built in stone, the latter with brick courses. The bell tower also had a chequered career. It was too high at two hundred and fifty feet; an earthquake damaged the top, and only in 1558 was the top of the tower rebuilt, adding another sixty feet and installing an imposing statue of Faith and a magnificent *tenebario* (branched candelabrum), which is also a weathercock (*giraldillo*). The cathedral was built by the Visigoths from Morocco, hence its magnificence. The Muslim tolerance was notable, until the bigoted Almohads came and demolished it, erecting in its place a great mosque, which in turn was demolished, except for the Giralda tower, by the equally bigoted Ferdinando and Isabella.

My favourite part of Seville is the Barrio de Santa Cruz, where the Jews were allowed to live in these early times. It is a maze of tiny streets, with such delightful names as Pimento and Pepper. The buildings are high with yellow or white painted walls, hung about with old soup tins painted in bright colours and filled to the brim with exotically coloured flowers, such as geraniums, also the herb basil plentifully sharing their living.

Then there is the Calle de Maimonides, with an excavation deep in the ground which has produced two large Roman columns, their feet encased in a deep pool of bright green shiny weed, an entrancing sight with its brilliant colours. They are bereft of capitals, taken many years ago to grace another patio, no doubt. The lamps are a joy in these twisting streets – wrought iron brackets hold them to the walls. Little courtyards, when there is room, make crowning points amid the tangle of these narrow streets and miniature squares. How delightful they are, sporting a small orange tree decked with their brilliant coloured fruit, or a myrtle tree dark green against the white walls, or a paved herringbone pavement of bricks worn to a muted hue. The place is noiseless except for the flutter of birds. Then, to me, is the *pièce de résistance*, the most exquisite small oriels with their latticed screens, bowing from the wall, a mere foot from the pavement. These are called *mushrabiyyah*, being used in the days of the Arab occupation for the dwellers in harems to spy on to the street without being seen. The atmosphere of the whole place is exciting, redolent with jasmine, orange, stocks and basil. Then there are a few grander small squares, one with a wrought iron cross amid the magnolia; another – the Plaza de las Croeces, which has three wrought iron crosses, one of which is Roman; then the Church of Santa Maria la Blanca, which is a converted synagogue.

We also went to the Triana. I think that it was here that we went into a factory shop to buy tiles. They were incredibly cheap, as the populace come to buy their wares here. I bought two small tiles, about three inches square. They are made to insert into all the pavements of Seville, a lovely custom. On them they have either a castle with a blue outline or a dragon. They have adorned my kitchen wall for many years. This area is rather run down, although it must have been a charming country abode, in years gone by. Then it was inhabited by potters, who became noted for their work, and the gypsies, who I understand lived carefree lives here already. It has the oldest church in Seville still in existence – Santa Maria – and which still sports some of the old *Mudejar* work; it is older than the cathedral and is said to be built by men from Burgos.

Another place we passed which was of interest to me as an ex-opera singer was the Fábrica de Tabacos, now a university. It is the famous tobacco factory, the setting for Prosper Merimée's opera *Carmen*. Grand though it is, it will never be my favourite city; many people will not agree with my point of view.

Another time when we came here we were only passing through Seville. By now there was a motorway to Cadiz and we could do the journey in a day. We did stop for a picnic lunch in the Parque de Maria Luis; this is an incredible place, built in 1929 for the Great Exhibition. Different parts of it were built by several countries, but everything is tiled, balustrades, small bridges over the stream, wells and all else, and the tiles mainly white with blue pictures on them, giving large splashes of colour to the whole. Everywhere were palm trees, citrus trees and flowers but, best of all, white doves, who dived-bombed one's shoulders, hands, and knees if sitting. It was delightful, their soft whirring wings spraying one with a soft warm current of air. These friendly creatures induce one to relax. The only other place I have known this to happen is outside Iona Abbey in Scotland.

When there with Geoffrey in the 1980s we had a most interesting trip to Italica, a very large Roman site. Our guide told us that in fact it was very much larger than it looked, because it ran under all the small fields and villages around the perimeter. They would have the hard task of deciding when, or if, they should reclaim the rest of this most valuable and unusual site, one of the largest known in this part of the world. They would need to demolish the entire buildings, ruining also the many fields of crops, causing much heartbreak and poverty.

Italica is outside Seville and was built by Scipio Africanus Major for veterans of the Second Punic War. It was also the first to be built in Andalucia. Interestingly Trajan was born here. Eventually the dreaded Visigoths took it over, which was the beginning of the end. It really is a most beautiful setting, surrounded by fields and small distant whitewashed cottages; trees grow amid the ruins. This is a silent halcyon place under the hot sun with exceptional bursts of birdsong. It is interesting also that Rodrigo Caro (1573–1647) wrote *A Las Ruinas de Italica* on seeing these very ruins, as we now were. He wrote: '*Estos, fabrio, ay dolor que ves ahora campos un tiempo Italica famoa; acqi de Cipion la Vencedera colonia fue.*' ('Alas, these solitary fields, this parched mound, that you see here, Fabrio, were once Italica the famous. Here was the victorious colony of Scipio,' in the translation by J.M. Cohen.)

Another time, about January 1968, Ruth and I entered Spain from Elvas, crossing into Spain to Badajoz, so as to visit Mérida. I had gone down with tonsillitis the night before, so was travelling with quite a high temperature and feeling very dazed.

The following morning we went to the Roman excavations with its renowned theatre. I could see it was well worth a visit so staggered out of the car. All I can remember seeing was a blur of buildings. We decided to hurry on to Seville and get me to bed, then the following day do the same to Cadiz, where the Sarazenas would get me their doctor. We had heard not very good reports of Spanish doctors at that period.

We got to the Sierra Morena, where Ruth fed me a little tinned Ambrosia rice, then announced that she needed a *comfort stop* and disappeared up the lower part of the mountain range. I sat in a haze in the car, my temperature rising with every minute. Then up the road roared a couple of *Guardia Civil* on magnificent motorbikes. Stopping, they shouted with many gesticulations that I must move on *at once*, as the mountains were full of bandits. I nodded, they roared away. It was very cold high up in the Sierras and Ruth seemed to be gone forever. However, eventually she returned and on giving her the instructions from the *Guardia Civil* we moved. We found out later from Spanish people that what the police had told us was only too true. There was much pillaging and harassment from the bandits, who called us all *rich foreigners*. These types of Spaniard were too poor to mind what they did for money.

We were now making our way down into the evocative Andalucia, seeing again its mixture of many disparate cultures – deep into Moorish Spain with its geometric architecture, entwining patterned stucco work of myriad blues and yellows. Arch upon arch, which stretched often it seemed into infinity, keyhole doorways, curved walls that never show a jarring line, where unnumbered fountains drip away their fluid lives, so rounded, so suave, smoothing one's thoughts into the unutterable softness of complete relaxation, when the body soon becomes the quintessence of unboned fluid quietness. All this mixed with the Gothic, typical newcomer – over-ornate and unfeeling, and eventually into the modern nothingness of box buildings.

Travelling one sees vast empty acres of countryside, dotted here and there with small eruptions – haciendas of the rich, remote and seemingly unpeopled in this dusty yellow earth. Bulls for the national sport graze unconcernedly in their heat-hazed pastures, and horses – they too for the bull rings – haughtily stalking and stamping the ground in an effort to create a stir of air in the stifling atmosphere. Every now and then one passes a quilting of silver-green eucalyptus trees, giving sparse shade to the sun-soaked road, stinging the nose with their well-remembered scent of nurseries and colds.

The small villages with their far-flung cafés with juke boxes of pop and flamenco, covered in signs denoting the forwardness of their living! *Citron pressé*, Coke and, magnificently, Nescafé, served on the latest up to date, much prized, plastic tablecloths and mugs. This is a country of deep feelings – joy and sorrow which one can see in the faces of the ever friendly peoples.

Eventually we arrived in Cadiz over the *tombola* and with difficulty found a hotel, the Hotel Atlantico, with its beautiful view of the sea and surrounded by gardens. This city, set as it is, has to have its drinking water transported to it each day from the mainland. It is a spit joining an island to the mainland. The *tombola* is a type of sand dune. Razed by an earthquake and subsequent tidal wave in the eighteenth century, Cadiz is more a *new* town by the standards of the ancients; narrow dark streets of high stone buildings, intersecting each other, dressed with small intriguing shop windows, like that of a toy town. Cars driving up these narrow streets scrape the stone walls on either side as they go, their horns warning pedestrians to jump into doorways to avoid the ignominy of being squashed to death, like an unwanted beetle.

Ruth left a letter stating our arrival in the Sarazenas' *aptado* box at the Post Office. Apparently mail was safer that way. Also we could not quite remember how to find their flat. I had thrown off my clothes and sunk, half conscious, on to my bed, my throat as bad as ever. The Sarazenas contacted us at once and came straight over with a charming doctor, who immediately gave me some medicine, the result being that in about three days I was very nearly completely better.

They are a truly delightful couple, so very interesting. They had been classical flamenco dancers, working all over the world, including the Theatre Royal in Bristol. They had their own independent group, which Pepita had started, before meeting and marrying José Luis, who had more recently become a dancer. Then with a guitarist and sometimes a singer they had toured the world, until, sadly, not all that long before I met them, they had been performing in Japan. There, very tragically, Pepita had damaged her Achilles tendon (she had had to practise on a cement floor), which meant that she could no longer dance, especially flamenco with its detailed and precise footwork. They didn't have much money, as it had always been ploughed back into their work, and now they didn't have a job. Now she teaches ballet at the Conservatoire of Cadiz, no piano provided and under other difficulties, whilst José Luis now has a job with something like an accountant's office. They later told me that they lived in Cadiz (he came from Seville), overlooking the harbour, to give themselves the feeling that they could sail away at any time!

Where they lived was a small flat, which was up in the heavens. The house itself was large, and owned by a delightful large woman who had run it as a brothel. She was now a retired brothel keeper. It was an unusual flat, with great character, as was its owner, who, when Pepita wanted an especially good meal (as, for example, 'Grouse Casserole') she asked her to cook it for her. The only trouble was they did not have a proper bathroom, so they had to carry up gallons of water along narrow dark stairs. Pepita said that, sadly, if they could find a reasonably priced flat they would have to move. That happened several years later and we actually stayed with them there for a few days.

They took us all over Cadiz, José Luis being a fount of information. He was very keen on poetry, painting and dancing. One day I mentioned that I loved Lorca's poems. He agreed, but thought that another Spanish poet, Rafael Alberti, was even better. With that he proceeded to write down for me a couple of his poems, which poor Pepita was asked to translate for me. José Luis spoke almost no English, and I no Spanish, but it is amazing how one communicates.

They also took us to many art galleries, one being the lovely Museo de Pinturas, which has a room devoted entirely to Zurbarán's paintings, which they are gradually acquiring as they come on the market. He is a painter (1598–1662) of many beautiful portraits, but also known as a religious painter. I had a collection of reproduction photographs of his work sent to me by a producer in the BBC who had become very interested in him after I had told him of my visit to Cadiz. It was fun; José Luis always stopped about twenty minutes and said that it was *tapas* time. You go to a taverna, order a drink and eat as many free *tapas* as you can. The tavernas were always interesting ones; for example, one of them where you always saw the famous bull fighters. They also took us one holiday (they have many religious day holidays) to a halcyon place. Sitting under the hot sun and dappled by the trees, they ordered the meal, a huge dish of many small fish, charcoal cooked. How delicious! The scent of the fish, the flowers and clear air were intoxicating. All around us were large families enjoying their day off, much laughter and joking, the children, as children all over the world, scampering about. I do think that this family outdoor living is a great binder of people.

We were also taken to see de Falla's house (Cadiz is very proud of his living there) and the cathedral, with its golden dome, the whole edifice seeming to be squatting down in the middle of the town. Another great joy was that they took us to a huge old building, which was now a home for old people. In its chapel were a group of Goya's fresco paintings, rather high above us, but quite seeable.

The seafront was near our hotel, and there was a small public garden, Parque Genoves, with a *dracoena drago* (a dragon tree), an unusual tree to find – extravagantly ornate. It was interesting, as Cadiz is so near Jerez de la Frontera, with its famous sherry bodegas run partly by the British. José Luis was a great connoisseur of sherry, going out every day – before each meal – and bringing back the appropriate bottle; also in the evening a sherry liqueur, a drink I have never found anyone to know about in this country. He was very generous and as we left on our last day gave both Ruth and myself a bottle, stressing that we 'must remember only to take a liqueur glass at a time'. I was very popular when I returned home and offered it to my friends.

We had decided to make our way eastwards along the coast, calling in at Algeciras. Ruth had said that she would like to go over to Gibraltar, but Spain had closed the frontier, leaving no way of getting to it, except that the travel agent in Bristol had said that one way was left open, but he did not know any details. On arriving at Algeciras we went to the harbour to find out.

I went over to a pleasant looking Spanish official and stated my case.

'Can we cross to Gibraltar?'

With a friendly grin he said, 'Yes.'

On enquiring how, his laconic answer was, 'Swim' and then he began to laugh.

His laugh was so infectious and without any malice that I joined in, mingling my mirth with his. From the car Ruth could not think what was going on. He then told me that in fact you could go to Tangier or Ceuta, then sail back to Gibraltar, repeating the journey on the way back. We decided to stay the night in Algeciras, then take the short journey to Ceuta, not going to Gibraltar at all, but sampling this small portion of Spain in Morocco.

The next day we were making for Ronda, a place we were both keen to see. We found that, if we got to Motril, we could make our way north from there. The day was dull and showery, the journey tiring and, as it was nearing lunchtime, we decided to find a place for a picnic. But, as it always is, nowhere seemed suitable. Eventually we saw an empty beach, except for a GB-plated Dormobile occupying one end of it. We always try to steer clear of the British while on holiday, but it was getting late for lunch so Ruth drove to the further end of the beach, well away from the GB vehicle.

We had started unpacking our meal when we heard two voices behind us. We stopped and had a pleasant chat with them. They said they must leave us to get on with our meal.

As they turned to go, Ruth said to me, 'Grisell, let's hurry.'

At that the woman swung round saying, 'Which is Grisell?'

I nodded and with joy they said that they too were Scots so would we go over to the Dormobile when we had finished eating, where they would give us a hot cup of coffee and a drink. We were getting cold, so we happily accepted.

They welcomed us into their van, which was very snug and well arranged. They said that they came from St Andrews and were called Doddington-Smith, but as a writer she used her maiden name – Steed. She told us that she wrote for the Scottish *Field*, the *Glasgow Herald* and *The Scotsman*. They had converted the van so that you opened one partition and there was a cupboard of reference books. They told us that it was so expensive keeping up a large estate, that they had bought the Dormobile and spent much of their life happily travelling and visiting friends and their children, even as far as Canada. They were such a charming, friendly couple.

I asked them if they could manage to entertain from their van. The answer was 'yes' because, as the weather is nearly always good they lay a table outside. In fact, she said, only yesterday they had had a great friend of theirs to dinner – a Diana Hay-Neave. In surprise I turned, saying that I had been at school with her, and in fact in the same form.

Later in the conversation they said that they were going on to Tangier in a few days as they had a friend, Michael Scott, there and would spend some time with him and his mother. Again I turned to her, saying, 'I know Michael Scott, whose mother – Lady Scott – is an artist and lives in Tangier.' What an extraordinary coincidence! I then went on to tell them that I had spent Christmas, a year or two ago, with great friends, the Greenhill-Gardynes, at Finavon Castle and that Michael and his mother had been in the house party. I also told them that Michael's brother, David Scott, and his wife Hester were great friends of mine, that I spent some of my holidays with them both in London and Mull. In fact we had been friends of Hester (Ogilvy, as she had been then) since youngsters and with her whole family.

We then said that we must go, as we were making for Ronda, and had heard that the road was difficult, in so far as it had many hairpin bends and a perpetual precipice on one side, quite beautiful but treacherous. As we were moving off she turned and said to me that she had been in my home town, Edinburgh, a few weeks before attending a

PEN Club meeting, and had met the most charming of men, Tony Chambers of Chambers Publishing.

I laughed, saying, 'He is my cousin!' With fond farewells we set off, rather belatedly, on our journey. It was a good encounter.

We arrived in the Serrania de Ronda, where on a plateau the little town of Ronda sits like a toadstool in the centre of it. Cutting through the town is a ravaging great ravine – the Tajo – very awe-inspiring, especially at night.

We stayed at one of the very few hotels, the Reina Victoria, which was comfortable and provided good food. But the best thing of all was that its garden, at the back, was the side of the chasm and, in the evening, the view from there over the hungry mouth of hell to the great jagged mountains beyond was magnificent. The sun sank lower and lower behind the range, silent except for the occasional last trill of a sleepy bird, or of the eerily silent flap of an eagle, who soared above the peaks, every now and then sinking in search of its last prey of the day. Eventually the stars flickered into being, leaving the mountain tops a stark unrelieved dense black, seeming to devour with greedy eyes the monstrous impertinence of the town for existing.

Not far from here grow the *pinsabo* trees, on the eastern range. It is said that these prehistoric trees are the only ones left in Europe; we sadly had no time to see them.

As we were leaving the hotel next day I spied a door marked with the name of the famous Rainer Maria Rilke (1875–1926); apparently he had stayed there for a while. I said to Ruth that I must see his room, as I was a great admirer of his works. I asked, as requested, for the key to his room, which was now a small Rilke Museum. It was not very large; the main items of interest to me were his books and pictures. It was sparsely furnished, very brown and rather depressing, but still interesting to me. He wrote many of his poems in Spain, and in *Duino Elegies* (translated by Leishman and Stephen Spender) he wrote:

> The Spanish landscape (the last I illimitably experienced), Toledo, pushed this tendency of mine to extremes' (he had become convinced that all existence was a task, and that ordinary pleasures only made new demands upon him to re-create) 'because the external thing itself – tower, mountains, bridges – already possessed the splendours, unsurpassed by means of which might have been represented. Everywhere appearance and vision came, as it were, together on an object, in every one of them, a whole inner world was exhibited.

There was a statue of him, a thin lonely figure, staring intently at the twin peaks of the Dos Hermanis.

Ronda is famous for its bullfighting. In fact its bullring – Plaza de Toros, 1785 – was the first in Spain; before that they fought in the streets. It is also the largest and has the distinction of being the only one that has two Doric columns and two storeys, each having a roof. Many famous bullfighters came from here, and still do. The magnificent Puento Nuevo, eighteenth century, spans this spectacular ravine. Its bridge is built into the base of the Tajo, so stands in the waters of the river Guadalevin four hundred feet beneath, where one stands peering down. The great massive rocks give one the feeling of might and awe, and thoughts of the precariousness of the town, which lives its life on the edge of its maw.

We went to Granada in our travels, crossing the snow-encased impressive Sierra Nevada. High up upon this vast and undulating mound the cool keen air threw its heady perfumes of rosemary and thyme, delighting unsuspecting travellers, while nearby on the uneven shawled snowline grew in profusion the brilliant deep blue iris, no more than four inches high. The saying goes that they will never grow anywhere else but on these long high slopes of the Spanish Sierra. Their roots have delved so many feet beneath this metamorphosed earth, just to prove that the mighty winter storms cannot upset their tenacious hold. These mighty mountain ranges stalk the brow of the country, an infinity of wooded or barren expanses, uneven and torrented, deeply gorged, an ever-tempting challenge to the climbers and skiers who stride their summits.

We arrived at Granada, sweeping up to the mighty Alhambra. This is a city of bells, which play the hymns of childhood on the every hour, none quite synchronising with the next, as if competing for favours.

The hooded withdrawn Alhambra gives as little as possible of its past. I arrived on my own, just an hour before it shut. The place was bereft of tourists. The Patio de los Leones – Court of the Lions – is so magnificent and compelling. Coming through an archway unexpectedly, the sudden confrontation of it transfixes one into a silent breathless wonder with its beauty, arched and silent except for the clear water spewing from the mouths of the ever expectant stone lions – lions looking as if one word from the right voice would release them from their rigid poses – a game of *statues* that has lasted far too long. The sun highlights the marvellous moulding on the silent stone and stucco work, while the birds sing their untutored songs on the small orange trees. Light, colour and shape make up this most wonderful fantasy of poetry; to see it alone was a miracle.

I then proceeded to the harem, dark and arched. Inside sitting in a dark corner was a tall Arabic custodian. Rising and bowing as I entered, he told me the history of this part of the Alhambra. It was interesting to hear of the lives of these women. I thought we had come to the end so turned to go, but he caught my arm, saying that he would show me how the rest of the ceremony was done! His now lascivious face bent close to mine as he tried to make me lie down on the couch. I pushed him away and made for the door. Realising that I was in earnest, with disgust he let me leave the building.

I continued my tour on my own. The whole place was staggeringly impressive, the beautifully crafted walls, fountains and elegant arches with the lovely Arabic inscriptions above them and elsewhere; no sign of a plant or person, this not being allowed in the Muslim ethics – only God is worshipped. I sat on a bench, facing one of the eternal strips of water, a great part of the Moorish ways of life, in contrast to their endless waves of sand in their endless deserts.

Among the Arabic lettering in the Alhambra are several poems written by the fourteenth century poet, Ibn Zamrak. I quote a few which I found in the *Companion Guide to Southern Spain*. Zamrak was a vizier of Mohamed V and his works were highly prized. A great many of the writings on the walls of the Patio de los Arrayantes are by him; and in the Patio de Mexual is a bowl, on one of its rims has been added a poem of Zamrak's, in which the fountain lords itself and in this way lords the King who ordered it to be made. Then in the Patio de las Leones, Zamrak has another poem of his carved on yet another bowl rim, which says that 'the garden offers a work whose beauty Allah did not wish to reveal'.

I moved on yet again. Now the sun was low and warm, the long buildings still with their imbibed heat, the long strips of water still as the proverbial sheet of glass. Only the sound of the distant fountains broke the silence with their spray, like crystal drops of tears – shivers of bubbles as they splayed on to the fountain's water. Birds sang their evening song – already gently sleepy – all this released the tensions in one's mind and body.

My friends and I came again the next morning, a Sunday. The whole place was crammed with chattering people. How very glad I was that I had had such an enchanting evening there on my own.

Our hotel was very grand, not our usual type, but we had heard that it was very near to the Alhambra, which is high above the city. We saw that the meals were expensive, so stealthily brought food from the boot of the car and locked our door in case any maid should come to turn down the beds for the night.

Quite near to the hotel, we were told later on, there was an *auberge* (inn) and also that St John of the Cross (1542–1591) had lived nearby when writing his marvellous poems. I cannot verify this, but it is worth a mention. He definitely lived in Spain, and there are still cypress trees there said to have been planted by him. In one of the small *calles* (streets) still stands the limestone doorway which sports the notice saying that St John of the Cross lived here in 1586. I believe that the Alhambra is the only Moorish palace left in the world.

Before leaving Granada we visited the Cathedral and the Capilla Real (Royal Chapel) where lie the coffins of two monarchs plus the Princess Juanca with her husband, Philip the Fair. This is a beautiful building, with many paintings and fascinating painted carvings, such a contrast to the cathedral, which, to me, is a vast gloomy Gothic-type edifice, overly full of monuments and memorabilia. I spent two days in the 1980s in Granada with my husband Geoffrey. Again it was the Alhambra that was our great choice. The saying goes, 'Whoever has not seen Granada has seen nothing' (*Quien no ha visto Granada no ha visto nada*).

We then went to Córdoba. What a bewitching place! We managed to get a room in a very minor hotel, which was L-shaped. At the front was a large area where in summer one could have drinks or meals. The usual painted tins hung all over the walls, with rather overblown plants – this being January. Our room was up some outside stone steps. The door was of heavy wood and led straight into our room, which had two large single beds and not much else. Accommodation was scarce, at our price.

We went out to explore or, as a small boy once said to me, 'Let's explode.'

We went first to the Juderie, the fascinating old part – again, as in Seville, a multitude of narrow streets, whitewashed houses, also hung with old painted tins but here filled with glowing flowers. I find these parts of Andalucia where time has stood still enchanting. As the name implies, this was the old Jewish quarter which blended in freedom with the Moorish religion, a way of life compatible, until the rabid narrow-minded Almohads came to Spain from Morocco in about 1150. There are also here the delicious small squares scented by their myrtle, orange or oleander trees, small versions growing in the centre of their minuscule squares. Another feature in these parts is the sculptures of various famous people who have lived here, such as Fernandez de Córdoba (1453–1515), he still being the one most people remember. He was known as the *Gran Capitan*, one of Spain's warring giants throughout the land. His equestrian statue is near the Plaza Mayor, but there are many of them scattered all over Spain.

The next most lauded person in Spain is still the great Maimonides (Moses ben Maiman, born 1135), a philosopher and physician whose statue is in the Juderie – the Plaza Tiberiades. This is a small plaza. The statue shows him seated, resplendent in turban and voluminous robes. The dates given on his plaque when the statue was erected are 1964 and 5724, in Spanish and Hebrew and says, 'Córdoba to Maimonides'.

He was a contemporary of the judge and philosopher Averröes (Abu-L-Walid ibn Rushd). Maimonides was banished to Fez in Morocco because of his Jewish beliefs, again by the dreaded Almohads; then he was sent to Cairo, where he became physician to the Saladin family. When he was eventually able to he went back to Israel – the Holy City. He was renowned for his Hebrew law and writings; amongst the Jews the Maimonides cult still exists. Averröes was also banished for the same reasons, being severely punished before he left.

Then near to Maimonides is a bronze statue of the poet Luis de Góngora (1561–1625), who is considered to be one of the most famous. His statue is where the famous Góngora House stood. Gerald Brennan says in his book *The Face of Spain*, 'seen through the perspective of the centuries, he must be called, if not the greatest Spanish poet – the term is ambiguous – at least the greatest and most enchanting artist of the language'. The bust of Góngora is considered to be a copy of Velasquez's painting of him (now in Boston). He is seen also in the great painting by El Greco, *The Burial of the Count of Orgas*, which is in a church in Toledo, where his face has been used as one of the assembly. One of the poet's poems was in praise of Córdoba: *'Oh muro, oh torres Coronades de honor, de majestad, de gallardia! Oh Gran Rio, Gran Rey de Andalucia, de Arenas Nobles, ya que nodorades!'* This has been translated by J.M. Cohen: 'Oh lofty wall, oh towers crowded with honour, majesty and gallantry! Oh great rivers, great King of Andalucia, with your noble, if not golden sands!'

The only other statue I mention is in complete contrast to the rest. It is modern and shows the great passion for bull fighting. It is one of the great and famous Manuel Rodrigues Manolete. Killed in 1947, he is still a Spanish idol. On the plaque of the statue it says 'Beloved Bullfighter'. Then of course there is the statue of the brilliant Seneca, the Roman philosopher, who was also Nero's tutor. His nephew was the famous poet Lucius Seneca, who himself wrote many plays.

The synagogue is one of the most interesting features of Córdoba, situated in Judios Street (or Calle de Maimonides). It is full of interest, small and dark, but with stucco panels and a fair amount of tiling, but it is the frieze which catches one's attention. It has, in Hebrew, quotes from the Psalms, and here also is a plaque commemorating the birth of the great Maimonides (1135) and says: 'Spain through its government expresses its homage to the immortal genius of Jewry. Córdoba, his birthplace, offers the veneration of its remembrance.' This is the only place like it in southern Spain.

Over the broad slow river, the Guadalquivir, is a low solid arched Roman bridge. Slowly the boats plough up and down. As the sun catches it, the unused large waterwheel rustles on the green weeds that are gradually taking it over. From the further bank one looks across to one of the most famous buildings, the Mezquitat (Great Mosque) and the Alcazar. I now thought that I must see these renowned buildings.

The Alcazar was nearest to me so I went to its entrance. One of the custodians was standing by the door and, in the usual Spanish way, gave me a smile, asking where I came from. He then told me that I would be particularly interested here, as one of their princesses had married one of our kings.

'Yes,' I said, 'Katherine of Aragon, who married Henry VIII.'

He looked at me in surprise, saying I was the only person who had known whom he meant. With that he told me I could go in without payment, and that he would personally conduct me around. What a bonus. He was fascinating about the whole thing, included many parts where the public were not usually allowed. He also told me that Katherine's father-in-law, Ferdinand of Aragon, used to send some of their best horses to Henry VIII, her husband, for his stables. These were called Barbs, an Arab Barb, which comes from north Africa to Spain. They were a highly sought after breed. It is also understood that most of the best stock in Britain still comes from this line.

Now for the Mezquitat (Great Mosque). On entering one is stunned. The whole vista has double-tiered arches and columns looking into infinity, and in fact it is often referred to as the Arco de las Palmas, arches which are horseshoe shaped below and semicircular above. These columns are all painted in uniform stripes of alternating cream and deep red. Silence is everywhere, the light giving a soft glow throughout. Off this long arched hall, with its keyhole exits made in slabs of marble and stucco work, are tiny columns and capitals, and again on the higher area it is finished with the cream and red worked stone, the lines everywhere being geometric. True to their religion, the ceilings often mould into a honeycomb. These entrances and exits lead off into other, equally ornate, rooms.

One of the strangest things here is built inside the Mezquitat – a Christian choir and high altar. It is a cultural shock, a Gothic-type intrusion, rather dark and sombre, with the worst traits of that European period, although impressive as a whole with its dark heavily carved wood choir stalls. As I am not very keen on Gothic work, and much prefer the Romanesque, I am probably a bad judge.

Spain is so full of magnificent sights, even in the small towns. We of course could not see all, but I feel I must mention a few, so many periods, so many conquerors, and so many artists and history of such disparate nations. *Ecija* – known as the frying pan of Andalucia – founded by the

Greeks, and owning a very strange square. Then *Marbella* – ex-haunt of deposed kings, and where I found the semi-precious stones (in masses) on the beach. *Zafra* – where coming out of a desert from the north one suddenly drives into a beautiful colonnaded square. *Vejer de la Frontera* – after driving up and up to this tiny town, perched on a high rock, you come into very small narrow lanes, white houses glinting in the sun, contrasted every now and then by small arched tunnels, which provide the most elusive semi-dark shelter from the sun – beautiful and a stupendous view of the surrounding country. The *Nerja Caves* – with their wonderful fairy-tale shapes and colours and where, I am told, one of the famous ballet companies once performed.

I also said how friendly the Spaniards are. One example will give you some amusement. One day I arrived at one of the great Moorish sites. On finding that it was locked up for the lunch break, and knowing that it would be another two hours, I thought I would have a rest. We had been very active. I found a bench under some trees, a lovely spot, and relaxed. Very shortly, a tall older-looking Spaniard in his long black cloak and black flat wide-brimmed Spanish hat came over to me and started to talk. He was very pleasant, very erudite and very interesting. We had so much in common the time flew. We suddenly found that the site was opening again. My companion said that he must go as he was helping with the guiding that day, but he suddenly took my hand, telling me that he had never met anyone so congenial and interesting before, that he had fallen in love and could he marry me? He had to rush, so quickly gave me his card, asking me to ring him in the evening. His card informed me that he was a professor, and his address was a place quite close, and beautiful.

'Please, please,' he had implored me, 'ring.' He said he did not want to lose me. It was getting late, the site having been closed. I hurried to keep my rendezvous with Ruth, who must have thought I had got lost. It had been a delightful episode, but we were leaving next day early. I never rang him.

Funnily enough, I had a similar offer from an Italian grandee a year or two before, who had only known me for two days. It must be the Continental temperament, although I also had a proposal of marriage from a Welshman, in the glamorous setting of the buffet in Cardiff Station!

The last time that Ruth and I went to Spain we decided to motor back from the south, up to the Atlantic, getting a ferry at Bilbao for Southampton. This was a very long haul, as I could not drive.

We did our usual rounds of Portugal and then Andalucia; again every place was a delight. We then started north, stopping the first night at Antequera, partly because I wanted to see El Torcal, which was a few miles from it, where there is an extraordinary geological formation over several acres.

We arrived there rather late. The journey had taken many hours and the sun was beginning to think about setting. When we actually arrived at the spot we were confronted by rocks, rocks and more rocks, many about twelve feet high, unadorned by any growth. It looked as if we were walking on the moon – stark and lonely. There was a sign to say that one could take one of two routes, the red one or the yellow. These were of different lengths, something like one being three miles, the other eight. I cannot now remember the exact figures, especially as both were too long for us to embark on. However, it was lovely even to see what we did see: an immensity of this rock – red limestone, weird shapes, even small waterfall-type shapes and remains of what looked like old stalactites, small uneven paths covered with broken stones of all sizes. The sun set, and we had to leave this now cold disembodied place with its grotesque rock formations.

We arrived in Anteguera and fond a hotel. As we were very tired we had dinner there, so did not see the little town until the morning.

Like so many Spanish towns, it had a small hill with an old castle on the peak and was fairly encompassed by fields and bushes, then a larger area sloping down to the countryside. The town itself was of no great note, but pleasant.

Our next main stop was Toledo, this never-changing place, its medieval buildings difficult to destroy owing to the narrow dark streets of high buildings. We arrived at the foot of this vast pile, the road curving up and up until one reached the town, this ancient capital of Castile. We had to park the car on the edge of the town, the streets being far too narrow for traffic. After parking we entered this magical place. It was hard to believe that this was in the 1960s: the small shops, many filled with tourist rubbish, here mainly Toledo swords (copies); world famous steel objects, their steel being one of the best in Europe; black spiked balls on the end of a chain for torturers; and the beautifully worked gold and silver Toledo jewellery and knickknacks, intertwining the silver and gold into fascinating patterns – world famous.

We found some digs in an old house, comfortable and intriguing, then went to see the cathedral with its incredible brightly coloured over-ornate altar. It is a massive building which, as usual, had first been an early church, then a mosque. This present-day cathedral was begun in the thirteenth century. Again it too has had many additions over the years.

One of its doors is particularly beautiful with its bronze panels. Here too, as one would suppose, is housed much of the work of El Greco, and well worth looking for. Interestingly the dome of the lower tower was designed by

Jorge Manuel Theotocopulos, El Greco's son, in about 1631.

There is also quite a lot of fairly early stained glass, which is of considerable interest, being produced in 1418–1570. The altarpiece itself was done in 1570 by El Greco, as well as much else, as I have already said. The lantern and spire interested me, as they are encircled by bands, the rays of which represent the Crown of Thorns. This was an added glory in 1422.

We then went to the St Tomé Church, built in 1300–1320. Here in an annexe we found one of the most famous of El Greco's paintings, *The Burial of Gonzalo Ruiz, Conde de Orgaz*. This has been cleaned, so every detail shows. We saw it in all its glory. The painting is hung on a white wall, surrounded by light. Seats are placed facing it, so that one can sit and study this amazing work. It was painted in 1584–1588. The episode it depicts took place in 1323. The figures carrying the body heavenwards are St Stephen and St Augustine. As Orgaz had been such a pious man he had a heavenly escort, honoured by these saints accompanying him. The citizens are all real portraits of well-known people from Toledo. They include a portrait of El Greco himself, while the acolyte is his son, Jorge Manuel Theotocopulos – which of course was El Greco's real surname. El Greco was a nickname meaning 'The Greek', given to him by the Spaniards when he came from Crete to live in Spain.

I then took myself on to Casa dei Greco (the house of Greco), where the artist lived and died. There were many pictures in this lovely house. When I arrived a Spanish guide came up to me and said he would take me round. I asked if he spoke English. He shook his head, saying very little. Nevertheless he came with me, discussing each painting in detail. It was amazing how much one could understand. I thoroughly enjoyed it. When we arrived back at the entrance hall I asked if they had reproduction postcards. This he could not understand, so I drew the shape and size of a card, pointed to it and to a picture. No success, but a flood of horror came over his face as he stuttered, 'No, no, no – we keep!' He had thought I wanted to buy one of the actual pictures. At this point he certainly did not understand me. When I got outside I laughed to myself, thinking of the size of my salary and the worth of any El Greco!

What a fascinating place this is. Perhaps one day I will revisit its beauties again.

Time was flying by, so we moved on to Madrid, driving over the great empty plain of Castile. It was no joke, the day was dull and very windy. Ruth had to use all her strength as her heavy car was buffeted towards lorries and all else. It is said that it is the coldest place in Spain in the winter and hottest in summer. We were certainly cold on this high plateau. Laurie Lee said of Madrid: 'Standing on its mile high plateau the city was considered to be the top rung of a ladder, reaching just this side of heaven.'

We arrived in Madrid about lunch time and found a good hotel for the night in a central street. We were hungry so went to a small bar close by and had what seemed very Bristol – elvers – delicious, then on to the famous Prado Art Museum. In those days there was not the other most interesting Thyssen-Bornemisza Collection, which is now nearby.

It was a great thrill to enter the Prado, a most beautiful heavily built stone edifice. What wonders there were. We knew we would have to decide which part we most wanted to see, so Ruth and I parted. I made for the early paintings, then the Spanish and Italian. The quality and quantity were astounding when one knew what was there, but even so in even one section there was almost too much to digest. I started with the *Master of Arquis* (1450) by Huesca, and went on until I was saturated by colour and workmanship. Later on I moved to the Spanish Room, where of course there were several Theotocopulos paintings with their long faces looking down at one. So many reasons are given for their shape, but as a mere amateur I think that, as he was trained in Crete, his home, as an icon painter he had always kept to that way of painting faces, long stylised ones. I also saw several Zurbaráns. I was lucky; I had seen many now, while travelling around Spain, a great pleasure.

Time was going yet again, the place was soon to shut, so I hastily made my way to the Velasquez room especially to see the one which had been cleaned of the *Infanta Margarita Maria*, with her attendants, her dwarf Mari Bárbola and others including José Nieto, Chamberlain to the Queen. Then, as a quirk, he has painted himself painting the King and Queen, but they are depicted in a mirror behind him so that is the only place you see them. Because of this the Prado has hung a round mirror (similar) in the wall facing the painting, into which you can turn and see it as Velasquez was seeing it, the mirror image reversed. On leaving I bought a large handful of postcards, mostly of pictures that I had seen there. We were exhausted, so went to a café for a cup of coffee and to discuss what we had both seen.

Dinner in Madrid starts at 10 p.m. at the earliest, so we went back and changed. We had been recommended to a restaurant that was especially good for Spanish food, which often was of partridge. It is also the emblem of Madrid. So about ten o'clock we ventured forth to the old part of the city.

The place we were looking for was the *Antiqua Casa Sobrino de Botin* in the Calle de Cuchilleros (cutters), which had been a muleteers' pull-up for carmen! Then in 1725 it was altered and now, still serving travellers, is a very popular coaching inn-type restaurant. It was good. The main building was still the same as the old hostelry had been, and it was packed with laughing hungry Spaniards; it was so good to hear nothing but Spanish being spoken around us – no English! The emblem, as I said, is a partridge – one sees it all over Madrid in one form or another – so I chose the partridge casserole, which came in a scalding hot brown pottery dish, and how delicious it was, better than I have ever tasted partridge, before or since.

We went back to our hotel when we had eaten. It was now quite late and we were aiming at an early start in the morning as we planned to reach Santander, on the north coast, the following day.

The only place we stopped at on our way north was Burgos, with one of the famous cathedrals of the world, which had been built in 1221. We stopped to eat and then I went in search of the said cathedral but, alas, on finding it the doors were firmly locked, the keepers of the doors were also having their lunch, so regretfully I never saw more than the façade. It, like so many, was a solid building with a lantern to which many lacy small spires had been added, a large rose window added to the decoration of the whole, but in general it was very much less decorated than many others. The only person of note who seems to be connected with this city is Rodrigo Diaz de Viva (1043–1099), known universally as El Cid or, to the Arabs, Sidi.

The weather was rather poor. One felt the usual British cold damp winds. What a change.

We arrived in Santander in the early evening. This is a rather dreary seaside town, with a long bleak beach. Our large and characterless hotel faced the grey wave-driven Atlantic. We booked in for our last two nights in Spain, before catching our Bilbao ferry. We had planned this as we both wanted very much to see the famous Altamira Caves with their very notable cave paintings. This was a little east, down the coast at Santillane del Mar.

Next morning we set off down the coast to the above. What a delightful surprise is this small medieval town, seemingly unspoilt, with its old fifteenth and sixteenth century stone houses; small streets with balconied smaller houses; many flowers and shrubs;. an *ayuntamiento*, solid and grand. It is renowned for being the one in the famous tale *Gil Blas* as his birthplace. Standing in a garden is an eleventh century convent of Regina Coeli, which is now a museum, and the lovely Romanesque Colegiata (Collegiate Church). What exquisite lines these Romanesque buildings have, what presence.

We went on to the Cuevas de Altamira. It was a cold dull day; no one was about but ourselves. We paid our entrance fee and escorted by a rather dour (unusual in this part of the world) solid young Spaniard, who first informed us that the cave had Magdalenian paintings. This is a period about 12,000 BC, where the people painted their caves in ochre and sometimes outlined them with flint scratches and shaped the drawings to fill the odd curves of the walls. These animals were remarkably lifelike; they were only discovered in 1879. We were lucky to see them, as soon afterwards no one was allowed into the caves, due to deterioration of the paintings and the atmosphere. I understand that there is now a replica in the museum in Madrid.

As we entered one by one, the guide holding a large torch led the way. He hurried us on, flashing his torch up on the walls every now and then. The pictures were fascinating and highly skilled. We reached a very narrow part when the man suddenly turned and shouted, 'Lie down, lie down.' We both conceded, lying on a cold damp slab of rock. He hovered rather menacingly over the top of us and lifted his torch. What was he up to? We were rather scared. Then suddenly he turned, flooding the roof with light. They were the most exquisitely done paintings of them all – staggering. We were now told to get up and he led us out. Both of us had been decidedly nervous when told so abruptly to lie down by this burly guide with his long heavy torch, and to be stood over in that way – as if to strike us! But it had been well worth while. I have never had the pleasure of seeing cave paintings before or since. We were lucky to see one of the best ones in Europe.

Next day we boarded a Scandinavian vessel to take us back to England. The food was delicious, including the smorgasbord that they produce, and the bunks extremely comfortable. All was well with the world, a good ending to our holiday.

Chapter Seven

Morocco

Casablanca, January 1969

It was the end of December 1968, in fact on the 26th, that Ruth Lovell and I set out for Morocco, a land so different from Europe, a place we both wanted to visit and mainly Marrakech.

The £50 limit was still in being, so we had to plan carefully. The only way that we could manage it on our money allowance was worked out for us by a very helpful tour operator. We had to fly to Casablanca, stay several days there, then fly to Las Palmas in the Canary Islands and stay for a few more days, then fly back to Casablanca and get a train down to Marrakech for the remaining time. This we did.

We set off from England, which was icy cold, in an Air Maroc plane, which was delightful, with sandscapes painted all round the cabin, and all in green and sand colours. They gave us each a French newspaper, then came the shock. Headlines in the paper stated that it was snowing in Casablanca, a very rare occurrence. We could hardly believe it.

On arrival at our hotel a smiling receptionist greeted us. As he got the keys, he said 'Americans?', a statement rather than a query. When we answered, 'No, British,' he handed us our keys, and never again greeted, or even smiled at us again. We were not money spinners – Harold Wilson had apparently put a stop to that, as we gathered all through our visit.

However, it was exciting being in a part of Africa for the first time in my life, with all its different ways and customs. Casablanca was not very exciting – an odd mixture of a European/African mélange. The great modern cathedral, white, as its name indicates (*casa* house, *blanca* white), its shape slightly reminiscent of the one in Palma, Mallorca. The side streets were filled with orange trees, but much of the fruit had fallen on the ground. We could not understand why no one picked it until one day, daringly, we picked one up and bit into it, but oh, the bitter taste! Our question was answered.

The people, when not aping European dress – usually in the poorer parts of the city – were so picturesque, with their long, usually brown *djallabas* and yellow, very soft leather slip-on slippers, the back of them invariably lying flat under their heels. The women were in their *haiks*, which cover the head and body, their faces hidden by veils, which only leave their large dark beautiful eyes to convey their expressions.
It is a great cosmopolitan, soulless city, that never seems to gel together: white, clean and untouched by any culture, but certainly aiming to succeed in business.

We went to the *souk* one day, an intriguing venture. There were stalls of so much, from plastic to old silver, in fact almost everything you could want, and much one coveted. We saw tumbles of necklaces, blue, orange and green, mixed with metal beads of all shapes with beautifully worked designs of geometric shapes, then enamelled and finished, often by a heavy amulet worked and again enamelled in the same glorious colours.

Inside the cathedral the Christmas decorations seemed incongruous. The Arabic script was everywhere, palm trees bowing in the wind outside the plain glass windows but, most of all, the crib, a rather gaudy affair, but as real to the congregation as our anglicised ones are to us.

This seemed a city that I could not personally come to terms with, ever – but?

We thought that we would take the short train journey to Rabat, the capital of Morocco and one of the four great royal cities of the country. We found that we could get there fairly easily and by going early in the morning would have a full day's sightseeing.

We booked our seats on a train recommended by the station and also bought return tickets. It was an interesting journey, watching the life being lived by people who rarely see tourists. They worked hard to gain a living in this hot land, but which nonetheless cultivates palm trees, apricots, roses – masses of them – and of course vegetables and cattle, a necessary commodity. There is much water in the High Atlas Mountains with their waterfalls and streams.

The train was modern and comfortable, the large windows permitting us some splendid views.

We were particularly interested in seeing the old buildings of Rabat, which is said to have many of the best. We made our way to the famous Chella Necropolis, which was built by the Merinides in the thirteenth century, and built on the foundations of the ancient Roman town of Sala. It is now a ruin, with storks nesting on top of its tower, as always an intriguing sight, for we seldom see these birds.

The famous Yacouth el-Mansour had in the twelfth century made Rabat a place of glory, with the most famous of all towers – the Hassan Tower – and a huge gateway. This is considered to be the greatest era of building in Morocco. The Tower has walls ten feet thick and is thirty feet high. You see it standing solidly and confidently, framed by the hot azure sky and lapped by the eternal scents of Africa.

After the snow scare in the newspapers the weather cleared and was perfect, thank goodness.

The city made a lot of leatherwork – pouffes, *babouches*, slippers and much more – in the most sensual soft leather in bright green, scarlet or yellows and tooled with gold designs. They are also matchless carpet makers; their sense of colour and design are particularly distinctive.

We next went to the royal palace. Passing its high walls we came to the entrance which took us into the grounds. No one was about, so we thought we would venture in, then nearer and nearer to the arched palace entrance. However, evidently the nearer and nearer was enough. Two military guards, dressed in colourful white, green and red uniforms, emerged with what, to us, seemed like rifles at the ready. As they approached us they asked what we were doing and why? We told them that we wanted to see their beautiful building. The men laughed, saying, 'We should not let you in but, as you have come so far and the King is away, follow us and you may see the inner entrance, and the interior of the hall of the palace, but no more.' What a treat – arched walls and a dim cool massive hall. How lucky we were to see that. We thanked them profusely and went on our way. The King lives here when in Rabat. Also the Government use part of the palace.

The mosques were beautiful. We were not allowed to enter them, but could walk around the gardens. Their shapes and colours were a joy to the eye; the sausage-shaped tiles of their roofs, often a glorious viridian green, under which one could see the intricately carved deep brown woodwork above the painted walls.

It is said of Fez, which we sadly had not time to see, that it is the most imperial of the royal cities: 'The pearl of the modern world, this is where, as in Florence and Athens, you come in search of a whole civilisation's treasures.'

We had brought some rolls with us, so made our way to the beach after seeing the mosques to have a quiet picnic, but – what a surprise – the rocky beach was strewn with rubbish and the rancid smells of everything unpleasant assailed our nostrils. No one was about except, in the distance, an Arab walking at the sea's edge. It might have been better there, but the thought of making our way over this unpleasant matter was more than we could contemplate. We later found a clean, odourless spot of grassy ground to have our much needed meal. Then, truly restored, we went over and entered the old *medina*, again, both to see the *souk* and to look at the beautiful white-washed building so reminiscent of Spain. We learnt that, in fact, in the seventeenth century the Andalusian corsairs had taken over and had built this *medina*. They were the Muslims from Spain, daring adventuresome men.

The *souk* was a delight, as always, and a temptation: spices and herbs in abundance. I was greatly tempted, but what would I do with them here, and they were not packed for travelling. Here too we sat with some Arabs and drank hot sweet mint tea, poured from one of their magnificent silver-like metal teapots, with its long neck and bulbous body. How lovely it was, cooling one's thirst, and talking to these most interesting hawk-nosed, handsome men, of all ages and types. It had been a long hot day. We had seen all the most important sights and decided to take an earlier train back to Casablanca than the one recommended.

We arrived at the station to be told that a train would be arriving shortly. On arrival it looked very full. However, we clambered on, the porter helping us up the rather steep step. We went down the corridors looking for a seat. This turned out to be a risky business. All we saw – and felt – were curtained compartments, the curtains being held back by lascivious looking Arabs, whose multi-hands, or so it seemed, were trying to pull us in, presumably to sit on their laps – there was no other space. We hastened on, but the whole train was the same. In desperation we stood by one of the exit doors. The wind had come up, cutting in its intensity, and also, for the first time, rain. The doors had no glass, so we became frozen and weary with standing. A train attendant came up the train punching tickets, looking in horror when he saw these two bedraggled females. He took me by the arm and tried to push me into one of the overcrowded carriages, where again the many arms and grinning hopeful faces lashed out at me. I pulled away from the ticket collector, who looked in surprise at my refusal to take up his kind offer of... a knee? He shook his head and went on his way.

This journey took much longer than the first one. The train was old, its compartments rather like stalls with seats, plus a curtain, rather dirty, over the door. We arrived in Casablanca dishevelled with the wind and rain.

Using some of our precious money on a taxi, we reached our hotel and warmth. The adventure left us with stiff painful necks which seemed immovable for several days, but it was worth it in hindsight.

Our schedule was now a visit to Las Palmas in the Canary Islands. Las Palmas itself was seedy, dusty and unkempt, its gimcrack buildings nodding against each other. Luckily now and then it surprised one with delight – a beautiful old Spanish façade faced with ornately carved wooden balconies, dutiful to its Canarian past. The more modern part, with its multi-storeyed hotels, was like an unmade up jigsaw of inferior materials.

The beaches were of a mouldering texture, destroying the flow of the pounding, indifferent sea and fronted by shops filled with an extravagance of cheap gifts, supplying – one supposes – these large stifling hotels that house some of the more minor brains of those who travel for the sake of – the Joneses?

Outside this town lay a most beautiful unspoilt island, with trees darkly shadowing the lush green profusion of growth. The lovely quilting of tomato fields decorated the landscape like an eighteenth century embroidered coverlet.

The Duchess of Arucas was the fabled queen of the banana plantations, which highlight this area near the centre of the island and with its pockets of large luxuriant growths, trees of mighty girth, omnisciently guarding the fertile massed fruit – bananas. Nearby there is the grandly ornate cathedral of Arucas, standing sedately against the ever blue sky – or rather almost ever; it rained well and truly one day while we were there.

On our voyage of discovery we passed an extinct volcanic crater, the Caldera, which plunges from the side of a winding road, looking like an old wound in the side of a wounded tiger. It houses a harmless one-cowed farm, we were told; ancient fertile lava luxuriated the growth of their crops. This is the area of hills and the large wine-producing industry. How lovely vines look, with their small child-like trunks and splayed branches. This is also an island of deep gorges, mountains and vegetation.

We then went into the hills to the Santario de Nuestra Señora de la Nieves (shrine of Our Lady of the Snows). This small white seventeenth century church has the most beautiful Canarian balconies, indigenous to the country. Sadly we had no transport to get us to this exact spot, but one of our tours took us to the Playa Las Nieva. Eerily shafting sunlight gave an ominous atmosphere to its troubled sea, which was surrounded by black silent hills, overhung by statically living clouds; a study in perpetual blacks and greys.

There was also a rum factory set into the hills and the ever interesting sugar cane plantations. It is certainly a bountiful island, away from its capital.

Hiding in one fold of a central mountain is the browny-green town of Teror. Its delightful old Canarian whitewashed houses slope down the narrow street to the tiny tree-massed square. There sits, hunched in on itself, the lovely Basilica of the Pines (Notre Dame du Pino), shadowed and secret until entry, then, high in an arched aperture above the altar, dazzling the eyes, Our Lady sits resplendent and brilliant, jewelled and glittering with unaccountable wealth, jewels given and dressed by the rich and poor alike. No lock or key guards this immensity of wealth, only the presence of God. In this present time this might not safeguard the treasures, I am afraid. This church was built to commemorate the appearance in 1481 of an effigy of the Virgin in the branches of a pine tree.

Our coach then took us away from this town: small winding roads (never a Roman here!), eucalyptus trees with their tangy smell, reminiscent of nurseries and colds. Again the landscape was lush.

We stopped for a drink and lunch, a welcome break as we had been going for several hours. When we returned to the coach with the scuffling and shuffling of those of us settling into our seats a peasant-type man arrived in the coach swathed in rugs for sale. No one bought any. He shouted in thick Canarian English, 'Where do you come from?'

When we answered, 'England,' he turned in disgust, shouting back at us, 'Oh that Wilson! No one has money.'

Wilson of course had cut our money to the £50 limit, and even this uneducated peasant, on top of a fairly deserted mountain in Las Palmas, was affected, an amusing episode.

Money really was short for all of us travellers, but we were lucky at one point. A friend of ours in England, Gillian Charde, had a Dutch friend who ran a very smart small pizza bar (rather unusual in those days in Las

Palmas). Gillian had written to tell her of our coming and to ask if she would give us dinner one evening in her bar. In return we were to give her the same when she visited Bristol, which she eventually did, I am glad to say.

We found her little restaurant with no trouble and introduced ourselves. What a delightful person she was. The décor of the dining room was charming. To give height to the small area she had had the ceiling painted a deep sapphire blue, pock-marked by small stars, then under that a wooden trellis across the whole area. About two feet beneath this pseudo-sky climbed a dark shiny vine, with its clustered green grapes. One felt one was out of doors.

We had a most delicious meal. Pizzas are so variable, but she was known far and wide for her prowess in that field. She sat with us for a little while. The place was full, so she did not have much free time. She told us that she had a young brother and sister, from a very poor family (they were aged about eight and nine) to do the washing up for her when they had finished their day's schooling. Several weeks before Christmas they had asked her if they could have all the empty wine bottles (you could get money back on them) as they wanted to buy their Mother a present. She told us that she had willingly assented, watching them each evening staggering out with their load. After Christmas when they returned to work she asked them what they had bought as a present for their Mother. Their faces fell. Apparently when she saw them arrive home with the money she had taken it from them, saying that if she did not have it there would literally be no food in the house over Christmas. The result was that they could eat for Christmas, even if it were a spartan meal.

She also told us that she had many Swedes eating in her bar. Apparently Sweden was very good in that, whenever the poorer factory workers were tired, depressed or unwell, they sent them to Las Palmas to recover – a marvellous idea, but they forgot that they did not have the money for food. The pattern as always the same. Two would come in, order one meal but two lots of cutlery, and that was their meal for the day. At least they returned home rested and fitter, even if hungry.

There was one particularly handsome building in the town. It looked like the town hall. Outside, guarding it, were two stone dogs well over life size. Flanking the entrance, they represent the Canaries, as *cana* means dog and not canaries!

It was a pity that the shore was so unappetising, but I understand the whole place has now been thoroughly modernised and cleaned up. The island is a great attraction for tourists as the weather is warm all the year round.

The last place where we ventured was Maspalomes, at the most southerly tip of the island. We took a coach, which meandered for an hour through the countryside. This sand-swept desert is said to have 350 days of sunshine in the year and is where the expected camel never arrives over the windy waste of grey sand dunes. We hired a couple of deck chairs, decrepit and wobbly, and cheered ourselves up with an ice cream cone. Again, I believe they have tarted up the place, and imported camels to give credence to their desert image.

The Gran Canaria was well worth a visit. This Island of Dogs – *cana*, as I have already said – leaves their statues to court their worth outside the often black, dirt caparisoned buildings of note, a wayward spreading of fame.

We flew back to Casablanca ready, at last, to go to our main goal, Marrakech.

The train journey to Marrakech, many miles, was fascinating. We had large picture windows on this smooth express and also, to our joy, air-conditioning. We passed, amongst much else, a fabulous camel market. These creatures, with their very superior look, flared nostrils and wide eyes with long filmstar eyelashes, seem almost like beings from another planet. They were restlessly moving around on their flat, soft circular feet, as the buyers took note. Some of a more relaxed nature were lying on the ground, gazing at the bustle with disdainful remoteness. The whole journey was a joy.

At last we reached Marrakech, the principal city of the eleventh century Almorabides. Our Moroccan tourist guide book had a lovely description of it. I quote: 'An oasis on the frontiers of the desert, a jewel at the foot of the Atlas Mountains, capital of Southern Morocco, and which gave the country its name.'

We took a taxi to the main part of the old town – red walls everywhere, no Reading High Street anywhere – tall date trees looking haughtily down at their green surroundings. The pavements were studded with orange trees, their perpetual fruit scattering the roads in gay abandon. The whole atmosphere assailed one: the Arab-laden contours, thrumming *souk* and *kasbah*, spice-laden dirt mingling with noise, history of the ages. Colour hit the eyes in strange discordant combinations, thrilling and stimulating, this half world of the *souks*. Candles nodded conversably with small lamps, which flicker in precarious existence, as do the penniless Arabs themselves, chattering mechanical rabbits unable to cease this burrowing existence. Vast warrens of clamouring life, the vivid yellow, green and scarlet soft leather slippers silently watching, to wean the passing foot from the murky dust. Fresh green mint titillating the nostrils, the eternal sweet tea, which links the barterers and buyers in a truced bond, relaxing the rich Arabic life of cushioned ease and shocking, with its incredible sweetness, the unaware tourist. This is a mirage city, stonily surrounded by arid Moroccan soil, burning under the tedious sun – Marrakech, its pinkly crenellated walls, like a baker's oven to the touch.

Superior tepid-green date trees are thrown into extra beauty by the black green brooding cypresses which guard the city's gardens. The wide streets themselves are like lace on a handkerchief. A thousand over-fruiting orange trees, so many that their fruit, falling abandoned, lie sweating their drops of tart globular juice where they lie. Deep orange, thick fleshy skins, pitted like the face of smallpox, their linings of white dry fur which had warmed the fruit as a child in the womb.

Women stroll, garbed in their black Arab habits (*haiks*), looking like badly upholstered armchairs, their black veils revealing only beautiful large impenetrable eyes. In one fairly empty part of the souk I saw a tall aristocratic looking man standing deep in thought. On his arm stood a passive, hooded hawk, its feet steady on the padded arm. I wonder where they came from.

A mysterious place, this Marrakech, thrown into relief by the majestic grandeur of the silent, snow-covered peaks of the range upon range of High Atlas Mountains.

Pink and patterned, the Koutoubia dominates the town and the deep blue sky, as it has done for eight hundred years, a straight and silent warning, mediating over the religious. Each of its façades has a different carving, showing up the designs done by the Almohads in the twelfth century. Nearby, also a holy reminder, are the famous Saadian Tombs, dust of kings, dust that all must become in death. Rosemary hedges – for remembrance – surround these vaulted repositories of the élite in this twelfth century *kasbah* mosque.

Every one of the tombs is plastered in intricate twinning blue, yellow, and black and white patterns, weaving, like life itself, endless designs, byways seemingly uncontrolled and lost, until the whole beauty of the pattern is ultimately revealed with its purpose. Storks stretch their mighty white wings from their nests on the high pink walls, the only life living with the lifeless. While there I picked a twig of rosemary – for remembrance. To my delight it still grows in my garden in Bristol, a reminder of the Saadian Tombs. I did the same at the beautiful monastery at Daphni, Athens, and from Jerusalem. All three grow happily, in peace together.

Clanging and raucous, cheek by jowl, is the great Djemma-el-Fna (Place of the Dead). What a misnomer for this ant-heap of perpetual motion, from the soft warm dawn until velvety night, the great world-famous market, a patchwork mazing its living with the excitement of the mundane: story-tellers of ancient tales, snake charmers, witch doctors, *blue men* (Berbers), the *G'laoua* and musicians. Round the rim of this exciting market square are entrances to the huge souk. We entered one of its darkly lit alleys, swarming with people. Here you can buy anything. It is a magnificent spider's web of money making, although the amounts changed rarely amount to much.

We arrived rather late in the afternoon, browsing through this incredible place for hours. Before we left, Ruth stopped to look at a narrow stall manned by a small ragged boy, no more, I should say, than eight years old. She was looking at their wooden stools and all else, taking her time. I was quietly standing watching. There seemed to be no adults in charge, so were presumably at home. As we eventually moved off, the young boy ran after me, pressing into my hand the short leg of a small stool, saying, 'For you.' Then with a beautiful smile he ran swiftly back to his post and carving. No money was exchanged or wanted. It was a marvellous gesture of friendship, the touching of nations. I was very moved and, to this day, always have it on my desk.

We managed to find our way out, having been told not to go without a guide, as it was so large and intriguing. However, luck was with us. We went once again at a later date, as Ruth wanted to go back to look at a beautiful silver bracelet she had seen on our first visit. As we were short of time we did get a guide, a tall lecherous Arab, who swung us through the alleyways, pinching my behind whenever he could. I said to Ruth, 'Please hurry,' but she was so engrossed with her various purchases she only half turned and absently asked, 'Why?' Like everything else in life, time went by. We eventually left the *souk*. The only reminder I had was a bruised bum.

The colours of this dim *souk* were staggering: again the piles of soft variously coloured slippers, pouffes, bags, stalls glinting with silver. The workmanship of the jewellery and belts was intricate and beautiful. The shafts of light that came from above caught the colours below. The many coloured dresses were like curtains of red, blue, yellow and anything else you could think of. Perfumes hovered in the slightly fetid warm air. Waterfalls of densely alive coloured wools hung from great racks, a feast of optic delight. We emerged again to the outside world of the Djemma-el-Fna, now set in the dusk of the hot evening, the intense sound of mingling voices, overhung by the vast dark blue sky and remains of a striking sunset.

We went to a café which overlooked this vast arena, treating our very thirsty selves to a drink of freshly pressed orange juice. The lamps were beginning to flicker on, small pockets of personal lights. Now too the music was coming from everywhere, the strange melodic strains of Africa and Islam, a haunting quality, Syria and Egypt contributing to the mixture of love songs, *salaran* clarinets and all those mysterious gay and melancholic rhythms of the Middle East. We were only sorry we never saw the *blue men* (Berbers) galloping in from their abode in the High Atlas Mountains. They only come now and then. To think this mass of life starts at six o'clock in the morning, only ceasing at three the next morning, every day of the year! The water sellers, brightly coloured in their red tunics embroidered with gold, have slung round their shoulders a long pad into which are hooked metal bowls, from which they give you their precious cold water to drink – for a fee. Their hats are large and conical. From the wide brims hang many four inch wool plaits, ending in tassels. Is it to keep the fly-life at bay? Under these hats they wear their white turbans, which hold the hat steady.

Another fascinating thing to watch in the souk is the tailor. He was sitting on a stool embroidering a long cream coloured tunic right down the middle of the front. Standing about a yard away from him was a teenage boy helping his father. The father was making a design down the front of the tunic, his thread and needle busy, while the boy stood about a yard away from him and every time the father made an incision the boy twisted the two long threads. The result was a beautiful long line of intertwining embroidery.

What is very evocative of the place too is the muezzin calling out to the people to pray to Allah several times a day. I believe that many are recorded now, but the feel remains the same. This is a wholly medieval world. I understand that Churchill said that Marrakech was the loveliest spot in the whole world.

One night we thought we would venture out to try a cultural evening's entertainment – belly dancing! We asked the hotel where to go. This hotel was good, well mannered and helpful. On the broad steps leading up to the bedrooms was a very large pottery Ali Baba's jar, full of delicious oranges. On it was perched a notice which read 'Take one whenever you pass', a tip we followed.

We tidied up for our evening, got a taxi (having asked the hotel beforehand how much it should cost) and ventured forth. The interior of the restaurant was delightful: one sat on couches or pouffes, with a low brass-topped table in front of one. The pouffes were covered with soft leather embossed or appliquéd in gold and primary colours. The décor was Arabic – drapes, rugs, scents and music.

We ordered our drinks, having eaten beforehand; it was too expensive at a place like this. I cannot remember what the drink was, but sweet and delicious is the memory. This is a Muslim, a no-drink country. We lounged on our cushioned sofa, relaxed and happy. Later the dancing began. The beautiful dancing girls wore lovely bras and long, full, low-slung gauzy skirts; their feet were bare but the ankles were adorned with bracelets. The exotic music and the supple movements of the hips and bellies were soporific, the footwork was minimal. It was worth coming to see this show, although some might have called it touristy.

Our cab came back for us at the correct time. On arriving at our hotel the driver demanded twice the price agreed. We refused, he demanded. We were beginning to get annoyed, so we went in and asked the hall porter to help us. He shrugged his shoulders, saying, 'Pay him.' There was no way out; reluctantly we paid him to save having any trouble. We were not paying an exorbitant price, after all.

The other place we wanted to visit was the foothills of the great silent snow-capped High Atlas Mountains. These mountains have never been conquered. The Romans failed and right up to the present day it is so; they remain inviolate.

We were defeated too, but by the buses. Huge long vehicles crammed incessantly with Arabs (for whom, after all, they were run) clinging even to the door rails, their feet on the entrance step. The roofs were filled with enormous bundles of cloth bags, though I can't imagine what was in them.

We took a taxi, bartering with the driver for a favourable price, and eventually we set off. Occasionally we could see a small village squatting on the red slopes of the mountain.

They themselves are the same red with square, flat-roofed dwellings huddled together in the intense heat, the cloudless blue sky like a blue sheet enfolding them. At this distance we could see no life. Our taxi never took us through a village. No doubt their smaller roads led to nowhere else. Our road was arid, with no flowers or growth of any distinction.

Eventually we arrived at a viewpoint, so beautiful, looking down over the way we had come and back over the higher slopes of the towering backdrop of these silent, unforgiving mountains. If only one had had time to explore even the high meadows and plateaux one could, I understand, have seen some lush vegetation. There are many rivers and waterfalls in the High Atlas, irrigating the lower slopes, which have palm trees, apricot trees and many other plants, masses and masses of roses, one of the joys of this country. I have read that it takes one ton of rose petals to make one litre of their famous rose extract.

We made for a small hut selling cool drinks, sitting on weather-worn chairs. What a breath-taking view. Our driver said that he would get our drinks for us. Gratefully we accepted, telling him to join us. However, he refused, and having served us went and sat on a solitary hillock nearby. We sat quietly immersed in the silent splendour of the place, the *champagne* air wafting through these lower slopes, also of the many peoples who had inhabited the place – Africans, Saadians, Phoenicians, Romans, Almoravides, and so on, down to the present day. This stream of cultures mingles down through the bloodstreams of the people themselves.

At last we started back. The sun would begin to set, then very quickly enveloped us in darkness.

As we started down the long tree-shrouded road there suddenly appeared several small Arab boys in their long *djallabas*, and clutching in their hands beautiful hunks of

A Short History of Morocco

1,000,000 BC	Origin of mankind in Africa, south of Casablanca, a million years ago
3,000 BC	Neolithic man – the Berbers, a word of Greek origin
1,000 BC	Phoenicians
146 BC	Rome
	Vandals – Byzantines
	Berbers
632	Death of the Prophet Mohammed
682	Ogba ben Nafi – conquered one part
705–710	Mousa ben Nassir – conquered the south
789	The Idrissids and Moulay Idriss – the latter a grandson of the great prophet
1042–1147	The Almorabides
1071	Youssef ben Tachfine
1147–1248	The Almohads
1248–1554	The Merenids
15th century	Portuguese Kingdom – began in certain parts
16th century	Portuguese – nearly complete control of Morocco
1554–1665	The Saadians – took Marrakech and southern Morocco
1682–1727	Moulay Ismail
18th & 19th centuries	Decline
1912	The French Protectorate
1956	Independent Morocco

amethyst rock. These are easily found, we heard later, in the slopes where we were. They shouted to us, gesticulating with their rocks, for us to stop. This we did. It was like a swarm of puppies around our legs. As we got out of the car they were trying to sell the amethysts to us. The prices were ridiculously small, but so was our money at that point. Our holiday was near its completion, we were leaving in the morning for London. One could have bought huge chunks of pure amethyst rock for about fifty pence. What a temptation! Still, with only sixpence to spare, I bought a beautiful small piece for that price. When I returned home I got a jeweller to set it for me. I told him to leave it uncut except for the top, which he levelled. Then, with the gold from an old ring, he made me a most unusual pendant, which I wear to this day and which is always admired when I do so.

Tired but happy we arrived back at our hotel. The food was good, as was all the food we ate anywhere in the town. The Arabic flavours are delicious and aromatic: couscous pots, with their conical lids and double pots, lovely cinnamon aromas, their haunting smells and tastes; many vegetables cooked in the lower part of the couscous pot, drowning all in the tastes of the whole. The most used meat is lamb, done succulently on charcoal. Their pastries, as in Greece, are often made with honey and almonds. The most delectable one is called *cornes de gazelle* (gazelle's horns). The great drink offered to one in shops – whilst bartering – and cafés and even socially is mint tea, served from a tall silver-like metal jug, which has a domed lid, then a neck, which leads to a large bulbous base curving to its flat base. They take handfuls of very fresh mint, stuff it into this glamorous pot, pour in boiling water and an inordinate amount of white sugar but oh, how delightful as a thirst quencher. It is, as always, given with much kindness and courtesy, and often free of charge.

We were leaving early next morning. The only consolation about the hour – six o'clock breakfast – was that everyone had told us that we must not miss the fabled sunrise over the snow crested High Atlas. We were lucky as our bedrooms faced that way. Our breakfast arrived; we speedily arose to be confronted with a miraculous sight. The whole of the sky was a deep pink, staining the snow and outlining the lingering black clouds, colouring and edging the sharp peaks and slopes. What a wonder, and to think we might never have woken so early to witness this glory.

We had to get rid of all our dirhams as we were not allowed to take any of their money out of the country. I had a certain amount left, so said to Ruth that I would spend them in the duty-free shop. We were to fly home from Marrakech.

We duly arrived for our plane. It was bitterly cold at that hour, and of course we were high up. Looking around, we seemed to be standing in a large earth-covered field. No airport building was visible, only a largish hut, which in fact housed the customs and passport office – not a shop in sight and me clutching my precious dirhams! Being a Scot I did not like losing out on money. I gave in my passport and was told to wait. Everyone else went through and were having their baggage opened and well searched. They were still discussing my passport. In those days this often happened for, although my passport was British, all my details had been to do with Malaya where I was born. Not a word was said to me, but eventually a group of officials decided that I was harmless, and so returned my documents. The customs men had been very busy; most people had now moved on. When I turned up with my suitcase they took one jaundiced look at it and passed me through – plus my dirhams.

Chapter Eight

Ceuta

1968

The only other time I have visited Morocco was from Algeciras.

We were touring Spain and thought we would go to Gibraltar for a day. I had never been there but, a few days before leaving Britain, a ruling was brought in that no one could go to Gibraltar from Spain. This was all to do with the British not ceding back what Spain thought was rightly her territory. We had heard that there was one way we could get there from Algeciras, so I went and asked an official at the harbour. He smiled broadly and said 'Yes.' Then there was a long laughing pause: 'Swim!' I did find out when his hilarity ceased that you could either sail to Tangiers and then return to Gibraltar or do the same from Ceuta. Tangiers was rather a long way, so we plumped for Ceuta.

The journey was a delight: a January hot sun, the sea blue and then, to crown it all, a shoal of dolphins started to leap around the ship. As usual, their faces had a look of sheer rapture. Their elegant bodies curved into the skies. Then, eventually and sadly, they felt they had done enough to entertain us and sped off.

We wandered around Ceuta, this hybrid town, Spanish and Moroccan in an uneasy mix. There was no outstanding feature that we could discern. We decided to return to

Spain. Gibraltar could be visited another time. We were not all that keen on an anglicised place – we could see England any day and even in the sun!

Chapter Nine

Germany

1960s

I did not go to Germany again until the 1960s. I cannot remember now the exact year.

I had taken up geology as a hobby (what a dreary word – hobby), going to the University of Bristol's extramural classes on the subject. Since childhood I had been fascinated by rocks; in fact ever since as a child I had found a lump of polished agate in our garden in Edinburgh.

Later on I also bought a monthly geological magazine called *Gems*. In one edition they were advertising a five day trip to Idar-Oberstein in Germany, one of the great rock-cutting centres of the world, and for only £35. It was by coach and the price covered board, travel and all excursions. What a tempting offer!

I rushed to my office in the Bristol BBC, looked at my diary and found that with a bit of juggling I could put my assistant on duty for the days I was away. Mercifully there were no plays on, no wig-fittings in London, no filming, just simple straightforward talk shows in the studio.

The magazine told me that I must be at Waterloo station by 6 p.m. on such and such a day. I was to stand clutching my *Gems* magazine, so that they could identify who was on their trip.

I waited, my heart beating somewhat. Who would be on such a trip? Soon someone came up to me, telling me the platform to wait at to join the Dover train, and that when we arrived there would be their coach waiting to take us down and on to the ferry.

I duly got into the train. In my comfortable compartment were a couple from New Zealand – still clutching their *Gems* magazine – and a tall nice looking man, also a *Gems* holder. We started talking; how pleasant they all were. The couple had read about this trip in the New Zealand edition of the magazine, been thrilled by the prospect of the holiday and booked up immediately.

After the ferry crossing, which was tiring, half-lying on a fairly hard seat, we clambered out and on to our coach – 3 a.m., sleepy but excited. The two New Zealanders sat in front of me and the single man came and sat next to me; interesting, as he knew all about this part of the world. We drove through a sleeping Belgium, with their overly neat lace curtains and spotless streets. We were to stop in the outskirts of Brussels for breakfast; so welcome, hot strong coffee and freshly baked rolls and butter. It also gave us a chance to meet some more of our party. Two were actually from Bristol; they ran a 'rock' shop in Gloucester Road – a strange coincidence.

Our next stop was to be Luxembourg, for lunch. On arrival there it was tipping down with rain. No one knew where to find a meal. It was Sunday and everything seemed to be closed, so although we were all hungry they decided to press on into Germany and stop at Trier.

We four stayed together for the rest of the trip. This started with our companion, who seemed to know the city well, saying 'follow me' and taking us to a beautiful restaurant, where he was greeted as a well-known customer. Chairs were pulled out, coats taken and menus brought. The food was excellent, accompanied by a delicious wine, chosen by him. In an hour we staggered back to the coach replete. Trier looked such a fascinating place that I was determined to return one day in the future.

Eventually we arrived at Idar-Oberstein, which in fact is two small villages joined up through their interest and employment in rocks and gem cutting.

It is a most beautiful small medieval place, in the mountains. Seemingly every second little shop was either selling the most interesting rocks, or rock-cutting equipment. There were also two museums and two skyscrapers, so incongruous! One was our hotel, the other belonged to the international jewellers, Ruppenthal.

These two villages, Idar and Oberstein, in the old days had quarried for agate in their hills, which were so abundant that the avid hunters found it eventually ran out. So many years of a steady job, finding, cutting and polishing, had ceased. Once the source had dried up they were becoming destitute, but after a while they found that South America had large sources of this stone. A deal was made, America would sell to Idar-Oberstein, which would then cut, polish and sell the rocks. The two little towns joined up and ever since have had one of the great names in the rock-cutting world.

We had lunch in the hotel next day; the dining room was on the twentieth floor. What a view over to the mountains, and the beautiful valley we were in, more mundane, but oh what delicious food. As we were setting off soon after lunch, I left the dining room before the others so that I could collect my camera, and so on from my bedroom. I got in the lift. Horror, it would not move and the door would not open. I had seen a play on TV several days before where a woman suffocated through lack of air in a broken-down lift! I rang the emergency button, a disembodied voice answered in a flood of German. My German vocabulary had vanished so I answered in English. More German flooded back over the tannoy, but I remained stuck and unmoving. More people were now coming out of the dining room. On hearing my frantic voice in the lift, those who knew me spoke, saying that they would wait and talk to me until I was released. Luckily I could hear them quite clearly. This they did, to my relief, as it took about twenty minutes.

The next place we were taken to see was a rock-carvers' factory, fairly small but very busy. There we saw them carving and polishing the rough rock; it was fascinating. We were then taken on to a small house, where the whole family worked on the preparation of rocks. It was so interesting to see it all being done on a small scale. There was a box of discarded polished rocks, all small, but beautiful. They were for sale at a modest price. I bought a delightful small piece of amethyst still attached to some of the country rock that it came from. Its colours were so beautiful. It is still a great treasure. I was fascinated seeing the dedication and love that these people put into their work and lives. Nowadays gem rocks of every type are bought and worked on.

We were then taken to a huge rock museum, near our hotel. Shelves and shelves of these shining, glinting rocks, many the size of a football, many even larger. They were so delicately lit, in this white-walled and shelved gallery, that their shapes, glorious colours and inner glow took one's breath away, and how staggering to think how these magnificent rocks evolve under the earth, and how perfectly structured, each to its own shape – in fact as we are. We spent many a long hour there, totally absorbed.

The following day we were taken to the other skyscraper building, where the famous Ruppenthal has its roots. These jewellers are established in all the main rich cities in the world such as Monaco, Paris, London, New York, etc.

One was taken round by a guide; each group had no more than about six people. We were, after all, looking at vastly expensive jewellery. We went first to the basement, where the large boulders of seemingly dull grey or brown rocks lay in silent splendour on the floor. When opened up, these would produce anything from rubies to agate, or in fact, to the uninitiated, anything of value.

The second floor was where rocks of a minor value, like agate, tourmaline and so forth, were carved and polished. The floor here and in the following floors had displays of jewellery one could buy as well as the exhibits, and here I spied a beautiful multi-coloured tourmaline necklace, each smallish bead in it so natural a shape and most beautifully polished. I was tempted by these lovely necklaces, but we had to move on to the next floor. Each floor had ever more precious stones; the second top one being filled with emeralds, rubies and such like, but it was the very top one that had the crème de la crème – diamonds – their interweaving rainbow colours reflecting in this huge brilliantly lit area. The cutting was so intricate and faultless, done by these superlative craftsmen. The room seemed like a shining heaven of colours in spite of the colourless stone.

With that we had to make our way down and leave. As we were departing we were told that we could come back any time and be taken to see anything we were interested in buying, a personal visit.

That night I went to my bedroom fairly late. I tidied up the mass of papers that I had collected – guides to museums, instructions on how to polish rocks, the history of Idar-Oberstein and much else. Eventually I thought I would have a shower and go to bed in this very expensive, glamorous hotel. I pulled the lavatory handle. It came away in my hand, but worse still the rushing water continued to flood down the lavatory pan. That would not have been so bad, but the noise was tremendous in this sleeping hotel. I rang the receptionist several times. No answer. I certainly was not going to try the lift on my own in these early hours and after my previous experience so I showered and went to bed, trying to sleep through this torrent of liquid sound. It was to no avail. Eventually I got up again but still no answer on the phone. I got out my small metal nail file and started working at the hand fixture. About half an hour later bingo. I don't know how, but I managed to stop the water running. Oh the blissful silence.

Next morning at breakfast my New Zealand friends, who had the room next to mine, said, 'We do hope that you too were not kept awake last night by some lunatic who left a water tap on half the night.' I thought I had better own up and tell the whole sorry tale and explain that in fact it had not been my fault.

On the next day we were free to do as we wished, so I made my way back to Ruppenthals. The young woman guide who had taken us round the day before saw me and came forward, saying with a smile, 'I thought you would come back.' She took me up to the tourmaline necklaces. Luck was on my side. I could just afford the one that I had coveted. When I took out my traveller's cheque and signed my name the girl laughed and exclaimed, 'You have the same name as me. I am Gisella.' She looked delighted and said in a whisper, 'I expect you need a fastening on the back of the necklace. We do not provide that but, as we share a name, I will go and ask the workshop to put one on for you.' No extra charge was added. It was a happy ending to the Ruppenthal visit.

As everyone had gone on their own that day we had decided, my three friends and I, that we would all meet up for dinner that evening. I had had a fulfilling day, for after Ruppenthals I had explored this fairytale town set in the mountains and decorated by a necklace of a river. The time had flown. What a marvellous visit it had been.

The next day the coach took us back to the ferry – Ostend–London – where we all said a sorrowful goodbye in, of all glamorous places, the station buffet.

The German people were, as always, lovely to us, as I have always found them. Yet every now and then one had a shiver of the dark tormented past, which many of them themselves had had to suffer. It intruded into the peaceful present. Gradually I forgot their horrific past and over the meals remembered the good of the majority of this race.

I will visit Germany again one of these days, I am sure.

*

My third visit was in 1986. By now I was married to Geoffrey Beauchamp, who, apart from being a wonderful man, also shared my passion for Greece.

This year we motored there, taking two weeks to get there, a month there and two weeks on our way back to enable us to sightsee as we went.

Chapter Ten

Germany

5th April 1986

We entered Germany from Luxembourg and made for Trier. As I have already said, I had been there and determined to re-visit it. My husband had never been to Trier. We planned the journey so that we could visit several places that we had always wanted to see and explore.

Trier is fascinating, as I had thought from my very quick visit before. The Basilica of Constantine, a building of great stature and sophistication, was actually built by Constantine in AD 310. It is 239 feet long, 93 feet wide and 108 feet high, before the over-decorated Gothic period and so much more telling with its great splendid lines and columns; mercifully, any later additions have not detracted from the whole. There seemed to be architecture of every period. The font was a modern iron design on an ancient capital, sunk slightly below the main floor; the floor itself was covered with mosaics simulating waves done in silver. All this was modern, as was the lovely pulpit, also covered with mosaics. There seemed to be every period blending into this ancient edifice.

Outside was an organ grinder drawing a happy crowd. How sad we never hear them now in Britain. It reminded me of my childhood. It was good to see the old Roman brickwork in many buildings, superbly restored so as not to spoil the whole.

Trier is said to have been there in 205 BC, the oldest town in Germany. It dates from 2,000 BC as a proper town, built by Prince Trebata, son of an Assyrian queen, who arrived and named the place Treberis. There is a very old house in the Hauptmarkt, which bears the inscription, '1,300 years before Rome stood Trier.' Diocletian made it one of his capitals; Constantine lived here for years, leaving his mark. When Rome collapsed it became an important centre for Christianity, and later one of the most powerful bishoprics in the Holy Roman Empire.

The Hauptmarkt is a lovely square, which has housed this market since earliest days. The market was in progress that day. I do so love them – stalls massed with many coloured fruits and vegetable and flowers, the bustle of happily chatting people, a world-wide occupation. I asked one of the stall-holders if I could take a photo of her stall. She blushed, nodded and tidied her hair, then I was permitted to proceed. There is also a very ancient cross of AD 958 in this square.

We visited many of the sites. One was The Three Kings' (*Drei Magi*) house. The whole square is hemmed in by the most beautiful pale pink, blue and yellow painted medieval buildings, its centre massed with the stalls, no cars; it is a pedestrian precinct.

All around the town are fascinating Gothic fountains, of varying periods. We had to go to the bank to cash some traveller's cheques. Near the dark louring Roman Gate (*Porta Nigra*) was a bank. On entering it a young assistant beckoned us to her part of the counter. When we told her what we wanted she leant confidentially over the counter, whispering that they would charge us 10 *Deutschmark*, but that if we went to the City Bank they would only charge us DM 1! Furtively she pointed out the way to us. We thanked her profusely.

We then went to the *Dom* (cathedral), an incredible building, very Baroque, not my choice. The white interiors are beautifully light, but they are so overly ornate; however, it did have a beautifully carved tympanum over the side door.

We went to several museums, sampled lunch at the noted McDonald's, sitting in the sun in a corner of the square. Geoffrey bought a new camera, his old one having fallen and disintegrated.

We had spent so much on a gorgeous meal the first night so this day we went to a modest *Wursthaus* (sausage café). It is good to try the different strata of society, and this place was excellent. What an incredible slice of history this city is, holding a great fascination over one.

We drove next day to Augsburg, about 290 miles on. The weather was mixed, but much warmer. We saw many of the large Bavarian maypoles as we passed through the attractive villages.

We managed to book into the Bayerischer Hof, on the outskirts of Augsburg, and were treated to a massive spectacular thunderstorm. The city was built 15 years before Christ was born and again has a mixture of architecture. It seemed rather a forbidding place, grey stone and unyielding buildings.

It was Sunday and we went in search of the *Dom*, our main reason for visiting the town. We knew that it had the oldest stained glass windows in the world. We had been going to lectures on the subject and become intrigued. Always the name of Augsburg came up in connection with their well-preserved windows. We found the *Dom*, St Maria, on a site where an Episcopal church had stood during the ninth century. After its destruction, in which the tenth-century crypt had escaped and also these marvellous eleventh-century windows, they are of five so-called Prophets – Jonah, David, Hosea, Moses and Daniel.

On entering the *Dom* we found the service in full swing, accompanied by an orchestra. We slipped in at the side, hoping that the service was nearly finished. We were not proposing to stay another night here, so wanted to continue our journey soon. It was a beautiful large light church, partly owing to the fact that all the windows seemed to be plain glass – strange. The seats were full and many people were standing in the side aisles. We were in the south aisle and were quietly and deviously moving our heads around, but no stained glass. At long last the service seemed to end, a few worshippers moved out, we quickly moved back and round to the north aisle. The service started again and we still could not see the famous windows.

Then, looking high up in the clerestory, we spied the five figures, quite large, but easily missed because of this height. We managed to move by a pillar, a more discreet spot, and looked our fill. It certainly was well worth the visit. These were what is known as *figure windows*, a single figure in each one and usually in a rather awkward stance, and very definite faces. We had not known, but they are usually in the clerestory! They are also one of the great treasures of the German churches; few now remain.

The colour is striking, although they are sadly becoming eroded, as happens everywhere. Their fascinating hats are each different and in various colours, their robes the same; in each right hand is held the sign that signifies their name, a wide scroll inscribed in the other hand. This is of course in Latin and falls to the hems of their garments. To crown it all, their soft large coloured slippers, like those worn by knights, have jewelled tops. What a pleasure to see them. It is thought that there had been a longer series of these figures. The ones we saw were thought to be still in their original positions, an interesting point being that their colour is so different from anywhere else. These are not primitive pictures. They were done by clever artistic cultured artists. They had worked from the Abbey of Tegernsee, a noted group.

We wanted to buy postcards of the windows but the church did not have any and sent us to a private house nearby, where a young man opened the door to us, then brought a shoe box of cards for us to inspect. On buying some and being paid he smiled and slammed the door shut. We could smell delicious food; we had disturbed his meal.

We then went through the quiet Sabbath streets of the old housing estate, known as the Fuggerei. The Fugger family had given money, in medieval times, for homes to be built for the less rich. They were likened to the Medici family in Italy.

Three famous people came from Augsburg: Hans Holbein the Elder, Leopold Mozart, father of the famous Wolfgang Amadeus, and Bertolt Brecht.

We now had to hurry, as we were making our way to Austria that day.

Chapter Eleven

Austria and Germany

8th May 1986

We arrived in Salzburg in the afternoon, having asked the tourist office outside the city to book us into a cheap hotel, and one from which we could easily walk to the sights. My hip had not been operated on yet. It was a folksy-type place, very clean, and provided a good breakfast of delicious hot strong milky coffee, cheese and rolls.

At breakfast we discussed whether we should now go through Italy to Greece, instead of Yugoslavia. The Chernobyl Cloud was passing up through Europe but, before we could decide, the news came through the radio that it had now hit Italy as well and was over Yugoslavia. The only sign we saw of it during the whole of the rest of our holiday was a persistent light mist.

We walked over the bridge to the old town, a marvellous medieval place with narrow streets, large squares and old world wrought-iron signs outside the shops in the Getreidegasse. These signs depict what the shop sells. They are now rather worn, looking even more attractive, becoming works of art. Even McDonald's has one!

We went first to the most famous place – Mozart's birthplace – a thought-provoking house, full of the atmosphere of his age. The architecture had been retained, a wooden interior, narrow stairs, panelled rooms. There was an exhibition in progress. It had many of the sets used in Mozart's operas over the years and coming up to our age, including some by Chagall, others by Oskar Kokoschka for *Die Zauberflöte*. We struggled up and down the narrow highly polished wooden staircases. It seemed as if the world and his wife had joined us there.

While Geoffrey continued his sightseeing I went to one of their typical cafés. This particular one was just near Mozart's house. You again climbed up a narrow wooden staircase, which led into a large panelled low-ceilinged room. Again, what an atmosphere! Its small paned glass windows, through which the sun poured, looked on to the narrow crowded street that I had just left. Inside were many tables and many people, but not overcrowded. It seemed to be a leisurely place, many of the men were lounging on their brown wooden benches with a stick on to which was strung a newspaper. I then noticed there were many newspapers of this type and which anyone could borrow. There were also many students, in deep discussions; the University was quite close. I took my time, feeling I was in another period.

After my coffee I went through a narrow archway which led on down a lane with the most lovely shops, again small and old, buying some postcards as I went. The temptation to buy more, and some books in a Dickens-like shop, was tremendous, but everything was so very expensive. This lane led me into University Platz, where there is the Kollegienkirche (collegiate church), a monster of Baroque art. The square was also filled with market stalls, hundreds of them filling up most of the central space, a riot of coloured fruit and vegetables, the happy incessant chatter of voices and laughter and where the church chimed out its hours. I was intrigued by the varied amounts of fruits and vegetables from many countries. This was May, but there seemed to be some of any species you could think of. Again

I was tempted to buy, but what would I do with it? One can only eat a certain quantity of fruit per day!

I then walked down a narrow street which led me to the Cathedral Square (*Domplatz*). The Cathedral was a huge dirty stone building. On going inside I found it was the usual Baroque style, everywhere white and gold, lit by many bright lights and ornamented over all. Its great bronze doors are one of its special features. It too was filled with tourists. I had arranged to meet Geoffrey there and then lunch.

We were on our way to lunch when we saw the notable *Pferdeschwemme* (horse fountain), a large light-hearted bit of sculpture, the large horses galloping (or so it seems because of the moving water) around in the spray, which has been caught by the sun, turning much of it into tiny rainbows.

After lunch it started to rain, but we made our way to the Cathedral Museum, which had only opened that day for the season. It was well worth going; so many of these priceless treasures were beautiful, but the rest unbelievably awful. Each to his own taste, I suppose. There was a marvellous cope with embroidered scenes and a cross on the back, a bluey/red material and embroidered mainly in blues, greens and gold. This was a large museum, which had probably been the bishop's palace at one time.

Geoffrey's walk to the Castle earlier had been a stiff climb, but well worth it for the fine view of the city, with its *Dom* in the foreground. There was a funicular which takes you up to the Castle itself, thank goodness.

That evening we made our way home, going through the Mirabell Gardens on the right side, then crossed the footbridge. The river under us was very fast flowing, but the swans and ducks were paddling away in a backwater, like rather grand ladies.

We had a rest at our hotel, bathed and then went dinner hunting. We had the meal both nights at the Wolf-Dietrich.

Geoffrey spied it, close to our hotel. It looked rather mysterious from the street, but had a good menu display. We went downstairs and found a delightful smallish area, lit by pink candles, looking in fact very Edwardian at its best. A rather stern elderly waitress came forward in her black dress and gleaming white starched cap, apron and cuffs. She showed us to a table, and there we had the most gorgeous meal.

As I said, the next night we thought we would return there. On entering, our stern waitress (the only one there) rushed forward with a smile, quietly telling us she had a table for four for us alone, that she would not put anyone with us. When we were leaving, she followed us to the door, saying what a great pleasure it had been to have us (we had told her we were leaving next day) and she told us that the woman who came to relieve her at ten o'clock had not arrived and, as her husband had had a bad stroke, she was worried about getting home to look after him.

What an enchanting city Salzburg is, so much unspoilt, and so full of history. I would love to go back for longer one of these days, especially when the Mozart Festival is in progress.

16th June 1986

Our return journey was through Austria and Germany from Greece. We took a different route, so as to see more places that we had always wanted to visit.

It was raining for a while, but we so enjoyed the drive to the Rottenmanner Pass. We passed an impressive Baroque church front in St Andrea where an important funeral was in progress. There were so many people that they were half across the road; all were in Austrian dress, beautiful colours, candles on the coffin and priests walking beside it.

Approaching Bad Aussee, Geoffrey decided to divert to Hallstatten See to look for a *Zimmer*. We reached Obertraum and decided to try at No. 39. It looked so pretty, with its typical dinky type architecture. A pleasant woman showed us to our room. She spoke no English but was very friendly. Our room had a carved dark brown balcony, smothered in scarlet geraniums, the garden had grass waist high and was filled with wild flowers of all colours. We booked for two nights, and that evening took ourselves down the short road to an inn. We had an excellent dinner at this Gasthaus Hollwrit. Austria is a very congenial place.

The next morning we awoke and, having bathed in the communal bathroom (there was no one else staying there), went down to breakfast: a cold hard-boiled egg and toast but oh the delicious hot strong coffee! We looked out of the window and saw mine host scything down the grass, flowers and all, and winding it on to hayricks, which were shoulder high poles. As Geoffrey said, they looked like headless men. Our view was tremendous – just a few similar type houses, then fields shadowed by the huge jagged mountains, and absolute quiet.

We thought we would go to the Hallstatt See and spend the day resting beside it. It was like a mirror, the smooth grey silky surface unmoving in the morning haze. All around it were the high mountains, the nearer ones forested up to their peaked summits. The more distant, gaunt, uneven light grey giants, with pockets of snow nestling in their breasts, soared into the blue sky. An occasional cloud flirted with their heads, showing, light-heartedly, their power of consorting with such majestic grandeur.

Across the lake from where we sat under the trees Hallstatt town looked like a tiny village, its centre revealing itself by the tall sharp black spire of its church, with a flapped cap, the earpieces clasping the tower in an effort to hold the whole together. The little town was reflected perfectly in reverse in the water.

Every so often a small tourist steamer revved its way past, the echoing voice of a commentator coming clearly over the water. The *Hallstatt* was doing the conventional round, for those who wanted to see everything in half an hour.

On the road above us was an occasional burst of chatter, as large groups of young people were marched past on organised hikes. Running up the trees where we sat was a small sparrow-like bird looking no doubt for insects. It began at the foot of the trunk then, with amazing speed and agility, ran up the entire length of the bark until it reached the leafy branches. It then flew over to another tree, dived down to its base and repeated the performance. This happened with about six trees before it, apparently happy, flew off to a destination unknown to us.

Running around the lake edge and darting through the trees was a small girl dressed in the traditional Tyrolean costume. What a delight: her white puff-sleeved blouse, dusky pink pinafore dress and pink and soft green flowered apron. Her fair hair was in two plaits. You could hear her laughing and singing over to her parents, who too were dressed in their native costume. What peace in this secluded spot in the heart of Austria and to think that a whole culture came from here, still known as the Hallstatt period, 700–500 BC.

As we were leaving we suddenly saw a sculpture on the grass, at least seven feet tall, made of black metal. It was a man, possibly a tramp, his head bowed so that you had to lean close to look up at his face. With great surprise it was the most beautiful face I have ever seen; the warmth and comfort that radiated from it. One felt one would have loved to talk to this man, and gain wisdom.

Later on we went to the little town of Hallstatt. This town hangs on the banks of the lake, surrounded by the sheer uneven sides of the great Dachstein Mountains. As Alex V. Humboldt says, 'the most beautiful lakeside village in the world'.

We parked the car at the beginning of the tiny town, walked up a steep path that went high around the first part of it and was absolutely beautiful. The path was narrow and filled on one side with tiered old wooden medieval alpine type houses, massed as usual with boxes of flowers – flowers of every colour. We eventually reached the Heimat Museum, a very tall old stone house, six storeys, very interesting, mainly photos of the old days; all the labels were in German. The photos indicated that the salt-stone rocks were quarried in the mountains and carried down these paths, on a sort of wooden frame, supported on a cushion on the head and back, mainly by women. The prehistoric section was incredibly interesting. The Celts had mined here, long before Rome had been built.

We eventually came down to the most beautiful square I have ever seen – wonderland. The square was in fact a triangle, the point being at its top, where a beautiful old Tyrolean type hotel stood – how I would have loved to have stayed there. Its balconies trailed masses of flowers and leaves. We were weary, and it was very hot, so we went to a small open-air café where we ordered a lovely hot strong coffee from the owner, who was dressed, as so many were, in his *Lederhosen*. When he brought the coffee to us he asked where we came from. On hearing it was Bristol he sadly said, 'What a terrible time you had in the War.' We asked him if he had ever been there but, shaking his head, he said, 'No, but as a small boy I was always hearing of the great bombing in Bristol.'

Round the square were beautiful little shops. One sold Tyrolean dresses, which were hung round the doorway, full colourful skirts – blues, greens, pinks and soft browns – then the lovely flowery long frilled aprons and white crisp blouses. How I wished I could buy one, but my shape did not permit. This is a magical town. I will never ever forget it.

On our way back to Obertraum we sat and read for a while by the lake, but soon we heard great peals and rumbles of thunder. The rain started. We sat for two hours in our car as water poured from every direction. I have never seen such rain. It was flooding down into the Lake beneath us, the road being under water by this time. We were in a lay-by. It was quite an experience.

The next morning we were off to Germany again, exploring its *Romantische Strasse* (romantic road). We had a good journey through a long tunnel so as to avoid Hallstatt Town, over the mountains to Gosan, quite beautiful, then a magnificent drive for about thirty-four miles, with a high but easy pass. We skirted Augsburg, then started up the *Romantische Strasse* itself; rather dull at that point.

On arriving at Harburg, a lovely small medieval town with gabled houses, we booked in for the night at the Gasthaus Goldener Lamm, where our bedroom looked over the Wörtitz River, with its gushing weir and beautiful old stone bridge. The town itself was spick-and-span, its medieval buildings marvellous and covered with flowers.

The road we took the next morning lived up to its name. Although flat, it was highly cultivated. We went into Nöck, where the American astronauts trained. It has a crater about twenty-five kilometres across, left by a falling meteorite some fifteen million years ago.

Our next stop was at Nördlingen, a delightful medieval town. Its outstanding feature was its great Gothic *Münster*, St George, with its great Daniel Tower, where every quarter of an hour except between 10 p.m. and midnight it gives out the message '*So G'sell so*'. This custom comes from an incident during the Thirty Years War. The old boundary lines are circular streets with St George in the centre. The interior of the church seems vast; at the back was hanging a huge circular mirror, which gave a delightful view of the church. It has also many beautiful paintings. The whole church was so light and airy, owing to the plain glass windows. In fact, through the mirror the place looked like a golden ball, topped by its enchanting fan vaulting.

There were also some unusual carvings on the benches. One was of an old man and one almost wondered if it had been carved by Riemenschneider. His left arm is holding his tired old face, which looks far into space, the elbow leaning on a wooden table. The whole feel of the man was immediate. His other hand clasped a small pear, or some such fruit – a haunting carving in spite of its small size. It is fifteenth century. In the chapel was a smallish *Pietà*, the Virgin holding an almost horizontal Christ with His wonderful face. This is beautifully lit and solitary. It is also fifteenth century. According to history, this statue wept in 1494, during some cruel war.

Just before we started this trip we had seen on television a programme about one of the world's great woodcarvers – Tilmann Riemenschneider, a German working in 1460–1531, known as Germany's master of late Gothic sculpture, one of the greatest still. He was born in Oesterode, but lived, worked and died in Würzburg. From a very young age his work became renowned, with its miraculous detailed carving, flowing robes, grace of figures, face and his incredibly beautiful hands. Small as they are, each detail shows: bones, sinews, nails and the feeling of moving life. He became a councillor and then a Mayor of his city, but in later life he helped in the Peasant Revolt of 1513, was imprisoned, tortured then eventually released, but his body and spirit were broken. His most famous altarpiece (of which he did many) is the one now in the Kurpfälzischer

Museum at Heidelberg. The programme also told us that much of his work was to be seen in the medieval churches on the *Romantische Strasse*. There and then we decided that we must see some of them.

So our next stop was to be at Rothenburg-ob-der-Tauber, said to be the best preserved medieval town on the Continent.

What a breathtaking place. One seemed to move back in time. It was larger than any we had been to so far, but completely in period, though sadly filled with tourists (like myself!). As I could not walk far because of my hip, Geoffrey kindly went in search of the *Dom*. We had had to leave our car on the edge of the town itself.

As I sat on a stone bench waiting for him, I saw opposite me a most intriguing shop called 'The Christmas Shop'. Now this was June, so well away from that festival. I crossed over and entered. Again my breath was taken away. It was like walking into wonderland. The tinkly sound of music boxes playing carols, Christmas bells, softly moving in the slight air current, snow and silver flakes everywhere. It was on two floors. Walking forward in the shop one came to a few stairs. Looking down there was everything you could wish to decorate a Christmas tree – no tawdry cheap stuff, but beautifully carved small items, crackers, a large Father Christmas (not real!), and what seemed like thousands of visitors all buying. Many were American. The whole atmosphere was so geared that everyone was excited and you could hear happy spurts of soft laughter and talk. I could not wait long, as Geoffrey would have wondered where I was, so I sadly left this magic place, and even more sadly, later on, wished that I had bought one or two of their delightful tree decorations. Nothing cost too much.

We then went to the beautiful Jacobkirche to see Riemenschneider's *Heilige Blut* Altar. One had to go upstairs and there was this masterpiece. It was on a low plinth in the alcove with plain glass windows surrounding it. In front were many chairs, most of them occupied by silent viewers. What a sight. Its two doors were open, they too (certainly on the inside) carved. On one was the *Entry into Jerusalem*, on the other the *Disciples asleep and Christ praying on the Mount watched by many angels*. The main centre had a carving of Christ talking to his disciples, the faces showing all the different reactions to what he was telling them. Christ himself was half turned away from us, but a postcard I managed to buy showed his face filled with sorrow. Between the legs of the altar was a small Crucifixion scene, and above the whole a Gothic arched top, with several angels watching these tableaux. The plain glass Gothic windows were lovely. All were circles of glass the size of the bottom of a glass bottle, only smooth and clear, leaded together.

One could have sat forever. I have never been particularly keen on wood carvings, but this was brilliant. Riemenschneider carved many life-sized figures. These he did entirely himself, but all his altar pieces were done in his workshop, where he employed several assistants. With the mass of work he was asked to do he needed expert help.

We then went on to Creglingen, where we knew there was another of his magnificent altar pieces.

We stopped for tea in a magnificent lay-by; this lovely spot had tables and chairs as is usual in Germany; they excel in this area. We always carried a Primus stove, tea, coffee and water. We sat under the trees in the blissful heat – some of the churches had been quite cold. A rather muddy river flowed below us. We were surrounded by birds. We did not know what they were, but they were about sparrow-sized and at a distance could be mistaken for them. In fact they were much more delicate, with white and yellow and dark-brown striped wings, darker brown on the top of the head and down their backs. They had a greeny colour and were rather beautiful and delicate.

We arrived in Creglingen, looking for a *Zimmer*. No luck, but we found a very nice *Gasthof* called Herrgottstal. The only thing was that it was their *Ruhetag*, so there was no meal in the evening.

This was a small medieval town and by one of the gates of the city we found a delightful *Weinstube* beautifully decorated (even the ceiling was carved), run by a family. We had a delicious meal. After it the young waitress and young cook had a long chat with us – we were the only people there. They told us that they had only been open one and a half weeks. They both spoke very good English, the chef having travelled a great deal. We wished them well. They had only been open on this *Ruhetag* because they were trying to attract trade.

We found that everywhere in Europe there was now a lack of tourists owing to the Chernobyl disaster. People were scared of the effect it was having on them. I later on got cancer, from which I am happy to say I have recovered. Whether it was because of that or not I will never know.

The next morning we set off a mile down the road to visit the Herrgottskirche (church of our Lord, 1390), where there is another marvellous Tillman Riemenschneider altar piece. This is quite a small church, up some steps and into a darkish interior. There you sat on the pews to look at this staggering piece of carving. The altar piece stood, again on a plinth, on top of the two steps up to the altar and was much the most spectacular thing in the church. It is known as Mary's Altar or the Altar of Creglingen, done, as I have said, by Riemenschneider, not like the medieval shrine-altar design, but an artistic conception inspired, it is said, by the thought of the beauty of a monstrance holding the wafer. This again, as in Rothenburg, has a very Gothic top to the altar piece with the Virgin Mary rising. The Coronation of

Mary above her is the risen Christ and angels. The figures in the main group are an unusual idea, the death of Mary and also her welcome in heaven. The figures beneath her again have the most beautifully carved faces and hands, full of expression and life.

Another man of note in the whole of this area is Walther von der Vogelweide, who died in 1230. He was the most famous of the legendary German *Minnesänger*, in the twelfth to fourteenth centuries, poet-musicians who always composed and performed songs of courtly chivalry to the élite of the time. These scores are still around, although not performed to the general public.

★

When I was staying in Southern Germany with the Braunfels, just before the War, a group of their cultured friends sang these songs. They asked the Braunfels if they would bring their young English singer friend to see them, so that we could all sing these old songs of the *Minnesänger*. I had heard of them but had not sung any. It was with great excitement I anticipated the event. They all lived in Süssenmuhler, where I was. The Braunfels warned me that they, like themselves, had hardly any money, no passports and were very short of rationed food – which meant all food.

We arrived at the house of one of them, and where the others waited. It was a most memorable afternoon just singing these beautiful songs. We sang in four-part harmony. The friendship and kindness exuded from them and enhanced our singing. I felt I did not want the time to end. We then went into the dining room, where there was an enormous tea laid out on a beautiful polished table. I was speechless, for these people had denied themselves food for weeks to enable them to make this meal. Also many of their other friends had also contributed to the feast. The thing of honour was one of their national dishes, a large *Torte* filled with gooseberries and topped with latticework and cream. These *Torten* are scrumptious; one never gets one in England that tastes correct. The whole afternoon had been such a joy, an unforgettable memory of the kindness given by suppressed helpless people.

I was now thrilled to be in the part of Germany that was so instilled by the long-ago *Minnesänger*s, and especially Vogelweide. He himself had broken with tradition in that, instead of only writing and singing to the grand ladies of the land, he sang to many of a lesser class and also wrote political songs – manifestos. He must have been a great character for his work was full of thoughtful questioning, often amusing and as always lyrically romantic.

21st June 1986

We arrived at Königswinter, right on the banks of the great grey river of the Rhine, and found a very unpretentious *Zimmer* in Hauptstrasse. It was an odd-shaped house, run only by a fat elderly jolly man, who gave us *Frühstück* (breakfast) in the morning. We had a mammoth washing session, as we had a huge bath and boiling water. When we were finished the bathroom looked like a wash-house. However, all was well, our clothes dried and would do us for nearly the remainder of our journey.

Everywhere we went there was a hot sun, but also everywhere this strange mist from Chernobyl had travelled, we now understood even to Scotland, where you could not eat much of their lamb because of contamination.

We went and looked at the large barges towing other barges down the river, a perpetual slap of backwash against the river's front wall. Then went to the Ali Baba for supper

– indifferent, plus a jukebox grinding away nonstop. It was evidently run by Turks, who looked happy and were very friendly. We finished up on the water front, each having a large gorgeous mixed ice cream, and watching the evening strollers, barges and pleasure steamers.

We started early as we had quite a way to go, circumnavigating Köln so as to have a reasonable time for sightseeing in Aachen and to find accommodation for the night, as we had planned to leave for Belgium rather early the following morning.

Aachen is a fascinating town. One is apt just to think of it as an entry from Belgium into Germany. The town has an unusual feature, known as *drei Fenster* (three windows wide) façades in their residences, a residue of when Charlemagne, the great military ruler, 742–814, came to Aix-la-Chapelle, as it was called then. Charlemagne's father, with the fascinating name of Pepin the Short, settled there to take the waters, the sulphur springs which came down from the Eifel Mountains.

Charlemagne was instrumental in making Aachen the centre of the Holy Roman Empire and, after his coronation in Rome in 800, stayed for much of his time in Aachen, where he built an enormous palace and the *Dom* (the *Chapelle*), which is an incredible hotchpotch of a place, filled with priceless treasures. People such as Barbarossa gave the most splendid chandelier, now hanging in the chapel. There is also a bust of Charlemagne commissioned by Emperor Karl XIV, which incorporated a piece of Charlemagne's skull, and so much else. It is interesting that thirty-two Holy Roman Emperors after Charlemagne were crowned in this *Dom*. He himself was buried in the choir, in a golden shrine. This place is crammed full of history and treasures, a great many of them Carolingian.

We could not find accommodation anywhere or for any price, so we decided that we would have to go on to

Belgium when we had finished our sightseeing. The streets were full of holidaymakers, the sun shone, and we were homeless!

We went to a large square near the *Dom*. It was enchanting, with a large circular fountain with life-size bronze figures around the edge of the basin, which was several feet across. Fountains seem a feature in Aachen, with their modern sculpting. Another had child-size metal figures of clowns and fancy objects, where the water spurted out on to the laughing young spectators.

It was very hot, we were tired and had seen all we had come to view, so decided to make our way into Belgium, the last country of our holiday. We were still partially enveloped by the Chernobyl cloud.

We had been to Köln (Cologne) before, so did not venture there on this journey, in spite of not re-seeing its fabulous Cathedral and all its connections with the Magi.

Chapter Twelve

Turkey

Early spring, 1970s and 1980s

I had always wanted to go to Istanbul, being fascinated by the Byzantine period and its Greek connections. Now was my chance. A notice in a paper advertised a trip there for only £83, with three nights at the Hilton Hotel. A friend of mine, Hilary Leeds, was keen to go with me, so we immediately booked the holiday.

We arrived at Atatürk Airport in the evening. The spring sunset was heralding in the dark. We were ushered into a coach to be transported to our luxurious hotel. Never normally could I have afforded such a place, but for a one-off it was an interesting experience.

Our guide on the coach was very good, pointing out the different places of interest as we went by them. What intrigued me was that, as we entered the new part of the city, over the Atatürk Bridge, he said, 'We have now left Constantinople and are in Istanbul.' A thrilling thought to think that they still refer to the old part as Constantinople.

Our rooms were very opulent, warm and beautifully decorated. As the weather was rather cold it was a joy to relax in this comfort.

The next morning we were setting off to see the various sites, so collected information about the places from the reception desk. I also asked how much a taxi would be to bring us back in the evening. This, they said, would be about eighty lire. We had already read much about the place, and knew exactly where we wanted to go.

We then took a taxi to the Blue Mosque with its distinctive six minarets. What a splendid place. The floors were covered inches deep in the most beautiful Turkish rugs; one sank into them. These have been donated over hundreds of years by worshippers who have received help from Allah. The interior is mainly blue and is so peaceful, the sounds minimal. The sun shone through their geometric, rather garishly coloured, stained glass windows, streaking here and there with bright red, green and whatever colours. The *mimber* was very grand, dominating the place. As usual the *mithrab* indicated where Mecca is, to the East but slightly more to the right than a Christian altar would be. When the muezzin starts calling all to prayer the place is filled with men kneeling and bowing time after time after time. It is very impressive.

Outside the Blue Mosque gardens is the great area of the Hippodrome, although now much smaller, with a road running at its side. This is where Justinian and so many others had had their great chariot races and circuses. Here also are several famous relics, like the great stone pillar (the Ormets) dated in the three hundreds and known to have been restored in the time of Constantine I. It had been covered when first made in bronze plates, grandly gifted to impress the populace. Also there is the obelisk (the Dikili). This came from Upper Egypt, being erected there by Thutmose III (1549–1503 BC), one of the Deir el Bahri. It was brought to Constantinople, where no one seemed to be interested in it, and was left lying in solitary state near the Sea of Marmara for over three hundred years, and only brought to the Hippodrome by Theodosius. The carvings on it are fascinating; on one side there is his family watching a chariot race, on another the Emperors Arcadius and Honorius, and much more, incredibly considering the age of them.

Then there is the curious serpentine column (the Yilanh Sutun), now fairly badly damaged, which had come from Delphi in Greece. At one time it had supported the heads of three serpents, winding themselves round each other, and were high on the shaft. It was not until 1700 that a Polish soldier cut off the heads, which shows what can happen when you are drunk!

During these early periods there were groups, or gangs, of people – the Blues, the Greens, the Whites and the Reds, these colours being taken from Earth, Sea, Sky and Water. They originated with the city guilds, but later on the latter two were absorbed by the Blues and Greens. The leaders mainly consisted of great landowners and, even more importantly, the Senate for the Blues and the Greens were the leaders mainly of trade, industry and courtiers from far-flung parts of the Empire. With both, the rest of the members came from any class of employment. The venue of the Hippodrome seemed over the years to be where, when not in agreement, they rioted.

We also went to the Aghia Sophia, of which the infamous Procopius in the sixth century wrote, 'The mind rises sublime to commune with God, feeling that he cannot be far off, but must especially love to dwell in this place which he had chosen.' I call Procopius infamous as it was he who wrote the incredible *Secret Diary* about the scandalous and terrifying activities of the revered Justinian and his Empress Theodora. The present Aghia Sophia was built by Justinian in 532, then it became a mosque.

I find this building daunting now as a museum. It is dark and dusty. There are four Romanesque-type pillars which break one's views. Two have marble urns, dark and sinister. The dome is built on the recognised Orthodox lines, huge and imposing; intriguing and clever how they built the circle on the square. Then there are what look rather like advertisements but are in fact eight large white painted discs of wood on which is written in Arabic the names of God, Mohammed and the two Caliphs of the time, then the names of the two prophets' grandsons. Later on they turned the mosque into a museum, an interesting progression – Orthodox church into mosque into museum. I think that it is rather amusing, in retrospect. They thought, when making the place a museum, that they would remove these rather unsightly discs. This proved impossible as they would not go through any of the doors, so ignominiously they brought them back and re-hung them. Apparently they had thought of cutting them up but felt that that would be desecration!

There is still the *mimber* (pulpit) and the *mithrab* (the small apse shape) which denotes the direction of Mecca. To me the most beautiful objects are the mosaics, one being of the Empress Zoë and her third husband, Constantine IX. Both are kneeling on either side of the enthroned Christ, a fourteenth century mosaic. Then there is a ninth century one of the Virgin and Child. Dotted around are many fragments which have been preserved, such as the large archangel, and then another complete one of John Comnenus (1118–1146) and his wife presenting gifts to the Virgin and Child.

As we left I saw in the grounds a long row of five columns. On each was a different type of capital – Ionic, Corinthian and so forth. It was good to see them all together and in period.

What an incredible city this is, said to be the longest continually inhabited one in the world. It was first lived in by Bygas of Megara in 667 BC, when he arrived from Greece, then became Byzantium, later Constantinople (when Constantine made it the second Rome) and lastly Istanbul.

The whole area is filled with the most exciting colour, sound, people, music and art – such a feast – unknown to most other places. The history rings with the clash of dagger and intrigue, ambition and myriad tales of ne'er-do-well and success. The feeling stays, the excitement, joy and anticipation you find in that fascinating history which oozes out of every pore of its buildings and people. The great rivers, the Bosphorus, the Golden Horn and the Sea of Marmara make geometric designs with each other seen when looked down on from our hotel bedrooms.

From our hotel we had to cross either the Atatürk or the Galata Bridge to get to the fascinating part of the city. The bridges themselves are very busy, fishing boats, men cooking fish over spits for passers-by, ferry boats setting out to go their interesting ways, crossing and re-crossing the Bosphorus, in fact crossing from Europe to Asia between each stop.

We visited the incredible huge area called the Grand Bazaar. Before leaving home friends had lent me a compass. They said that once in this renowned place many people got lost. There are many exits and entrances. Inside there is no shape or plan. It is an enormous exciting souk; stall upon stall, men bent low with furniture on their backs – porters. There is no traffic except the hundreds of people and these human porters. The place was a mass of colour. Scents of spices and perfume, beautiful Turkish rugs, and glorious colours of the clothes all mixed and blended together.

We thought that we would have lunch here. There were no cafés, but we found a clean plank of wood on a trestle, plus two chairs, and sat down. We were served a large tumbler of freshly squashed orange juice and a kebab. Oh how delicious and thirst quenching.

It was late when we left, but every minute had been an adventure. Also because of our compass we found the way out – where, in fact, we had come in.

The next day we went to the most notable Topkapi Palace, much of it built by 1462 and situated partially over the ruins of the old Grand Palace, now no more. The Topkapi is situated high above the water, a huge rambling building with many parts to it. Around are smaller, some very oriental, buildings, beautiful shelters for sitting and watching the ships on the river; libraries and of course the harem.

The museum's wealth is staggering: huge lumps of emerald, diamonds, gold and silver, swords and china – so much in fact one could never see it all in a short time. But we went to the small restaurant to revive ourselves with a snack. This place has a lovely setting, its windows overlooking the Bosphorus and the Sea of Marmara. Later we took ourselves to the secretive harem. What a place – long high stone, very cold corridors and rooms, interspersed by ornately decorated apartments for the Emperors and such like to take their delights. Each of these rooms had an enormous throne covered in beautiful coloured damasks or silks, the woodwork gold, the backs padded. They were about three times the width of a chair seat and at least twice the depth. How did the girls exist in this gloomy, bitterly cold place? No central heating in those days.

We thought we would take a taxi back to our hotel. It was getting late, everywhere were crowds and we were not too sure about dolmans. We were then near to the Blue Mosque, where we had seen a taxi rank. A young taxi-driver came forward, asking us where we wanted to go. We said, 'The Hilton.' His eyes glistened.

I asked him how much it would be. On being told two hundred lire I firmly said 'No' and began to walk away.

He shouted after me, 'What price you give?'

Knowing what the Hilton had told me I said, 'Sixty lire.'
He laughed, 'Rubbish, far too low.'
I again started walking away.
Again he called out, 'I take you for eighty lire' (the price that the Hilton had told me).
I nodded to him and we began to get into his taxi but as I was about to enter he touched my arm, saying, 'Why you say sixty lire and accept eighty?'
I answered, 'Why do you say two hundred and accept eighty?'
He laughed.
On the way back to the hotel he was most interesting. He told us that he was a student and doing this in his spare time to see himself through the course. He also told us that if we wanted he would guide us all over Istanbul the next day, quoting quite a low charge. But I explained that we were off to Britain in the morning. Another thing he told us was that the rich bring food every day to the mosques to feed the poor. As you might say, to gain Brownie points to get to Heaven.
The next day we had to wait several hours at the airport. We were told that many of their planes had had to go unexpectedly to bring hundreds of refugees back to Turkey and that they could not delay this job.

1975

I have been to Turkey three times. The next time was when I was on a Hellenic cruise. We left Greece for a short while, being taken to Ephesus (what an enormous, fascinating place) and to Side, an old Roman site. The drive to the latter was interesting. A coach took us through the flat countryside, with the Taurus Mountains in the distance. Every now and then one would pass a man with a camel and bullock pulling a plough. Everything still seemed to be very primitive. Unfortunately Mount Ararat is miles away, otherwise we might have gone investigating for the Ark. Side was a typical Roman/Greek site and, while there, we sat in the old stone theatre and listened to Sir Mortimer Wheeler lecturing about the now ruined buildings. What an excellent lecturer he was. He made things live.

I love unusual jewellery. By the harbour were stalls, many of them selling harem rings. They were fun. Apparently the girls of the harem were given them by their patrons, one ring with a tiny precious stone in it. Then when he acquired another girl she got two rings with stones. This went up to six. He could only legally have six wives, so the last one did well – a lovely six-hooped jewelled ring. Those being sold were only silver gilt and the size of the stones fairly infinitesimal. Mine was tiny chips of sapphire, but I was happy with an interesting memento.

1980s

The third time I went to Turkey was with Geoffrey, my husband, in the early 1980s. We went with a group from an adult education place in Bristol, which arranged trips abroad. This time I went for a week and it was November. Everyone said that the weather would be like our spring, so 'do not bring warm clothes'. We believed them, arriving in the snow! We shivered about the first two days, but then luckily the weather changed and it was beautiful.

We stayed this time at a hotel, again on the Istanbul side of the Galata Bridge, but decided to go by bus to the old city. This was an experience. The first time they turfed us off as we had not bought tickets at a kiosk in Taxim Square. The next time the great long bus was crammed full and it seemed hundreds were waiting to get on. We relaxed to wait for the next, but lo and behold the crowd more or less lifted us on to the vehicle, the tightly packed occupants being even more squashed together, and still they surged on. By this time we were halfway down the interior, hardly able to breathe; no need to hold on as we were packed tighter than I have ever been to another human being. We were helpless with mirth and trusted that we would manage to escape somewhere near one of the sites we wanted to see. Gradually things eased. Someone asked where we wanted to disembark. We told them, only to be answered that we were on the wrong bus, so at the next stop they all literally pushed us down the centre and off. What an experience! This happened many times during our week there, but usually at least on the right bus.

We went to see the Kärye Chora, a church now turned into a museum. This Kärye Diani, or Chora, former church of the Chora monastery in Istanbul, had all this incredible mosaic work done by a man called Theodore Metochites about 1315, as a devotional exercise. The ceilings are completely covered with the most staggeringly magnificent mosaics. It is lit by electric light so all the gold and brilliantly coloured tesserae gleam and move, or so it seems. It is as the light catches the pictures. They are in perfect condition, the colours of the clothes on the people, landscape and faces seem alive, all as usual telling the illiterate the stories from the Bible. We stayed immersed for hours. People came and went. We did not want to leave, but all good things come to an end. This place remained a church until the Turkish invasion. This place is in the suburbs of Constantinople. As we left we saw women drawing water from the well. It was a drizzly wet day, so we did not stand for long, but did see a donkey with milk cans hanging from its back.

We also visited the magnificent Süleymaniye complex, with its four minarets. Süleyman was the fourth Sultan, and had ten serifes (balconies on a minaret), the tenth of the Ottoman line. The mosque itself is the most beautiful one in Istanbul, designed, as usual, by the great Sinan in about 1550. Even some Frankish infidels were struck dumb in admiration of the building. It has, as do all large mosques, a complex of other buildings – a hospital, caravanserai and living quarters, several *medreses* and an *imaret* and a marvellous garden.

Sinan was a most remarkable man. It is thought that he was born in 1469, definitely dying in 1588. It is also thought that he came to Istanbul as a dervish. These dervishes were Christian boys who, on being accepted to become a janissary or to be given a job in the Palace, had to convert to Islam. The *bektashi babas* (Sufi leaders) were the chaplains of the janissary regiments. From this he became a janissary in the Turkish army. Coming as a dervish was quite a usual Ottoman custom, but all of this is just reportage. The janissaries were a special force, gathered from the children of Christians, living in Turkey, of any nationality. They then trained as fighters and also, as I have already said, to be members of the Sultan's guard. In 1539 he was made chief of the Empire's Corps of Architects and completed his first mosque, the Shenzado, when he was in his fifties. He lived to a very great age, having during his lifetime changed the geometric architecture of mosques. He made 477 buildings and there are still 196 in use.

One of his most famous ones is the magnificent Süleyman mosque in Istanbul, an incredible place, a great complex that Sinan had devised, comprising every feature. He was abandoning the old Byzantine methods, or rather incorporating his new technology with the old, and even noticeable so it is a great excitement of half-domes, the unusual levels of some areas, arches, in some cases pointed, the beautiful stalactite embellishments, leading to the whole, as a perfect conception. After that time he did not use the Byzantine plans, evolving his own inspiration for better and better results.

At the time we were there the military were in charge. Our hotel had two soldiers posted at the door, rifles at the ready. Many shops had the same. As with other notable buildings, the result was that it was very safe to walk about, day or night. Even as our plane arrived about six soldiers with rifles surrounded it. At night it was a pleasant feeling, as we explored the city for small cafés, where one would see the local people. In fact one evening we went to a self-help place, small and clean, painted white and furnished with hard chairs and plastic covered tables. As we were finishing our good and cheap meal, a youngish man came over and sat down at our table. He looked slightly unkempt in his clothes but spoke English well. He asked if he could sit and talk so as to practise speaking in our language. We happily agreed. The conversation went on the lines of, 'Why are you here, what are your politics, how do you live?' So much so that we in turn asked him about his views of life, country and politics. None of which he would answer. He was very pleasant and we were glad to have talked to a native.

Money was so very scarce for the Turks while of course for us the exchange was excellent. We had a coffee one morning at a café near the Blue Mosque. It was bitterly cold and raining. The owner was a man in his late thirties. No one else was there, so when he brought our tea to us he stayed to talk. He told us that even with two wages they could hardly make ends meet. His wife was a matron in a hospital, her wage just paid for their food, while he was a mechanical engineer, helping out in his spare time in the café so as to keep a roof over their heads, and occasionally buying some much needed clothes. He asked us if we knew anything about Australia, as they were going to try and emigrate. We unfortunately could not help him on this point. A charming man, and what a plight – for all of them.

We have some charming Balkan friends, though in fact she is English, who asked us if we would bring them back some *loukoumi* (Turkish delight) from a famous shop in Istanbul, the only place where they make it correctly. Great instructions were given as to where the shop was, and its name. We found it was like an Aladdin's cave. It had serried ranks of shelves filled with delicious confections, in all colours and flavours, which when bought were put into beautiful boxes. We bought theirs, some for ourselves, some delicious halva, again with different flavours and colours. We were so glad they had asked us to do this, as we might never have found this world-famous shop.

When he was young, he told us, amongst many other fascinating stories, that he and a friend had heard that one of the best restaurants was in one of the railway stations on the Bosphorus. At that time he lived in one of the beautiful large houses on the Bosphorus. They set off and, on arriving at the restaurant, asked the head waiter for a table for two. The place was packed so the man answered how sorry he was but that there was no table left. With that our friend said he told him that he could see a table for four in one of the corners. The man, very politely, began to tell them it was booked when a hand came down on our friend's back, a voice saying over his shoulder, 'These two men will give me the honour to dine with me.' The waiter bowed and escorted the pair of them to the said table. The evening was a marvellous success, the conversation flowed and it was not until later on in the evening our friend found that he was being entertained by Atatürk, who even had his chauffeur first drive them home. This was nearly into Istanbul, which was another surprise, as apparently Atatürk hated Istanbul so much he would never go near it.

I must say that I keep talking about drinking coffee, but actually one could not get coffee anywhere, only hot tea in a long glass with lemon. We had wanted to stay in the famous Pera Palace Hotel, but unfortunately it was closed for residents. This is the hotel that was built for the Orient Express visitors in the old part of Istanbul, and where Agatha Christie had set part of her book. *Murder on the Orient Express.* We did manage to get in for a cup of tea, sitting in a vast half-lit lounge with rather oriental fittings, entertained by a single man being filmed, giving a commentary presumably on the hotel.

I said to Geoffrey that I would go upstairs to the lavatory, as I might then see more of the place: sumptuous carpets everywhere, and a loo fit for a Queen, thick Turkish hand-towels, gold fitted taps and hangers and subtly scented hand soap.

One day Geoffrey and I, instead of taking the organised expensive trip, went on an ordinary ferry boat that was to go up the Bosphorus, nearly as far as the Black Sea. It was a fascinating trip, they zigzagged from Europe to Asia the whole way, whilst we sat sipping glasses of hot tea to warm us.

We passed the large sprawling Dolmabahçe Palace, on the European side, then many grand houses with piers private to the owners which were being lapped by the water, as at Yenkoy. Also we saw the mighty fortress of Rumeli Hisari, where there seemed to be a bonfire, again on the European side. A bridge was built near here by Darius I in 512 BC at the narrowest part of the strait. The fortress was built in 1452 by Mehmet II, and in 1097 the Crusaders crossed by boat at this point. The Janissaries are stationed at the fortress and show you round it. We did not get off the ferry there. It was interesting going under the magnificent bridge that is there now, to watch the many cars speeding across from Europe with its known traditions, good or bad, and into what used to be – and still is in parts – the mysterious Asia, where still many unfathomed customs hold sway under a veneer of modern western thinking.

We stopped eventually at the last place on the ferry route. It was not allowed to go up to the mysterious barrier of the Black Sea, although we saw many great Russian tankers pounding up and down there each day. We stopped at a place called Anedolo Kavagi (Asian side). A tiny little café was on the edge of the water and here the captain of our vessel disembarked, then sat down at a table for lunch. We did the same, settling at a table under the trees, and choosing some fish from a tank for lunch. The air was now warm and sunny. We relaxed, trying to work out if we could actually see the Black Sea. Forbidden places always have a peculiar fascination. As it was, we could not; it was round a slight bend.

On the way home we thought we would get off at a small town on the Asian side to see what, if any, difference there was from the other. We got off at Çengelköy (Village of the Hook), so named as Mehmet II had found an old anchor on the shore there. It was fairly primitive, the people poorly dressed, the shops very drab, but it was interesting walking about the streets. In one we found four cows having a butting match right n the middle of the road. No one took any notice, though I must say there were few people about.

We finally arrived at Üsküdar, which is a large town. The old oriental part of the place was much more interesting and attractive than the newer European part. It also still had lovely wooden houses, narrow twisting streets and flowers. If one is interested in the Emperor Constantine I, as I am, you will be glad to know that he defeated his great rival Licinius here and so was able to found the city of Constantinople.

It had been fascinating to watch at all our ports of call the people moving on and off the ferry, to see the different small piers, some, as I said, private ones, some decorated with flowers, others purely basic; but the people, as all over the world, were so individual and well worth watching.

We also took a ferry to the Asian side another day to explore Üsküdar, and found running between two busy roads a long widish Muslim cemetery. I am always fascinated by tombstones, what other countries produce and their decorations. We managed to cross the road and enter the top and older part. The grass and weeds were knee-high, concealed stones ready to trap the unwary. Many of the tall tombstones stood at a drunken angle, but it was a marvellous search, the search being that we had read in one of our guide books that, if one found the head of one of these tombstones laid on the ground by the side of the column, it meant that the man had been decapitated! The usual tombstone for a man is a column, about four or five feet tall; carved on the top was either a turban or a fez. When the turban was banned the fez was introduced. Later that too was banned. The tops also indicated what rank and sex the person was. The women's graves have flowers and garlands engraved on the top upper half of the column or slab and sometimes a shell. The men have, as I said, either a turban or a fez, on which are several tassels. The number of these denotes one's social status. So this was our search, either turbans and fezzes or garlands, but most of all as we had seen the above before, was the grave of a decapitated man! I must in all honesty say that I was keener than Geoffrey in this grisly hunt. Sadly there was no beheaded man buried here. As we passed the lower portion of this cemetery we saw a big funeral taking place.

We then went on to the Mosaic Museum, both being particularly interested in that work. It was a small place, an enclosed street with these ancient works of art on the walls and pavements. There was a small house at the entrance, where we paid our fee. The young man spoke English and told us to look round. We took quite a while and also took some photos. We passed one part which seemed to have a staircase going into the ground, but there was a rope preventing entrance and a large notice 'Warning, no entry'. As we were passing this the young curator came up to us, saying that he could see that we were really interested, and asking us if we would like to see the Grand Palace mosaic floor that was being restored. We were delighted, so he said, rather diffidently, that if we could give him a note (money) he would let us in. We hastily gave him a pound note. He lifted the rope and down we went. What a marvellous experience – great floors of mosaics and of very great age for the Grand Palace was much older than the Topkapi. It was about the seventh century, the site where the Byzantine emperors had their palace. It had had a thousand square metres of pavement in one covered passage, filled with these intricate Roman/Hellenistic mosaic floors. It is now thought that this building had been used as a basilica or an audience chamber. For us this was an incredible bit of luck.

When we emerged at last the young man was waiting for us and asked us to come to his house and meet his wife. We went to the house where we had bought our tickets, took off our shoes, leaving them outside the door, then entered a large darkish room where the wife, in beautifully coloured Turkish clothes, welcomed us. She did not speak English, but kept giving us handfuls of walnuts, with a lovely grin on her face. She also sat us down on the edge of an enormous double bed. It took up most of the room. Also dancing and smiling round us were four delightful small children. The young man then asked Geoffrey how much the pound note was in their coinage. He was most upset when told its worth and said he collected notes for interest only, not for their worth. He then showed us one which had been brought out in the German slump. It was for thousands of marks, but in fact worth almost nothing. This did not worry him. He then put the pound note into the glass-topped table with great pride.

As we left the delightfully smiling wife kept filling our pockets with walnuts, while the young man thanked us profusely for honouring him in his lowly home. It was an interesting lovely interlude.

We also went to the Military Museum, as we had heard that the Janissaries had a band which performed there once a week. When we arrived we had a quick look round the museum itself, then back to the entrance hall where we stood at the top of a double staircase to watch the show. Many others were arriving, but our perch was perfect. The band stamped in. What a glorious feast of colour and sound, their fascinating Byzantine uniforms, yellows, reds and blues, white gloves and mainly tall hats. They seem to have chosen the fiercest faces they could find. The music was fascinating in a slightly tinny, prehistoric way, the rhythm was splendid. The instruments consisted of bells, drums and strange, never-before-seen instruments, while the leader, a tall Cossack-looking gentleman, had a long stick which had a bell attached to the top which, as they marched, he thumped on the stone floor, and more than that, when turning to the audience, gave a large knowing wink to any woman he could attract – quite unofficially! There were about eight of them, the floor by the stairs not very vast, so they all walked with rather mincing military steps. We enjoyed it so much that we asked at the door if they had any cassettes of the music. They said, 'No,' but smiled and told us we would get one at a music shop up the road. This we did, after walking up an extraordinarily long street of shops, nearly missing the music one, as it was tucked away in an arcade. However, it was worth the trek.

It was now coming to the end of an exciting week in Istanbul. We thought we would finish off our visit by sailing up the Golden Horn in order to go to Eyüp, where there is the most sacred mosque in Istanbul – the Eyüp Mosque. Off a courtyard there is the grave of Mohammed's standard bearer – Aba Eyüp Ansari – who had died in the first siege of Constantinople, killed by Arabs (672–679). Future Sultans altered and then rebuilt this building.

As non-Muslims we were not allowed to go into Eyüp's burial chamber, but were allowed to view the grave of the Standard Bearer through a gilded copper lattice window, which was in the adjoining courtyard. The courtyard was beautiful. The façade of the tomb building is covered with the most lovely blue and green faience tiles, the factory making them being on the same site. The courtyard itself had plane trees, a fountain (obligatory for cleansing oneself) and was occupied by a lovely gathering of herons, pigeons and storks – how delightful.

As usual time flew. We made our way back to the ferry. The boat was just ready to leave. We rushed forward, Geoffrey managing to race up the gangplank but before I could get on to it they lifted it. The boat was still aligned to the pier, but moving very slowly. Geoffrey and a sailor shouted to me to jump over the rail of the deck of the now really moving craft. As I had the beginning of an arthritic hip and was a goodly age – sixty-six – I nearly hesitated. Instead I grasped the rail and, with no more ado, jumped. The sailor and Geoffrey hauled me over and on to the deck. I must say it was probably one of my most inelegant entrances! My legs flew out at an angle of forty-five degrees, my head down to the deck. However, I managed with their help to obtain an upright position before crashing completely to the deck.

The journey back was like a dream, sailing quietly up the Horn, the sun setting with all its clashing colours, which ranged from pale blue and pink to a deep harsh orange and mauve. This was outlining the many mosques, particularly the Süleymaniye, their minarets and domes black cut-outs against this raging heaven. The water was streaked with paths of light and speckling the wave tops. The millions of houses on this Constantinople side were pinpricked with light reflected from their windows. Never will I forget it. What a stupendous ending to a holiday in this magical city.

Samuel Johnson said, 'When a man is tired of London he is tired of life.' This is multiplied when you are in Istanbul.

Chapter Thirteen
Yugoslavia

1970s and 1980s

I went several times to this enormous ill-fitting, jigsaw-puzzle-like country with its disparate peoples. The sorrow, exasperation and affection one has for Yugoslavia is immense, and for Tito a great respect in his ability to keep these unhomogenous countries in a mainly peaceful cohabiting existence – and even for so many years after his death – but now?

On the first visit I was only passing through on my way to Greece – travelling by coach from Marylebone Station, London, to Athens, Greece, and all for only £36.

I was travelling with a friend, Hilary Leeds. We arrived at the Austrian/Yugoslavian border and went on to the border town of Maribor, on the beautiful wide Drava River. I had the name and telephone number of friends of a young Bristol girl, who worked at the BBC there with me. When she heard I was going to Maribor she immediately wrote to her friends there, suggesting that we should meet.

We arrived at our hotel about six o'clock then, having eaten, I asked the receptionist to ring the Bristol girl's friends for me – hardly anyone spoke English and I certainly did not know any of their difficult Serbo-Croat language. He got through and handed me the telephone. All I could hear was a rushing babble of unrecognisable words. After strivings on both sides to communicate, she laid down the telephone. Shortly a young male voice spoke in English. He seemed delighted that I had rung and said that he and his girlfriend would come over to my hotel for what was left of the evening. He also apologised for his mother, who only spoke her own language.

The two of them arrived about 8.30 p.m. They were delightful. We talked solidly until about 2 a.m., then, as I had to get up at about five the next day, they left, but not before making me promise to ring them on my return journey, when they would collect me and take me to his parents' house for dinner. It had been such an enjoyable evening talking to these two students about their country, their aims in life, relaxations (mainly sport) and much more that I agreed. His last remark to me was that I would find the rest of Yugoslavia very different from where they were.

Sadly, when I did return, for the one and only time, our coach was very late in arriving. It was May Day and all was out of kilter. I asked the hall porter to ring them for me, but all I could get was the voluble Serbo-Croat speaking mother. In desperation we both rang off. I later heard from the couple. Apparently they had waited but, as the hours went by, they thought that I was not going to contact them this time. As it was the first of May, the great holiday day for that part of the world, they had gone out celebrating.

Hilary and I went for a stroll in the dark to view the town. Every shop window had a photo of Tito swathed in laurel leaves. It was a handsome mid-European-type city. Its massive stone buildings had been built for prestige, but grown depressingly worn and uninspiring with age, colourless and often forbidding.

A few years later I was also in Maribor with my husband, Geoffrey. We stayed in a delightful riverside chalet surrounded by flowers and trees, an idyllic spot, woken up by bird-song, sunshine and the sound of the river. We walked around the town looking at all the fascinating pediments and ornamentation on the buildings, a lovely day. Next morning we left early. Stopping later for a picnic lunch we turned on the radio. Disaster had struck northern Italy in the form of a bad earthquake, the effects being so widespread that Maribor had had many of their famous pediments knocked to the ground in smithereens. We were only too glad that we had missed it – and by a hair's breadth.

Another year my husband and I went to Stobi, an ancient Roman city, near Titov Veles. First it had been a town called Perseide, at the time of Philip of Macedon (197 BC). The Romans had taken it over later on, when it became very prosperous. It had a varied career until an earthquake destroyed it. Now it is a pleasant area of country, studded with ruined buildings, a basilica, the usual columns, an amphitheatre and much else. It also has some very good mosaic floors. It was so peaceful and far from any town or village. We walked on the uneven grass down to an iron roofed area where there was a great deal of activity. The excavations are ongoing; there seems much still to be discovered.

As we were leaving one of the custodians asked us how we knew about their site. On being told 'from our English guide book', they looked in amazement telling us that they had no guide books about this particular place and that they did not know that any existed. With that we passed ours over to them. With great joy, surprise and many exclamations they perused it then, as thanks, they gave us each a cup of lovely hot coffee and some postcards, accompanied by overwhelming thanks and good wishes.

We also had a marvellous week at Ohrid, renowned for its Orthodox churches. There are so many there that it is almost bewildering. We arrived with, as usual, nowhere to stay. Geoffrey had read somewhere that the best place to go to was a flat, more entertaining and cheaper.

We stopped in a beflowered square facing the lovely greeny-blue sea. As Geoffrey went off to find the tourist office I sat in the car with the windows down, taking in this splendid view. I had not been there more than ten minutes when my reverie was interrupted by a reasonably dressed man leaning on the window edge of the car. He spoke good English, having, I learnt later, lived in Australia for a while. He asked me if I were lost and, on being told that my husband was looking for a room for us for a few nights, beamed into my face, saying that he and his wife had a room to let, 'very clean, very comfortable and cheap', and that he would take us to it. I told him that by now my husband had probably found a flat for us. However, he decided to wait and see – as his room would be much better!

We waited and waited. I was really rather worried at what had happened to Geoffrey. My companion was getting impatient, but would not leave. He then asked me which way my husband had gone and said he would go and find him. I told him that Geoffrey had gone to the tourist office, which I gathered was not far away. With that he took off on his bike, only to be back in about five minutes,

'Has your husband a shock of grey hair?'

'Yes,' I said.

'Well,' he said, 'he is on his way back. I saw him.'

With that, luckily, Geoffrey did come back, saying that he had a flat for us. I introduced my companion to him. He started offering us his room again, saying that the flats were no good. He was now getting angry but eventually we got rid of him. During the next few days of our stay there, every time we saw him he ran his bike in front of our car, shouting something or other about his room.

The flat was fun, very cheap, a large sitting room with a tiny stove, bedroom and bathroom. We got a mound of clothes washed. Every time we came in or out the children rushed forward shouting "Allo, 'allo,' or 'Bye bye!' with great pride and giggles.

The old streets of Ohrid are beautiful, narrow and twisting. There are beautiful old houses of every shape and size, usually painted cream and with roses and greenery clinging to their fronts. We set off to have a glorious glut of domed, iconed and frescoed churches – a veritable feast. The atmosphere was serene, the warm sun flaking through the early green leaves of the trees.

We went first to Svet Bogorodica with its beautiful exterior but sadly, owing to a local power cut, it had no lights. We could see little, the church being naturally a dark one. So we went on to Sveta Nikola Bolnicka; it too had very little light – not a very auspicious start. It is a smaller fourteenth century church. In its dim interior we could just make out some of the frescoes and the entrancing iconostasis. This church is known for its frescoes. To cheer ourselves up we went to a delightful café in a flower-filled square facing the sea and had a coffee, relaxing in the sun.

We then went to Sveti Naum, a most beautiful drive, about twenty-eight kilometres, driving round the Lake of Ohrid, the whole thing backed by huge mountains necklaced with cloud, the lower slopes covered with fresh green scrub. The lake itself was edged with trees. We passed small villages (*pestani*) with colourful fishing boats bumping each other with a tired muted sound and everywhere people going about their business. In one village we saw a Sarakatsán woman with her black skirt, stockings and shoes, a felted white tabard-type top with black designs embroidered on it, finished off with a black headscarf. Unfortunately she turned into a narrow side street before I could take a photo of her.

The Sarakatsáns are a nomadic tribe from Northern Greece – the Roumeli. They have no fixed abode, as have the Kouzovlacs and Karagoums, who are attached to villages. These Sarakatsáns live in the mountains, some often on the same one, but always on the move, using wicker and rushes to make a shelter, just returning to a fold or cordillera where they find a spot to graze their sheep. During the Balkan Wars the changing of frontiers and forbidden zones caused them to change their habitat, but it was still in the mountains though spread far. They were clever people, outwitting the enemy, and eventually infiltrating as far as Albania, Serbia, Russia, Constantinople and the Middle East. They are still elusive people. The women always wear black and white clothes, hence Geoffrey spotting this woman near Ohrid.

We went to the car park at Sveti Naum, to find it looking like Cheddar Gorge during a summer holiday period – horrid. However, we parked and then took the winding tree-lined avenue to the bridge and the monastery itself. We had been told that hundreds of youngsters were in Ohrid on a three-day cultural tour. We kept our fingers crossed, paid our money and entered, although the man tried to cheat Geoffrey out of his change.

We wandered up the cobbled path to the monastery, so beautiful, with its green area and its old country-type buildings. It was built in the tenth century by Sv. Naum. He had been a disciple of St Clement. It has a small church, a magical mysteriously dark place, the only light being the numerous candles, which still could not penetrate its lost corners. Enclosed by it is the secret tomb of Sv. Naum. The walls have mainly, sadly, lost their frescoes. I believe there are still a few monks in residence here. The setting of the whole monastery complex is a joy: green fields, trees, and of course the river and lake.

Our next port of call was Sv. Kliment. He was documented as a man with such energy that he seemed to electrify the whole of the countryside, teaching children, reading, writing day and night, taking services with energy and absorbed in everything. He was even said to affect the beasts and birds, who would show him where to build his churches, altars and all else. This church (1295) was been built with ornamented bricks and has amongst its frescoes several by the famous Mihajlo and also by Eutihije. They were followers of the great painter Astrapus (late thirteenth and early fourteenth century). In fact many think that Mihajlo was his son.

The Cathedral is Sveta Sophija, a magnificent frontage, with frescoes reminiscent of Renaissance work in their style, with healthy chubbier virgins and angels. It is a beautiful building situated in the town, originally 5th century, now much added to, with its triple apse and three naves. It was turned into a mosque by the Turks, then after 500 years was returned to the Christians, the *mimber* removed and an altar installed, the minaret having disappeared many years ago. This place has such a marvellously calm feeling to it.

One place quite near to Sv. Kliment was the intriguing tiny church of Constantine and Helena (fourteenth century). The continuation of the names of these two belatedly baptised Christians and founders of the Christian religion in Turkey is interesting. This small church was begun by a monk called Partenije and contains a portrait of him.

We had a meal at a small restaurant. Sitting on the balcony the view was splendid. Away below us was the lake, its tiny steamers cutting through the deep blue-green water, the foam bubbling behind them like a strip of bubbles and froth. The sun was warm on the nape of my neck and the birds seemed to be having a quiet conversation, each to each, that they did not wish us to hear.

Later on we saw a strange tomb, a stone with a ram and a ewe carved on it. We were reminded of a stone on the wall of the refectory at Sveti Naum itself, of a sculpted donkey.

During one walk we went on we saw a large house. It could have belonged to Albanians and, because of this, we did not take any photos as they are exceedingly touchy about any publicity and things could have become very nasty. Passing their border country you can see small roads leading into Albania itself. All have notices saying 'Forbidden to travel on this road'. Everything is sealed off to their country, so much so that one had a shiver of fear even looking at the notices. One knows from past times how vicious and cruel they can be. Now of course anyone can visit there.

The next day we took a road to the great towering mountains where bears and boars still live. Luckily we did not meet either, although it would have been exciting to see them in the wild. We had our picnic on a flat piece of scrub and grassland. Everywhere was silence. The scent of flowers filled the air, mingling with the pungent smell of herbs, which were covering the ground in their many colours. Here and there small bushes, also many with coloured flowers, broke the level of one's gaze. In the distance we heard a cuckoo, while nearby listened to the muzzy drone of some bees which were seeking the delicious pollen on all these sun-warmed flowers. Apparently it is the only place in Central Europe where this flora is found.

After lunch Geoffrey decided to walk up into the mountains, leaving me to wander about these lower slopes. Time went by. He had said that he would not be long, but now all I could imagine was that one of the bears was having a splendid unexpected meal of my husband. Eventually he returned, having gone further than he meant to. No bear had ever been in his sights. Oh for imaginings!

About six o'clock, after a rest in our flat, we decided to go and see the thirteenth century Church of Sveti Jovan, Kaneo (St John the Divine, Kaneo). This church is built on a rocky headland, solitary in its splendour, and very difficult to find but eventually we succeeded. Far below us was the blue-green lake, rocking fishing boats of bright blues, greens and white, lying at ease after a day at sea. A rim of light was settling on the far edge of the lake, speared by the setting sun. Cypress trees were cloaking a small irregularly built village, which tumbled down to the water's edge, interspersed on the way by pale aesthetic willows and other trees. The whole gave a cold lonely feel in the now setting sun. On the further side of this narrow headland, some well-worn stone steps wound down to the ancient church of Sveti Jovan, which stood on the point of the headland overlooking the water. Against it the last of the blue sky, with its shimmer now of pink, mauve and orange, warned of the encroaching night. It showed up the church like an immovable block crowned with Byzantine domes, the uneven stonework solid and unforgiving. The inside with its paintwork is still glorious to see, with Christ, his saints and many others jostling together in praise of their ultimate God. Newer paintings lit up the walls too, comparing well with their ancient neighbours. The holy lamps and many icons, silver encased to protect their surfaces from much kissing done in reverence to their deities, glistened, candles and incense permeated the atmosphere, used as the Chinese do their joss sticks, the whole place holy and remote and yet personable and believable.

It was dark outside, the interior now had a ghostly floating feel to it, the wavering candles giving an unsteadiness to these solid forms. The place was a revelation, an experience I will never forget. We walked into the dark but star-lit night in silence.

We thought we would explore the oldest part of the town for a taverna where we could have our evening meal. We wanted to find a restaurant called The Orient, much praised in our guide book. However, when we got there it was closed – how unusual. It is in a street that has shops that look like glass-fronted stalls. Close by was a mosque – the Ajdan Pasha Mosque – one of the oldest in Ohrid (1490), which contains the tomb of the Pasha who founded it. As we went the streets grew narrower and narrower, for after all it is on the side of a mountain and about two thousand feet up. At the end of our street was an enormous tree. We were told that a barber once set up business in its hollow trunk, which shows its size and his enterprise.

We found a café patronised by many locals, always a good sign of good food, and round this particular street were families taking their evening *volta*. They were washed and dressed in their Sunday best, the girls in frilly starched beribboned dresses, the small boys looking rather incongruous in miniature men's suits. It is always fun to watch this ritual. The young girls, still tied to the family's apron strings, looking back and smiling at any fairly handsome boy who was doing the same, although they were in a gang of boys. The traffic is stopped daily for the *volta* hour, about seven o'clock, a good custom in many countries.

The restaurant we had found was in the square of the hollow tree. The cobbled streets gave one an uneven walk there. The view of the tall thin delicate minaret pierced the navy blue sky. Little shops selling flowers and other goods were everywhere; especially lovely were the beautiful masses of roses. We had a French-speaking waiter, so he and Geoffrey were able to converse. Our meal was delicious, *Specialité de maison* done in wine, a gorgeous casserole and a cheese-covered salad. By this time the lightning was flashing over wide areas of sky above the mountains – most spectacular. Walking through the streets glimmering with the heavy rain we saw an oriental cake shop. We treated ourselves to one each and brought them, slightly sodden, to our flat, a worthwhile idea.

During the whole of this holiday the World Cup had been in progress. Every evening, whatever country we were in, the tavernas, shops and squares in the towns were strung with large TV sets. It was impossible to find a seat in any of the tavernas to have a meal unless you went at about six o'clock. An hour later everyone was sitting glued to the sets, a glass of ouzo clasped tightly in their hands – all men, hardly a woman. It was funny because both of us, being completely sport-illiterate, had wondered why they were all watching what we thought to be their local teams so avidly – we soon learnt. At one church we met a group of ten year olds who asked us where we came from. On saying 'England,' they then referred to England and the World Cup. I clapped as I thought we must have done well, only to watch the boys sorrowfully shake their heads.

We tried to find the elusive Ohrid Museum. Eventually finding it, we read the notice which told us that it was open from 7 a.m. As it was then 10 a.m. we tried the door but to no avail. We knocked loudly, but no answer. We felt like Walter de la Mare's *Traveller* – '"Is there anyone there?" said the Traveller, knocking on the moonlit door' – the only difference being that it was in broad daylight. Next door to it we found the nineteenth century Church of Sveti Nickolas Gerakomia. Its interest, we found, was the collection of wall paintings done in about 1864 by the well known artist Dico Krstevic, who came from a village near Debar. This peasant naïf painter, with his strong fascinating fairground-type of work, had been much sought after. Certainly whenever we saw one of his we were intrigued. We also glimpsed Roman tombs in the back street near Sveta Sophia – how incongruous.

On our way west as we were returning to Austria we went to Debar, a fascinating, almost purely Albanian occupied town, tree-shrouded with narrow, rather pot-holed roads. The men wore, as ever, their white brimless felt hats, the women, again, almost without exception, wore the beige long waterproof coats and on their heads cream-coloured scarves, worn peasant-wise. The Muslim women wore baggy Turkish-type trousers and brilliantly clashing coloured scarves on their heads, brought well down on their foreheads with the ends all tied together under their chins. Many of them looked to us like gypsies. They all treated one with nervous, yet arrogant, glances. Never do they look you in the eye.

We visited the nearby Painted Mosque at Tetovo. It is a large, wall enclosed building surrounded by trees, the exterior covered with large oblong panels, with painted designs in muted pinks, greens and blues. Its minaret, again as so many seem to, spearing the deep blue sky. We found a gate and entered. Everywhere were men, who indicated that we must leave, while groups of women sat around on a grassy slope.

Earlier on we had been to Niš and Skopje, which had suffered a large earthquake not long before, its station clock still registering the time it happened. We had done the long hundred-mile journey from Niš and were ready to find a comfortable hotel here. Everywhere was full up, so we went to a caravan site on the edge of the town. What a perfect setting. Each caravan sat enclosed by trees. There was a good restaurant on the site, candlelit tables, again under trees. The caravan itself was somewhat cramped, with two small sleeping areas and a minute passage between them. Geoffrey found that we had only hired half, a daunting thought, so he went back and said to the owner that we would like the whole caravan. Mercifully it had not been taken yet. We each had a bed, which was comfortable. We used the narrow passage to dump all our luggage, which necessitated a certain amount of mountaineering. We were leaving in the morning to continue our journey.

Geoffrey went to his jacket to get his wallet so as to pay our bill. With a voice of doom he announced that it was not there. We searched everywhere, then rushed to the car. Still no sign of it. We were both feeling panic-stricken. He had no cheque book, traveller's cheques, or credit cards – none of the valuable things that he keeps in such a place. This was a disaster. We went to the reception desk, explaining what had happened, and could we used the phone. He telephoned through to Niš, asking the chalet owner if by any chance the wallet had been handed in. A miracle – it had. We nearly danced with delight and, leaving our bags as security, went off to drive the hundred miles back to the chalet site. We were so delighted that the extra hundred miles there and hundred miles back seemed nothing.

We had had a chalet with a glassed front wall. Everyone passing could have seen in and what was in it. Also it was in a secluded spot amid trees. When we arrived the manager handed Geoffrey a neat bundle, which included his wallet, everything documented, the traveller's cheque numbers, the tickets for our ferry home, and all the money – mainly notes. Apparently a cleaner had found them, immediately handing them in to the office. With relief Geoffrey left her a good tip for her honesty.

We were so happy that we spun down the road leading eventually to Skopje – so happy that we were on the wrong side of the road and about to go through a red light. We were stopped from committing the last sin by a policeman on the further pavement, whistling hard at us, a great grin on his face. We collected ourselves and, without more ado, reached Skopje in safety.

The last trip that we made to Yugoslavia was also in the 1980s – 1986 to be precise – when we booked for a Yugotour holiday organised to visit the monasteries of Serbia. As you will have noticed, we are very interested in icons, mosaics and frescoes of the Orthodox churches and monasteries. We arrived at Belgrade (Beograd) Airport to be met by the handsome young man who was to be our guide. He turned out to be a particularly good one, erudite, explicit and with charisma, which enabled him to get us all the best treatment everywhere we went.

We approached the coach that was to take us to our hotel – the Intercontinental – the most expensive one in Beograd. It turned out to be a very small one, holding ten people, We asked our guide, Jewka, where the rest of the party was, to which he replied that the tour had been very badly advertised, especially in England, and that only seven of us had applied – hence the smaller coach. We were waiting now for an American couple to emerge who had apparently been on our plane.

When we all met in the lounge of our hotel for a briefing we were introduced to the others: Raymond and Louise Gadea (he being Spanish but brought up in Puerto Rico, now living in America; they became friends of ours, subsequently coming to stay with us in Bristol); an elderly friend of theirs; the couple off our plane were Dick and Louise Mallard, he being a rather jolly Methodist minister and his wife a quiet elderly good-looking woman, with a nice sense of humour. This small party was perfect, as we could always hear our guide; also there was no crowding round sites, so we were able to see everything. Our guide lectured us round the sites, then left us for about an hour to go round on our own, and buy cards or whatever.

We set off the next morning – Saturday, I think – driven by an amusing, energetic driver, who spoke no English nor any language other than his own.

On the first day there was to be not a monastery but a good-for-your-soul visit to Tito's Grave. This is at a place called Avala in the outskirts of Beograd. When we arrived we saw a queue winding up a steep hill four abreast and found out that Tito had asked to be buried in his beloved garden house.

We trudged up amid a rather hot sweaty crowd, but it was very pleasant. On reaching the top of the hill we wound round a circular bed of flowers; it was most attractive. The building was white and surrounded by flowers. A red velvet curtain was clipped back from the entrance, which was guarded by two very young, very earnest soldiers. Here we were told that we must take our shoes off before entering and that, when in, we must not speak. In fact, to be as quiet as possible. As one stepped in one got the impression of happiness and serenity. Stationed at the four corners of the tomb were another four young soldiers, heads bent. The large white coffin lay on a plinth surrounded by flowers and, instead of any vulgar eulogy, there was simply plain gold lettering saying 'Tito' and his dates. The people walked round fairly quickly and you found yourself out again in the hot sunshine. We had not particularly wanted to go and see it, but we were both moved and glad to have had the opportunity. It was also interesting that so many people were still visiting this place, so many years after his death in 1980.

We then proceeded south, reaching Oplenac near Topola in the early evening. Without delay we were taken to the church of the Karadjordjevic royal family. The church is not very impressive, a mixture of Byzantine/Serbian architecture, built in 1912. Its interior is a mass of mosaics, mainly copied from old Serbian churches, but the darkness and depressive atmosphere resulted in our spending very little time there. It is now a mausoleum.

The next day we went to the fifteenth century Ljubostinja Monastery. As it was Sunday we had to view the interior between services. It looked much more like a European church from the outside, very impressive in a kind of Town Hall style but with a tower, and is in fact pre-Morava style. It is also said that it was built by Princess Milica on the spot where her husband Prince Lazar, of great fame in Serbia, proposed to her. The interior has many good frescoes. What a feast of delight these places are. Following the Bible stories through the frescoes and mosaics, identifying, if you can, the hundreds of saints in the icons. This particular monastery had beautiful warm colouring.

Then on to the thirteenth century Zica Monastery. Here there are thirteenth and fourteenth century frescoes. It is a tall red brick building, with the required amount of domes, set in its own grounds, peaceful and distant to life. It was there that I went to buy some postcards of the buildings and on my way was accosted by a young woman holding a baby. She asked if I came from England and, on my assenting, said that she was married to one of the young priests there and how very happy she was and that, in fact, she had not been home to England for four years but that her parents had come out to see her. I later met the young husband, looking grand in his black tall hat and black robes. His hair of course was cut; only the monks are not allowed to have their hair short. One can always tell them apart, as the monk invariably has a small bun, usually held back with very unromantic kirby-grips. It was there also that I found some incredible unusual gravestones. Each one had the outline of a large face with outlined eyes, nose and mouth. I was thrilled as I collect photos of gravestones from every country as well as our own. They are a fascinating subject. I still have not found anything out about them, not even from our guide. You find this type all over Serbia and, for all I know, elsewhere. An exciting find.

We were then taken to the famous monastery of Studenica, the coach going up the most alarming hairpin bends; at one point the back wheel became lodged over the very edge of the precipice. But what a staggeringly marvellous drive – gorges, ravines and rivers tumbling down the rocky surface in a desperate attempt to reach some stabler level. Eagles soared high above the tops of those mammoth mountains, dark against the blue sky. Eventually we reached the monastery. Twelfth century Studenica is renowned for its fabulous icons and frescoes. It is the richest of these great Serbian monasteries, having three churches in its walled enclave. The oldest is the thirteenth century Sv. Bogorodicna, which houses the most beautiful thirteenth century frescoes, with their sapphire blue and gold backgrounds, which are said to be some of the finest early thirteenth century art. There are also many done by an artist from Peć, called Longin. These are sixteenth century. His work is found in many parts of this church. His painting of faces makes them come alive. The whole church, built of polished white marble, has the usual domes, the bases of them painted deep red and then crowned with light blue roofs, a curiously satisfying picture. It is built in the Raska style.

Our guide gathered us together after his talk in the church, saying that he would give us half an hour to look around by ourselves. Then one of the priests, a friend of his, wished us to join him on one of the balconies, where he would give us a drink of his home-made *slivovica*, a plum brandy indigenous to Yugoslavia and not enjoyed by all. Jewka, our guide, asked us not to be seen gathering for this drink, as he did not want all the stray sightseers to join us. He also told us an amusing story of how this priest had once boastingly said to him that he was the best *slivovica* maker in Yugoslavia, to which our guide had replied, 'No, you are the second best.' The priest could not agree to this, so the next time Jewka came to this monastery he brought a bottle of the wine made by the one he thought was the best. He gave it to the priest, who sipped it slowly, then with a dejected face had said, 'I am the second best.' We had our drink with him, a charming middle-aged man, who spoke little English but you could feel his warmth and friendliness. It was an interesting interlude.

We have a Dutch friend, Catherina Gaskell, who lives in Weston-super-Mare. When she heard we were doing this trip she asked if we would deliver a photo to Father Simeon who lived at Studenica. They had been there the year before and had become friends of this monk who, when his photo was taken with them, asked if he could have a copy. This we did. On handing this very old monk the photo his creased face wrinkled even more into a grateful smile.

After this interesting visit we were then driven nearly to the top of the highest mountain (six thousand feet), where there was a hotel for skiers, now nearly empty as the snow was melting fast. There we stayed the night. Our meal was good – much meat, which seems usual to the Slavs – the dining room very large, occupied by our group of seven and several larger parties of Russians (this we had in several hotels). They must have been Commissars and their wives, no one else being permitted at that time to leave Russia.

The next morning Jewka had arranged for the chair-lifts to take us up to the very top of this mountain where, he told us, you could see over to Rumania, Albania and Bulgaria. With my arthritic hip I nearly missed the chair. As the chair-lift did not stop I had to leap on, landing half on and half off. However, I righted myself during the journey up. There were only patches of snow left but, better still, down under me I could see dark brown squirrels darting under the scrub and the bushes.

We stayed up there for about half an hour. Sadly it was fairly misty, so we could not see the entire view. It was chilly, in spite of the warm sun, so Geoffrey and I decided to go back to the hotel. No one seemed to be on the ski lift. I managed to clamber on, with Geoffrey on the one behind me. As we slowly descended I saw a man and woman coming up. I looked over. The man passed but when I looked at the dark-glassed woman I shouted, 'Sheila!' I could not believe it. They were Sheila Rivers-Moore and her husband, who go to our church in Bristol! She shouted back, equally surprised, then, as she passed Geoffrey, she shouted to him, 'Have you been to Sopoćani?'

When we arrived at the hotel again no one was about. Geoffrey said to me, 'Some strange woman shouted over to me had I been to Sopoćani? I can't think why.' I laughed, telling him who they were. What a strange coincidence.

We all gathered in the coach, which Jewka said was taking us a little way down to where he had arranged a barbecue, the hotel staff bringing down all the equipment and food required. It was a most beautiful flat grassy spot, with a small river nearby and then a narrow road. Everyone helped with the barbecuing. The scent of charcoaled meat in the air, the birds singing, the water gurgling, how idyllic.

We had just started our meal when Jewka turned to me, saying that he could see our friends' Dormobile driving down the road. I told him it could not be so, as they had converted a Japanese van into a sort of caravan. 'Yes,' he said, 'then it is definitely them.' The road was quite a little distance from us. We shouted and waved. Our waves were reciprocated. Jewka said, 'Tell them to join us for lunch.' This we shouted over to them and, without more ado, they stopped, took off their shoes and waded through the river and up to us. It was lovely and only after a good chat did we part company. I also managed to collect some small lumps of gneiss to bring home. It shows how old these mountains are. Another trophy for my rock collection.

Just before Novi Pazar, and right in the country, we were taken to a small charming church. Sporting only one dome, it is ninth and nineteenth century, called St Peter and Paul, and said to have been built by the apostle Titus, or by the Romans – strange. Treasures have been found by its walls – Greco/Illyrian – valuable treasure trove, now in the Beograd Museum. It was a fascinating church, where I managed to go down to the crypt. There were several unusually old gravestones against a wall. I was just taking a photo of them when Jewka came in. He said, but with a smile, that it was not allowed, but added, 'Take another quickly, as the guide of the church is outside at the moment.' I then wandered outside, where I saw that most of the church was surrounded by small gravestones, small stones with a broad main part and then, strangely, a broad crossbar. Each was inscribed with Cyrillic script. It is one of the oldest churches in the country.

We went on to Novi Pazar for the night. The hotel was very modern, much of it balanced on what looked like large threadless cotton reels, the whole painted cream and orange, a truly incredible looking place, very modern and very plastic. Inside was a huge circular reception area, with enormous plastic plants. A large fountain sprayed all in its vicinity. Upstairs was still circular, its balconies looking down to the ersatz hall, where you could, if you so wished, watch everyone doing their transactions at the mammoth reception desk. Every arch and every conceivable space had climbing plastic plants, in fact in many cases trees, growing up them, nailed strategically to any available wood – a real triffid land. Our room was a good size with very Moorish-type furniture. Our window gave us a good view of the River Ras, where many women in Turkish dress promenaded with their husbands, who were up to date in slightly limp tight suits, many with the Albanian white round hats.

The dining area was unbelievable. It was huge with only a large open-work metal screen between it and an incredibly loud disco, so noisy we all ate our dinner at record speed, Geoffrey with bits of torn white paper napkin stuffed in his ears, a sight to behold. Meanwhile, Jewka was being arrested by the police. He had left his jacket at our barbecue site, where one of the hotel waitresses found it, bringing it over to our coach at Novi Pazar for him to collect. When he did so, the police saw him and thought that he was stealing the coat, hence he was arrested. It took many arguments in the hotel before the police believed him. He was furious, partly because he thought his status had been assailed; he hated anyone to contradict him – very nice but arrogant. This was hard luck.

The next day we were off to the thirteenth/fourteenth century monastery of Peć and then to Dečani, both fascinating monasteries full of treasures. Peć is the best preserved medieval monastery, with four churches, much influenced by the Ottomans who ruled Kosovo in 1455. It stands in a most beautiful wooded valley, a most imposing sight with its three heavy domes, being a huge complex in the Raska style. This is the Holy Apostles. Later on in the fourteenth century they built Sv. Demetrius and then Sveta Bogorodica (Mary). Later on still was built Sv. Nicholas. The churches of Demetrius and Mary have the most lovely frescoes, like the Palaiologos type, even having in the Demetrius some painted by the famous Jovan.

In the old town bazaar there is also a most beautifully preserved mosque (Bajraklicarsi), with very early Islamic-type architecture, about fifteenth century. The interior, I am told, is decorated with flowers and geometric designs. Dečani is considered to be one of the most outstanding Serbian monasteries in the province of Kosovo, medieval in nature and eclectic in composition. The sculptures, architecture and paintings are thought to be done by Fra Vita of Kotor and the master builder may actually have been Fra Vita of Ravenna – nothing but the best.

Passing through Pristina, capital of Kosovo (much in the news, sadly, these days), we stopped fleetingly to see the neolithic sites by the Glacanka River. This is a quiet impressive site. When you think of the age of it, one is reminded of so many past lives and settlements. Then we saw the magnificent Imperial Mosque (Carska/Fatih/dzam, 1199), which was built in 1461 by Mohammed II, the conqueror of Constantinople. It is one of the largest built entirely of stone – a beautiful sight with its slim minaret pointing to heaven.

We were being glutted by these magnificent monasteries – one after the other, several I have not talked about – Gračanica, Sopočani, fourteenth century Ravenica and many more, each one perfect, fascinating and set in idyllic places, where one could spend days assimilating all truly majestic buildings and their precious ageless contents. Each one has its own unique atmosphere.

Before we left that area we were taken to Niš, to an incredible monument of skulls. These toothless, eyeless heads seem to sum one up as one walks by. It is a remembrance of a fight for freedom in 1809. The Turkish commander ordered the skulls of the 952 slain Serbs to be built into this wall in 1832. The famous French poet Lamartine was so moved by this event that he wrote the message: 'Serbia... a song of freedom – it is a song of freedom and glory that the mountain wind sings to the tower of Serbs that died for their country.'

We stayed that night at Svetozarevo, a fairly modern town, but with many old Turkish houses in various states of preservation. On many of the trees lining the streets were postcard-sized bits of white paper embellished with black writings. These, we gathered, were put up by people of the town when a relative died, in the same way as we insert a notice in the *Times* or *Daily Telegraph*. Some also had photos and a eulogy. As in all good obituaries if a Christian it also had a cross, if a Socialist a star and, if a non-believer nothing, this goes back to the thirteenth century.

When we arrived back in Beograd the coach took us to a fortress overlooking the wide River Danube, which joins the Sava River at this spot. Above it is the great fortress of Kalemegdan, standing in a beautiful green park. Originally this was a Roman fortification, as with so many places, and this was in the Roman-Celtic period. It has had many changes over the years, culminating in this large expanse of extensive building and ruins. Because of my leg trouble I stayed in the coach, getting out my book for a happy twenty-five minute read. However, our driver thought differently, insisting that he would take me for a coffee in a nearby taverna. It was a very kindly friendly thought, but oh what hard work! He did not speak English and, as I have said, I had no Serbo-Croat. The result was that for the whole twenty-five minutes I had to converse with him in sign language. Are you married? How many children? and so forth and so on. I actually managed it, but it was with an enormous sigh of relief I saw our party return, and we all went to the oldest café in Beograd called 'The Question Mark'. Apparently, as it was built quite near to the Cathedral, they called it the 'Next to the Cathedral Café' but, as soon as it opened, in walked a priest who objected to the name. By the afternoon of the same day its name was changed. To this day it is known as 'The Question Mark Café'. It was lovely, a small darkish place. Everything was wood and, to complete the picture, it was an old man in local dress who brought us our coffees. You felt that Dickens might walk in.

There is one thing more I must mention. This is about the hundreds of partisan statues, dotted all over Serbia. They are magnificent pieces of art, many being in metal, and in memory of the many who died when fighting the Germans in the Second World War. They all seem to have been particularly well placed – on the skyline of a hill or a sward of grass, against a lovely wall, and so on. Their shapes are beautiful, modern but telling, often giving the feel of the struggle that had ensued with their sharp angular shapes, many beautiful rounded creations full of sorrow. It would make a fascinating subject to photograph them, adding their history. Also these tragic grassy mounds, some seven or eight feet high and longer horizontally, are literally mounds of Yugoslavian bodies shot by the Germans and thrown into pits, which built up and up, resulting in those high mounds, which the ever encroaching living grass has made just bearable to look at.

We found Jewka unyielding and deeply angry about both the Turks and the Germans, both of which devastated their land. But he also gave one an insight into the Serbs as we have been seeing them. They are a relentlessly passionate people, who will not tolerate interference, ceding nothing back to an enemy, even if they themselves had wrested it from them. I understand why he should be like that, but not why they should never give back what is due, and forget. It seems an ineradicable part of their nature.

As this was our last evening it was arranged that we should be taken to a restaurant in the Bohemian part of Beograd for dinner. The restaurant was called the Skadaliya and was most picturesque. We arrived soaking wet. The rain had started a really heavy downpour with lightning zigzagging up and down the small street. We had no coats or jackets and had to run through a very narrow street to reach the restaurant. It seemed too that we had to sit outside, but luckily with a wooden roof over us.

We settled at a long table for nine people. As we were handed our menus our driver got up and gave each of the women a beautiful long-stemmed red rose – a lovely gesture. During the meal a plump Arabic woman and a man sang the most evocative soul-stirring songs, something like the Fado singers. They were accompanied by an accordion, double bass and a guitar. The only trouble was that the amplification was too loud, resounding on the wooden roof. The place was packed with other diners out for a happy weekend evening. It was a marvellous ending to one of the most fascinating holidays I have ever had.

Chapter Fourteen

Lantau

Lantau Island, February 1975

I had gone with a friend to stay in Hong Kong for three weeks with friends of hers, he having been with the BBC in Plymouth where she had worked with him.

We had been there a while when one day he asked if we would like to stay a couple of days at a Buddhist monastery on Lantau Island, a much larger island than Victoria Island (Hong Kong), and very beautiful. There was a guest house and restaurant, he told us, saying he would get his secretary to book us a room. We were delighted, and duly the room was booked.

Several days later, we got the minibus down to the famous very busy Star Ferry, a fascinating place in itself, myriad crafts of every sort and size milling about the water between Victoria Island and the mainland, Kowloon, and also the many ferries to the islands and Macau.

These ferries themselves and the other crafts were a revelation. One just wondered how they did not collide – jetfoils, private ships and yachts, junks, ordinary ferries, large steamers, then hundreds of tiny sampans, lastly huge cargo steamers, too large to come close to land, but discharged of their cargo by working junks which are said to be unsinkable.

We found a seat on the ordinary Lantau ferry, one which gave us a good view of the scenery, then sat watching the other passengers arrive. It was absorbing. An old Chinese woman was clambering on board, with a long bamboo pole across her shoulder from which dangled several very dead ducks. How beautifully she managed over the softly moving gangplank. This is a very useful way of carrying one's goods. There were also people carrying long sugar canes; others with good old dreary plastic bags full of vegetables and much else, which were being swung precariously on their arms as they chatted, or rather shouted, in their high pitched singsong voices, a sound one came to love. How sedate we looked in our English slacks and blouses. With delight we watched too the small Chinese children darting here and there, with their lovely small oriental faces which lit up the whole of their face when they laughed or smiled – such intense joy.

The journey was also a joy, sitting on deck in the sun with a welcoming breeze to cool us, surrounded by deep blue sea ruffled by the following white wake of the ship.

We stopped at many islands, such as Cheung Chow. Each one seemed a cosmic entity in itself. Their small ports had many stalls set up selling the usual, but attractive Chinese cabbages, tomatoes, greens of all sorts and other brilliantly coloured vegetables and fruit, also inevitably many hens running between the quick moving feet of the stall-holders, always missing them untouched, to live another day – hopefully.

We arrived at Lantau at about 11 o'clock. Walking to the bus that would take us to the monastery high in the mountains, two Buddhist monks came to us. Addressing us by name, they informed us that they had been sent to fetch us from the ferry. Surprised, we followed them to a car, where they sat in front and we seemingly in the back. Although they spoke English, they did not talk – perhaps it was prayer time?

The journey took about three quarters of an hour, rising all the time, with stupendous views on either side. The hot air was getting cooler with every rising mile. The countryside was beautiful. It could have almost been summer in England – in fact it was January in China.

Every so often we looked down, catching sight of the blue sea between the mountains, tiny boats bobbing like toys slumbering on their anchors, and our, by now, tiny ferry boat getting up steam to return to Hong Kong.

We arrived at the top of this great mountain range. Ahead of us stood the most staggering sight, a red and gold ornate archway covered by the most beautiful Chinese carvings. Driving through it, we saw many buildings scattered about, also with these fascinating colours and designs, as well as houses, all amid delicate trees.

Many Chinese, clutching large handfuls of joss sticks, were surging round a sort of circular dais covered thickly with sand. The ones close to it were murmuring prayers at a great rate, while pushing the many joss sticks into the sand and lighting them. In the centre of the dais was a god surrounded by flowers and fruit.

This was a special festival weekend, many having come to this particular place of worship – we had noticed how packed the ferry was – to add their sticks to the many already there; no one seemed to have less than twenty or thirty sticks. The spicy scent was so evocative amid the haze of the wavering smoke in the brilliant sun. All were honouring their gods, these hundreds of small colourful Chinese men, women and children in their lively coloured tunics and trousers, which added so much to the festive scene.

By now we were also familiar with the singsong cadence of the language and, as I said earlier, came to love it.

The car arrived at the front door of one of the buildings and framed in it was a most distinguished, beautiful, elderly, slim holy man. He was dressed in a blue silk embroidered robe, black slim silk trousers and a small round black silk hat. He sported a traditional delicate shining beard. His white beautiful slim hands were pressed together.

We left the car carrying our two small suitcases, to be greeted by this seemingly very important monk, who told us to drop our cases and follow him into a room. His dismissal of our cases was as if he were saying how trivial and unimportant they were.

We literally dropped our cases where we stood, following him into a most attractive large room, with a highly polished long table in the centre. On sitting down at the head of it, he motioned us to sit on either side of him.

He then proceeded to tell us in his soft cultured voice that he was going to instruct us in the Buddhist faith, a faith I personally have been very interested in for a long time. We were speechless but delighted, and sat listening and learning from him, so many words of great wisdom and common sense.

After about an hour, a Chinese woman brought in three delicate cups of fragrant China tea. The cups were painted porcelain and handless. He took his cup in his elegant frail hands, so gracefully used you could almost see through them, held it in front of his face, drank slowly, never speaking or looking one way or another. On putting it down, he turned to us and said in perfect English that what was so sad with Europeans, and in fact with much of the modern world, was that we never relax, never have time for anything, to appreciate what we are doing, to gather in the force round us. We had a so-called *better life*, which was leading to all the terrible strife in our world.

He said that he had had the heads of most of the states in the civilised world coming to him, to ask what they could do to save their countries from the tragic state they were in. 'I told them,' he said gently and sadly, but of course it is ignored, and it is happening all around us as well. No one would give up so much for a state of happiness and prosperity in its true form.

Taking his cup up again, he said, 'This is a small example. I have taken up my cup, I am relaxed, I think how beautiful is the cup, I sip the tea, concentrate on the delicious fragrance, taste and the gentle warmth of the liquid. I never look around or hurriedly think of a hundred things. I put down the cup slowly and gently, feeling refreshed to go on with our talk. You people,' he said kindly but firmly, 'never give yourselves time to relax, to gain peace and composure.'

He went on with our instruction. Now, several years later, I am ashamed to say I cannot remember much of what he told us. We had been so surprised and unprepared, our minds were not ready for such an experience, but the substance has lasted the rest of my life.

He then said that we had twenty minutes before lunch, and would we please come with him, as he would show us the living quarters of the monks. This he did, actually taking us into one of the small houses, where the monk gave us a biscuit to nibble as we four sat and talked. He was a part-time monk who had a small firm in Kowloon. He had come here this time for the celebrations. He too spoke good English and said that he often came and stayed at this monastery.

Our guru told us that he had been detained on Lantau, as he spoke English, to instruct us, and that he was the head of a monastery at Lion Rock in the New Territories. He asked who we were, what special people? He said that the Hong Kong TV studios had rung them to tell them we were coming, so they understood that we were people of substance, who wished to learn about the Buddhist religion. How awful, they had misinterpreted the telephone call, we should just have been booked into the guest house. We told him of the mistake, apologising profusely, but luckily he did not mind and later continued with our tuition.

He then said that we had five minutes to wash and then to present ourselves in his dining room.

On entering the dining room, exactly on time, as were the others – our guru of course, the electrician monk plus another monk, who did not speak English – we were served a most delicious meal by a Chinese woman, one of the most delicious I have ever had. It was vegetarian, many beautiful bright green greens and other coloured vegetables, the colour of them all retained although cooked, and with it many other tastes that I did not know, but how delicious. We had seen the cooks all sitting on the ground outside the kitchen, preparing this marvellous feast, on our way to see the monks' houses, their great round baskets full of freshly picked green produce, tomatoes and other coloured plants, as well as many varieties of fruit. They had all been chatting and laughing whilst working. Buddhism certainly seemed to make for joy.

We had to use chopsticks, of course, helping ourselves from a large central dish into our bowls. The china was that beautiful white and blue patterned one, with rice actually baked into it, making the pattern; you see much of it here nowadays.

I had been lucky and been taught how to use chopsticks before I had left England, strangely enough by Arthur Negus of *Going for a Song* fame. His daughter and her husband lived in Singapore, so he and his wife went regularly to stay with them. He borrowed two of my paint brushes to use as the chopsticks. How glad I was now that he had shown me the technique.

At the end of the meal our guru told us to go with the Chinese woman he had summoned to see our bedroom and to take our cases with us. Again he gave us the precise time to be back – in ten minutes – as he was taking us to the large hall where the religious ceremonies were taking place.

We followed the woman as directed. She took us up quite a steep rise to a house, then upstairs to a bedroom completely empty except for two large double beds – one each. The beds were very thick planks of wood, polished by wear, a small straw-filled pillow each and a straw-filled duvet each, plus of course a mosquito net each. She told us that she would wake us in the morning at about five-thirty to give us time to get back to the ceremonies, and that she would leave us a small jug of cold water so that we could wash.

We then went promptly back to our guru, who took us to the hall of celebrations. It was filled with Chinese, who seemed to be jogging round the hall, in the middle of which was a lovely Buddha in a glass case. Round the edge of the hall were long benches against each wall, and round the hall floor was what looked like a well-worn stair carpet laid fairly near the Buddha, again right round the hall. The rest of the floor was bare.

Our guru told us to go and do whatever the others were doing. He too then plunged into this moving mêlée. Everyone seemed so petite and graceful I felt like a very heavy lumpy giant.

We joined the joggers, tiring fairly soon, then getting our second – and third – wind. There seemed a curious timelessness about the movement; one's thoughts became calm and peaceful. After about half an hour everyone, at the sound of a gentle gong, started running; this again lasted for about half an hour. We learnt later that they had started by walking for half an hour.

It sounds unbelievable, but more and more one had an extraordinary feeling of wellbeing, a strong exhilaration of the whole being in time with the universe.

After that half hour was over our guru came over to us and indicated that we were to sit on one of the benches. People moved aside to let him through to them – everyone tries to get to the benches before they fill up. Everyone else, which was the majority, had to sit on the carpet, legs crossed Buddha-wise and palms up on either side of them, no part touching the ritual floor. Then the gong sounded. We sat down, by now fairly exhausted physically, but still with the same mental agility. As we sat a man gave a sermon while walking slowly round and round the room as he talked. His soft Chinese cadences were peaceful yet forceful. We of course could not understand it, but were fascinated watching the absorbed faces of the people around us.

This went on for yet another half hour. When it ended, in this absolutely silent hall, we had to arrange ourselves in the position to meditate. For us that meant placing our hands palms up on either side of us. We could not cross our legs as we were on a bench. We totally relaxed our whole bodies, closed our eyes and started to meditate. Again I personally found this a marvellous sense of release, limbo, and yet one's brain was following the thought – the mantra. I found a sort of *cotton wool* bodily detachment, and yet still the brain concentrated.

This too lasted about half an hour. The gong went softly in a recess. We all sat and chatted, while a small cup of China tea was handed to everyone. The whole ceremony had taken nearly three hours. We found the whole thing fascinating, although to read about it may make it sound very strange.

Ruth and I got up to go, but on reaching the door our guru came over and said, 'You go back and go through the same ceremony again.' We turned tail back to our places, listening for the gong to tell us to start again. This ceremony we did three times, nine hours in all; the only difference being that at the end of the second one we were given a small delicious cake instead of the tea, and the third time a special festival small bun.

After the third time we said to our guru that we had no energy left to go through another session. It was now about 10 p.m. Reluctantly he agreed, but said that we must be at the 6 a.m. session, where he would be preaching, and that every time he came to where we sat he would speak in English. He then went back to do yet another session – a man who must have been well in his eighties.

We staggered up the hill in the pitch dark, no stars about on this cloudy night, only the sweet and pungent scents of the flowers and herbs. We stumbled, exhausted, to bed. The night was very cold on this mountain top, no hot water, no drink, nothing except a very hard bed and straw-filled cotton pillow and duvet, plus a very dim small lamp.

We crawled into our beds and slept with sheer weariness. During the night I turned, slapping hard down with my body on the unforgiving bare wooden base, then slept on. In the morning we both agreed it had been the most peaceful comfortable night we had ever had.

It was twenty past five. We washed in the cold water from the small jug, dressed and went outside. The light was just beginning to break, the cool clear air was beautiful and the birds were giving sleepy twitters in the trees. We made our way down to the hall – six o'clock on the dot – joining the crowd that was surging into the hall. The gong went and we started walking round and round the hall as before. As promised, when it came to the sermon our guru spoke in English as he passed us.

We were not so comfortable this time round, as we did not manage to get a seat on any bench for the sermon and meditation. We tried to curl up our legs crosswise – no limb must touch the floor, but only the carpet.

My friend was rather arthritic for her reasonably young age, so could not sit with her legs crossed Buddha-wise, or in fact any other wise; a little Chinese woman next to her helpfully grabbed her one leg and tried to push it into position, all in vain. Eventually she looked over at me, shrugged her shoulders with a half-apologetic, half-resigned smile on her face and went on with listening to the sermon.

At the end of this ceremony we were allowed to go and look at the other beautiful temple-like buildings, and then meet our guru for our last meal before we left.

We saw in the distance the large visitors' restaurant, but went straight to see the temples, so exotic and colourful. Various rich men in Hong Kong over the years had given money to make the gold roofs. These roofs are splendid, curving down from the straight top and covered at certain parts by strange dragons, Fo dogs and much else, all of great significance; inside, wreathed as usual with the incredible smoky haze and smell of incense, a fantastic sight. In one of the temples was a huge (much larger than life-size) Buddha reclining on an ornate bed, on its soles were inscriptions. Sadly we never found out what they said.

There were still hundreds of Chinese everywhere. These people did not attend the festivals in the hall. I don't know on what criteria you could attend. They were still offering up their bundles of joss sticks. The sound of their voices was more intense to us now, after our silent engrossing hours, the sound was more penetrating.

Again these people had only come for the day from Hong Kong, the islands or even from Macau, to take part in these religious festivities.

At the appointed time we met for lunch, which was as good as that of the previous day, and with the same charming company.

After lunch we were going to catch the bus down to the harbour, but before we left we asked if we could take a photo of the guru, his electrician friend and the other monk. My friend elected to take the photo, so the guru asked me to join the group as well. Sadly out of all the photos we took that one did not come out – perhaps the Buddha intervened!

Our guru gave us a book he had written, sadly only in Chinese, but we were delighted with our gift. We had a very warm friendly farewell. On our return to Hong Kong we told our friends and others about our experience. It was greeted by all with jealousy (kindly) and astonishment, a thing they would all have given anything to do.

Chapter Fifteen

Far East Tour

Heathrow, 10th November, 1977

We arrived at Heathrow for our journey to Singapore – or, as the orientals say, Singapura, the Lion City. I was doing this trip with a friend of mine, Ruth Lovell, a producer in the Bristol BBC.

As luck would have it, the plane was late in leaving, the mechanical luggage ramp having seized up. All the luggage had to be manhandled on to the Jumbo jet. This took two hours, including having to wait for Concorde to leave. Being a prestige plane, it was allowed to go off on time, leaving us poor relations to wait on its pleasure. It stood next to our plane looking like a beautiful haughty bird.

As we whiled away the two hours incarcerated in the static plane, my spirits got lower and lower. I read the instructions telling one how to save lives if the plane should crash, first on land – a preferable way as with certain pre-knowledge one would be killed outright, whereas on the sea we might come crashing down on the hungry maw of the sea. I cannot swim, I had visions of gulping for air as I sank. I looked surreptitiously, but with no luck, for the lifejacket, said to be under my seat. I have still never found this seemingly mythical jacket, in all the journeys I have made. I read the instruction card. It said, 'Do not inflate until out of plane door.' But what good is that to me? By then I would be drowning.

I thought I must do something more cheerful so searched further into the pocket of the seat in front of me. What did I find? A large bag which said, if you feel sick, do use this bag. All so encouraging and welcoming! The pocket being explored, I now put on my safety belt, yet more doom and gloom. Now I was ready for a stiff drink but, woe betide, we were not allowed one until we were in the air.

Eventually we left. The flight was uneventful to start with, broken by dinner and a blissful strong gin and tonic to steady the nerves.

We arrived at Zurich but were not allowed off the plane, all in the aid of security. Still one hour is not unduly long for refuelling. It was now time to take to the air again. The bell tinkled and a voice came over the tannoy: 'We are so sorry but one of the engines has failed. We will be delayed for another two hours.' The passengers took it well. At least it had not happened when we were in the air. Time goes as time will, and we again took off. We were fed, and as everyone was by now sleepy, they put the screen down for us to see a film. I invested in a pair of earphones, settling to enjoy a film everyone said was marvellous, *Rocky*. Well, either I have no sense of humour and style, but I thought it terrible – fighting, and punching and sorrow.

We arrived at Muscat. Again we were not allowed out of the plane for security, so we all crowded round the exits to get a breath of fresh hot air. It seemed to lap round one; what a change from icy London! Meanwhile, an army of little Arab gentlemen with cotton crochet caps (signifying that they had been to Mecca, I am told) swept round our feet, changed all the towels and antimacassars – what an old-fashioned world – loaded on tray after tray of yet another meal, then, like a stream of processional ants, they flowed out of the plane, into a transport bus and on to the next plane. What a life, from one dirty plane floor to another in a noisy petrol-laden airport, no doubt for a pittance. But still it was a job, which for many countries is something, not like our cushioned spoiled society, who think that they are at starvation's door if they do not have a TV and three meals a day.

The plane was now taken over by the most beautiful Indian women in glorious coloured saris, their graceful movements and smiles such a contrast to the business-like English crew that had just left. We were all set to go, when, yet again, the tannoy tinkled and a voice cracked through, 'We are so sorry but another engine has failed. We are afraid this will take two or three hours to repair.' It was unbelievable; there certainly seemed to be a jinx on this journey. To soothe us, the sari'd girls came round with bowls filled with shocking pink and apple green facecloths which had been dipped in cool rosewater. They proceeded to hand one to each passenger with, most incongruously, tin meat tongs. Oh how cool and refreshing in the heat of this earthbound plane. One lingered with it over one's face, neck and hands, but all too soon they came back, scooping the cloths up and disappearing into the galley; only the scent of the rosewater lingered in the still air.

Outside was the most stupendous dawn, great smudges of orange and yellow being torn across the sky, dispersing the grey clouds of night, the white rooftops of the unseen town catching the glow, as birds and cocks were making their presence known.

Eventually we took off. We turned our watches forward even more, leaving gaps of unused time behind us. We had been given menus for all our meals on boarding our plane at Heathrow, so that we could savour what we would have on the flight. We took these up to give one something to do; the cabin steward came up saying that, as the passengers had been so inconvenienced by the breakdowns, the captain said we were all to choose a drink. As it was after Zurich where the drinks were free anyway, we were clear of ABTA.

We arrived eventually in Singapore in the hot glaring beautiful sun. Everywhere were trees and flowers, their fragrance hit you as you breathed. It was a funny little airport then (1977) for what is such an important place. I believe they have now enlarged it; I am glad I saw it in its toytown days!

We hailed a taxi to take us to our oriental hotel, the 'South Asia', in Bencoolin Street, where we booked a room for the night. It was fascinatingly primitive, the shower being a small portioned-off part of the room, the floor sloping to a small hole, a spray tap over one's head to sluice one down. The hotel was filled with Indians, Malays and others, sitting around the corridors on the floor, dusty though it was. The heat was intense. We were now nearly on the Equator.

Before leaving England a young couple I had met several years before in Hong Kong had sent me an intriguing parcel; it contained a small hand towel to tie on to my handbag as a de-sweater, and a malaria coil, to put on the windowsills of hotels/doss-houses where we happened to stay that had broken mosquito meshes across their windows. Both items were most appreciated during our seven week journey.

We took ourselves out sightseeing. The hot air hit one like a blanket as we stepped into the street, almost stopping one's breath. Singapore is a fascinating place, an enormous, very clean city, so clean that there is no malaria there. Every drop of water is sprayed and cleaned and any dank unnecessary water cleared away. You can also eat anywhere. Even the food that is sold in the streets is perfectly pure.

I was particularly interested in this city, as in 1914 my parents were married in the large English cathedral, my mother having arrived from England to marry my father, who was a rubber planter. On arriving at the Singapore port, she was greeted by a note from my father saying that he had gone to fight in a mutiny and would be back soon! Not what a well-bred sheltered young girl from England expected. However, the ship was docked there for several days, and she was able to stay aboard until his return, which luckily was quite soon. At their reception, my mother said you could see outside the hotel windows Malays with rifles at the ready in case of more trouble.

The Indian temples are strange, over-ornate and rather scruffy, every inch covered with carvings of animals, people and symbolic gods, the roofs often covered with sacred cows and other odd creatures. They did not mind one going inside as long as no special prayers were in progress. They are rarely empty; people are in and out all the time praying. Oh so alive and vibrant.

We saw a great many temples of all persuasions. It is odd at first to see these mixed types everywhere – Muslim, Taoist, Buddhist, Chinese and many more – of course all the dark dreary legacies of missionaries for good or otherwise. The more I travel, the more I wonder whether we should interfere with other faiths. Surely it all reaches the same god, under different names, and who are we to say only our way is right or 'no heaven for you'?

There was a huge, splendid temple in the suburbs of Singapore called the Temple of One Thousand Lights, in Racecourse Road. It has an enormous Buddha fifty feet high surrounded by lights. Also in a room behind this is a huge reclining Buddha. Both are covered with gold. On the soles of the feet of this reclining Buddha is written a prayer in Chinese. I find these Buddhas strange. There is a sense of dusty cheapness about the temples but, when you look at the Buddha's eyes, you get an odd feeling that they are watching you and following you, sensing any derogatory or otherwise thoughts. You also get a marvellous feeling of calm, the insignificance of oneself. The Buddha seems to say, 'You might have much to say about my religion, way of life, my philosophy, but the way I lived brought a peace, and stillness, a closeness to god that you westerners seem to fail to achieve.'

In the corners of these temples you see the curator-type people, male and female, going about their domestic duties, busy cooking on tiny stoves for a sprawl of children around their feet, or selling incense sticks to those who want to pray. Life is certainly lived in these places.

We had a meal that night in an area called 'The Satay Club'. We had been told about it but did not know what to expect. We arrived at an open patch by a sea wall. From several crippled-looking trees hung garish lamps. Around one circular piece of worn grass were lots of tiny stalls, plenty of Malay and Chinese music, and the eternal high singsong chat of the people gathered there. Strewn around the grass were logs to sit on and planks on which to lay our trays. We went over and looked at the stalls: delicious steaming satays, kebabs and Indonesian foods made with meats, fruits and hot spicy peanut sauces, the owners cooking on tiny charcoal braziers. You went round these stalls and chose what you wanted, ordered and sat down. In a very short time it arrived with a smiling flourish, costing literally pence. You then went to another stall and chose your drink; what exotic fare, a passion fruit drink or cane-sugar one or yet again perhaps a lychee, Ionian or papaya one, absolutely delicious, and oh so difficult to choose from so much. One usually ordered one or two different types. It was so hot one had to keep drinking... what a good excuse.

We then decided we were still hungry, so went to another stall. They were selling something called *popia*, which turned out to be like a very thin pancake spread with chilli and sweet sauce, then piled up with turnip, bean sprouts, prawns, chopped nuts, cucumber, and more chilli sauce. It is then rolled up neatly and handed to one. It was absolutely delicious.

We walked back to our hotel past the famous Raffles Hotel. What a name to be conjured with: a Raj-type looking building surrounded by palm trees, whose leaves grew out of the top like a fan. We thought another evening we would go there for a drink; it is such a historic place, one of the world's famous hotels. However, time flew and we never made that visit.

It was so hot at night as well as during the day, but for a blessed twenty minutes each evening when the cool wet rain came down. It was bliss to be in it, as one dried again in a very short time, also it washed all the grey-greenery green again.

Another evening we were coming back to our hotel – by then we had moved to a slightly better one across the road, trundling our heavy cases on wheels through the ever rushing traffic – when we saw an Indian hotel. Ruth suggested that we go there for a drink. We went through a large gate, leading to an open space before the house; there was a tall Indian smothered in hair, who eyed us oddly. We then went into a murky looking hall, where a little old Indian came out of a back room and asked us what we wanted. We asked for a cool drink. As we waited for it to arrive, the large bewhiskered man from the garden came in and whispered in my ear, 'Come, have some brandy with me!' After much refusing, he eventually left us. The Indians of course do not drink, their religion forbids it – food for thought?

Next day we went to see St Andrew's Cathedral, where my parents had been married, a dark grey edifice among the brilliant colours and sunshine of the East. The British seem to manage to make their places of worship extraordinarily sad. We then explored the district around there. Shopping, when not done in their fascinating markets, is done mainly in big multi-storeyed supermarkets, amazing places with even play centres to leave your children while you shop. They are open from eight in the morning until ten o'clock at night. We ate our lunch several times at a small outside restaurant in front of one of these emporiums, called the Plaza Singapura, where they had cheap but delicious meals. I bought in the store there a man's most attractive jade-green batik shirt; one could only wear cotton in this heat. I travelled everywhere with just two voluminous blue and white Indian dresses, so cool and easy to wash, and bra and pants. Another day I was out shopping and sightseeing on my own and saw the most beautiful silk material in the window of a small shop. So I went in to price it. The youngish man told me how much it cost, far too expensive for my purse. (It was not the type of shop where you bartered.) On telling him that I could not afford it, he said, leaning confidentially over the counter, 'If you come out for a drink with me, I will knock down the price for you.' He still has the material!

Later on Ruth and I met and went on to a covered market, one of the most fascinating places, I think, in any part of the world. Unfortunately they were sluicing the floors down and gradually shutting up the stalls, but luckily we did find a spot with chairs and tables of much worn wood, where we were introduced to the most delicious drink called *chendol*, made from coconut milk, brown sugar, crushed ice, and a stringy jelly-like substance of green pea flour. How we wished we had found it sooner. It has an Indian yoghurt base.

Another day we thought we would go to Sentosa Island, off the southern part of Singapore Island. We caught a local bus, which took us to the ferry from Jardine Point. There was also a cable car over to this island, but we thought we would rather trust ourselves on the water. The island is an incredible place; the whole of it is dedicated to pleasure. It has small buses that do a circular tour. You get off and on them as you come to the places you want to see, all with the same ticket. We went first to the Coralarium. I may say that luckily when you buy your entrance ticket to the island they also give you a map with all the things on it that you can see. This also includes the bus trips – as many as you want.

The Coralarium was fascinating, a huge building, open at one side, and with large maps of all parts of the world showing the shells and coral of each country they came from stuck on the appropriate places. It was in a beautiful setting too, surrounded by palm trees sloping down to the deep blue warm sea. As I came out of the building a group of Malay schoolchildren were entering. One of them was a most beautiful girl of about twelve, who in fact had sat next to me on one of the buses chatting to me all the time. She now came running over with her friend and said, 'I see you have a camera. Will you take a photo of me and then send me a copy?' I duly obliged and she gave me her name and address – Fausiah Sapar, 6 Veterinary Station, Lim Cu Kang Road, near Singapore. I told her I would not have it developed for several months, as I was travelling around. When I arrived home 2 months later, there was a Christmas card waiting for me from her. I later duly sent her the photo.

After the Coralarium we saw a notice saying, 'This way to the Whales'. With great effort in the heat and no shade we followed the notice, which took us up a great many concrete steps, each one seeming harder than the one before. With great expectation we reached the top but, lo and behold, there was a huge concrete pond and in it one solitary, tiny baby whale swimming desperately around. So we left it and went for a meal under the trees. Everywhere were birds about six inches high, dark donkey brown in colour with vivid yellow beaks and feet. There was also a cameo centre, a maritime museum and much else.

On Sunday we took a bus to Tanglin Road, where there is a tourist office with a large crafts centre complex. We found, surprisingly for the East, that nearly everything was closed except an Indonesian shop where I bought a fascinating group of bamboo pipes for a little Swiss-Indian girl I know in Bath – Indira Varme.

The large Botanical Gardens were near here too. Ruth went off there, as she is very interested in plants, and I, with my 'temple' interests, went to the other side of the city, by bus, to see a famous Hindu temple. As I waited for my bus a lot of lorries passed by filled with soldiers wearing strange hats and carrying small shrines and flowers. It must have been some special holy day. Later on in the town a Chinese funeral went by. The hearse was decked with flowing streamers and garlands. The Chinese with it were playing bright music very loudly. No one but me took the slightest notice of them.

The bus I eventually caught was very full. I asked the driver to let me out at the Sri Mariamnan Temple. He waited until I found a seat, the last at the back of the bus, only then starting; such manners. Then all the way, about a twenty minute journey, he shouted down the bus about all the sights I was to look at on the journey. Marvellous, except that his broken English was almost impossible to understand. On reaching my destination we did a beautiful bowing and thanking act together.

The temple was fascinating. The front, with its high pyramid-type edifice, was carved into a multitude of shapes. Like so many others it was a dirty multi-coloured building but also, like all the others, it was filled with the devout – a living vital feeling throughout the whole place.

Later on I went to one of the many fascinating markets, teeming with chattering smiling people, a riot of colour with its oriental flowers, fruit and vegetables, all looking most tempting. What ambience a place such as a market has, whatever part of the world one is in, filling one with quite a different feeling of the country, watching the animated sellers bartering and laughing as they worked. I tried many of the fruits in this market – papaya, mango, starfruit, jackfruit, rambutan. Luckily durians were not in season, as I would have felt I must try one. My father had told me that the smell of them is so dreadful and overpowering that you have to hold your nose to eat them, but that it is well worth it as the taste is so delicious.

I explored that part of the city, walking over a bridge spanning the dirty, sluggish river with its old derelict houses and small working boats. Behind all this, are the tall new, even ghastly, high-rise buildings of the modern world, the kind found in New York, Sheffield – in fact defacing the whole of the so-called civilised world. The only consolation was that there were no dreary useful but soul-destroying Reading High Street type of shops and grey crowds.

I met Ruth at the Plaza Singapura. I thought I would try and see if they had the delicious *chendol* drink that we had sampled earlier. The young Malay waitress brought it to us. She laughingly whispered to us, 'We call this green maggots! But we are not supposed to tell our customers that.'

That evening we thought we would treat ourselves to a reasonably priced cultural show which demonstrated local dancing, singing, etc. It was billed at the Hilton Hotel, a great edifice that is like a no man's land in every major city of the world. One has almost to ask, once inside, what country am I in?

This show was called the Instant Asia Cultural Show and, as it was at the Hilton, we donned our long dresses, fractionally tidier than our day-cum-travel-ones – in fact a dress that had just been washed and ironed! Carefully we combed and lacquered our hair, and equally carefully did our make-up, then to keep ourselves reasonably tidy we took a cab – very cheap in that part of the world. He drove us to the big hotel he called the Hilton and on being paid drove off. We took his word that it was the Hilton, walking into the most magnificent foyer, only to discover that we were in the Mandarin Hotel. It was well worth the mistake. It was like an enormous Aladdin's cave. It has the most fabulous décor that I have ever seen, à la Chinese, a marvellous high domed gold ceiling, beautifully worked with mouldings and Chinese-type chandeliers. All the furniture, carpets, pillars and curtains were on the same sumptuous scale, an exhilarating riot of golds, blues, greens, oranges, and glitter. In no way looking cheap, it looked most grand. I usually hate these big hotels, but here I would have given my eyeteeth to have stayed for one night.

We asked at the desk where the Hilton was, to be told it was only three minutes down the street. We set off to walk the three minute distance, that became ten minutes, then fifteen. At last we saw it starkly against the sky in the distance; it was now very dark.

Having arrived, we asked for tickets for the show and a meal, only to be told that they had just sold the last one and that the show had started. We sat for a while in their large opulent lounge – who would want to stay in these soulless places? Quite impersonal, with no stamp of the country in which it was situated, so why not stay at home! The lounge was crowded with the nouveau riche of the Asian and European world: all dressed alike, flashing their gold and diamonds in competition – no minks, too hot.

Having rested we walked back down the street and found an Indonesian restaurant in Orchard Street, in a block of flats with the ground floor arcaded shops. It was a delicious meal; Indonesian is my favourite of all Asian food, as long as it is not the very hot variety. I had *pendang lembu* – beef stewed in coconut milk, *gado gado*, a most delicious mixed vegetable dish done in a sauce with fried bean curd, then added to it a sweet sauce called *ketiab tahoo*, cooling it all with two large glasses of pure orange juice. The young waitresses spoke a little English. She thought us very funny and was explaining to me what I was eating, so that I could write it down. By now other waitresses had found us, and then the smiling manager and some of the Asian customers, who all became hilarious watching us. Feeling very well fed and exhausted, as the heat never abated, we walked back to our hotel in the Bencoolin.

Our bedroom looked on to a Muslim temple, a great bonus. As we as women were not allowed to enter it, only men, here we could see right into the temple, which had no side walls on two sides. Men came and went, dropping on their knees, brows on the floor, then up, murmuring their prayers as they knelt or stood. The open arches gave an added atmosphere to this kneeling and bowing reverence. There were no chairs and only the *mithrab* which faces east, as our altars do, out to Mecca. If you go into a Christian church that has previously been Muslim, or vice versa, you will see that the *mithrab* is situated slightly to the left of the altar. Outside the mosque at the back was an earth-covered garden, no grass, and there were clothes lines, where occasionally men would come out and hang up dripping wet white garments. The large mosques usually have the floor covered with rugs, about four to six deep, given by the faithful in thanks for some heavenly satisfaction. They also have a small part of the building reserved for women to come and pray.

Next day we were leaving for Malacca. We paid our bill, this time by American Express so as to save on cheques and money. The manager gave us two cards to give to friends in England saying that, if they came to Singapore, they could contact his hotel and they would be given a reduction on their rooms. I know not why, as his business seemed to be flourishing.

On looking back at my visit to this incredible city of mixed nationalities, one is stunned by the colours – the vivid magentas, oranges, blues, yellows and every other hue possible all mixed together, not a drab one among them; by the people, the streets ringing with life and laughter, the fruits and flowers but, most of all, the kindness. Another thing for me was the incongruous mixture of fascinating temples of every Eastern religion – mosques, Hindu temples, Chinese temples, Buddhist, Armenian, Thai, and even the occasional grey English church. Spilling everywhere were the fragrant beautiful flowers, plumbago, bougainvillaea, the red and orange flowers clashing together on the same bush. Oh those exotic names and so many more excitements.

The temples and mosques were my greatest interest: the Otian Hock King in Telok Ayer Street, which is mainly used by the Hokkien; the Buddhist Temple of a Thousand Lights on Racecourse Road, which I have already mentioned; the Hindu temple of Sri Mariamran, also mentioned earlier, in South Bridge Road; Subramanian Temple (or Chittiar) in Tank Road, which was especially noted for the Thaipusam celebrations, also a Hindu temple; the Sultan Mosque, it too in South Bridge Road, splendid with its domes (it is the largest in Singapore); then the Siong Lim Temple at Jalan Toa Payoh (it is a very large and most beautiful temple). I could go on and on, which would become tedious for the reader.

We had to get up early to catch the 6 a.m. bus to Malacca. As always it was intensely hot and carrying our cases did not help. We had brought fairly large ones as we had been told that by the time we reached Hong Kong it would be quite cold, nearly Christmas.

We arrived at the street from which the local bus left. Being a little early, we bought some fruit from a nearby stall – delicious little green bananas – also some Dr John Collis Brown's Mixture, just in case. It was now not obtainable in Britain, but oh how useful it is if one is upset by any food.

The bus trundled up on time, quite small, but it was air-conditioned. We also found we had a very good driver – something to be thankful about in these parts.

The passengers were a motley crew: Indians, Malays, Chinese and a white South African girl, who told us later on that she was twenty-eight and thought she had better hitch-hike around the world before she got too old. I laughed to myself, being all of sixty-one years. She was on her own but did not seem to be enjoying it as much as she should; more as if it were a duty to be done. She had already been to most places in the Far East, carrying only a rucksack and staying at student hostels.

We reached the causeway that joins Singapore to Malaysia. Now it was all Malay dollars instead of Singapore ones. They would not accept the latter, not like Singapore where you could almost use any currency. But of course it is one of the famous free ports of the world. The difference in value of the two dollars was exactly two centimes!

On arriving at the border post, Johore Bahru, we carried our heavy bags into an open-sided shed with long trestle tables. We waited patiently for one of the many little Malays to come and pass us through. A very young official kept asking me questions, seemingly quite unnecessary, then told me to open my case. He at once gave up being conversational and watched me with great curiosity unpack my overfull bag. The contents of an elderly white-haired woman being of no interest, he asked me to hurry and helped me push everything, rather unsuccessfully, back into the case. By this time Ruth was well ahead and our coach was waiting impatiently for my return. I had still to go through Passport Control; nearly everyone by this time was through. Then I was asked, in very bad English, where I was going. On saying Malacca he said, 'For how long?' I answered, 'For two days.' On that he gave me a form of entry and stamped my passport. I just caught my bus in time. I could hear it revving up as I staggered up to it.

We started to move. I got out my form of entry and, to my horror, on reading it saw it gave me permission to stay in Malaysia and then leave the country in two days. The man Ruth had dealt with had been much more explicit. They were very strict in Malaysia about this sort of thing and I was staying there for at least three weeks. By going to a large municipal building in Malacca and queuing for hours I finally got the correct document without any trouble.

The journey was quite fascinating, through hundreds of miles of rubber plantations, reminiscent of all my father's stories of his plantation. The tall quiet trees slowly dripped their sap into small cans tied on to their trunks, where a circle had been cut around the trunk to release the latex. Here and there stood men in typical coolie dress and hats matching the colourfully dressed women emptying the already full cans into a large container. There was a dark stillness about the whole land, which was slightly eerie.

Everywhere now were miles of thick jungle, the green growth densely packed, among it coconut trees, durian, palm trees and even banana trees – those small green delicious bananas you buy everywhere. Darting among all these trees were brilliantly coloured birds, bright greens, vivid blues, scarlet, yellows, birds of all shapes and sizes, and among them parrots in all their gay plumage. The others I am afraid I could not name.

This was a four hour journey we were taking, during which we had one stop for lunch and, as the National Trust say, a comfort stop. It was a small village where we stopped.

I never knew its name and could not have read a signpost anyway as their script is entirely different from ours. It consisted of a clearing in the jungle, with shacks and stalls selling a brilliant array of strange fruits, nut biscuits and vegetables. Some of the passengers went into a strange and dirty looking shed and had something to eat. We had already bought our bananas and cartons of passion fruit (grenadillas) and milk drinks – how delicious and cool and mercifully thirst-quenching. The heat, as I keep reiterating, was so intense we bought some more cartons to drink on the bus, this time fragrant mango juice and soya juice. We lived on these cartons throughout our visit to the Far East; a great boon, they had the added delight of being hygienic and cool.

Moving on, we noticed small clearings among the trees, with small wooden one-storey houses on stilts. Underneath they stored the inevitable products of modern living, bright plastic bowls in garish colours and much else, while around them were playing their beautiful naked children. The Malays, I think, are the most handsome race of people we saw or have ever seen in any other country. The women are quite lovely, slender and small in stature, so graceful in movement, but above all those beautiful faces; the men likewise, with in general soft good-looking faces. They are not a people who like to work; as in Spain, it is *mañana* always, whereas the Chinese are the great workers of Malaysia. My father had told me that, when he had a rubber plantation in Malaya – Kemandore, near Malacca – he had to employ Chinese entirely, so as to get the work done properly and efficiently, but that it was the Malay people he loved.

We eventually arrived at Malacca, the town where I was born in 1916. It was very exciting to see it, having heard so much about it from my mother and father.

It is a bustling town, people, cars and rickshaws everywhere, and as usual the fascinating mixture of old-type Malay houses, Portuguese buildings, and lastly modern, fairly monstrous odd edifices.

We had nowhere to stay so, with difficulty, managed to hail a taxi which took us to the tourist office. Laying down our luggage, plus our hot steaming selves, at the foot of the steps leading up to the office, we got our breath, then, as I guarded the luggage, Ruth went up to see if the tourist people could help us. She asked a very pregnant young girl, who was busy knitting garments (I can't think why, as I am sure the child would never use them) for the name of a good cheap hotel. She stopped knitting and rang up the Valiant Hotel in Jalan Bendahara, and was told that they could have us.

We trundled our cases to the edge of the pavement and again started hailing taxis, but to no avail; they were all full. We thought we would try a trishaw. I always like to try anything new at least once. One stopped for us; with many gesticulations we managed to get two as one was no good for both of us and our luggage. Our trishaw driver had hailed a friend to come and join him. Ruth got into one plus her baggage and I got into the other. It was a strange vulnerable feeling rushing through all the heavy traffic in this slight tricycle and carriage, especially as they went quite fast and wound in and out and roundabout the lorries, buses and anything else.

We had given them the name of our hotel and we started off. We seemed to go far around the town, stopping at every hotel that came in sight. We were convulsed with laugher as we passed and repassed each other. I do not know how they do it, peddling for dear life. Eventually we arrived at our hotel, which was only about two minutes from the tourist office. As we walked to the reception desk the man said, 'Where *have* you been? We saw you pass us nearly half an hour ago. In fact you passed us several times.' Our trishaw man carried our luggage in for us. They took their fare, but refused a tip.

It was a comfortable small room, quite adequate for what we needed. Downstairs was a small restaurant. Most important, it too was quite cheap. Ruth had brought an electric tumbler heater with her which we used, quite illegally, every morning to make some coffee for breakfast. None of these cheap hotels served breakfast. It was unbelievable the amount of times that the plug had to be changed to fit this multitudinous variety of sockets. It seemed eventually that we had more plugs than luggage to carry!

The shops around were mainly smart shack-type places, although there were one or two small supermarkets; small in comparison with ours in Britain. Our great joy was an amazing fruit and vegetable market by the river where we shopped several times during our stay, acquiring luscious fruits and fruit drinks of many varieties.

Behind the market was a delightful mosque. I think these domed buildings are particularly beautiful against the vivid blue skies and under the hot sun; their cream and mixed colours look entrancing. I walked into the garden where a turbaned gentleman sat. He came over to me saying that I could walk around the garden but must not go inside the mosque as it was the praying area for men. As the sides of the building were open arches I could see these worshippers bowing and bowing, their foreheads to the ground, praying quietly to their god. They all wore the most lovely coloured clothes. It was a fascinating experience, backclothed as it was by brilliant flowers and trees.

The town was, as with everywhere here, filled with the happy faces of Chinese, Buddhists, Taoists, Thai, Muslim and all else – this multitude of varying temples making intricate designs against the skyline. Also there were, as always, the sad-looking grey buildings with shut-in faces of the British churches.

The museum was the most interesting I had seen so far. It included many Portuguese themes, for of course Malacca had belonged for so long to them and the Dutch, as was also seen by the deep maroon painted outer walls of the buildings. One part of the town, near the tourist office, is nearly all this type. The clear-cut rounded fronts of the buildings were most pleasing to look at. The Malaysians now use these old colonial places as offices and such like, although, of course, the church remains a Christian church.

I went to see the church where I had been christened sixty-one years ago – Christ Church – again a dark red building with a typically Dutch frontage. Inside it was quite beautiful, very light with white painted walls and dark, well-polished woodwork. On the wall was a long brass plate with the names of all their vicars, including, I am happy to say, the name of the one on my birth certificate – John Smith, rather common or garden, but at least I knew I was truly christened!

Later on I bought some postcards from a small shed-like shop, one of these being of the church. A very pretty young Malay girl served me. As she counted the cards I had chosen, she came on the one of the church. Turning to me she said, 'I go to that church.'

I said how pretty it was and with that she smiled and said, 'I was christened there.'

'So was I,' I answered, and with that she flung her arms round me, asking me to go to church with her next Sunday so as to meet all the congregation.

Sadly I could not, as we would have moved on by then. It would have been interesting.

As I was leaving she said, 'Please remember me, my name is Violet.' I have the misfortune to have a middle name Violet, so I told her this. She was so delighted she nearly knocked me over hugging me and we parted eternal friends.

The sea front is charming, pale apple-green sea, an expanse of dry yellowy grass flanked by stalls selling tourist attractions; as the world over, horrendous. These stalls do not seem to detract from the scene luckily, mainly I think because of the brightly dressed Malays and Chinese running them.

There were several tiny palm-covered islands further round the corner, with more bays with boats unloading cargo. Everywhere was fragrant with frangipani, bougainvillaea and other intoxicating scents coming from the trees which grew everywhere. As usual there seemed to be friendliness and warmth to lift the heart. No problems seemed so great or dire. The sun is a great comforter.

That evening we had our meal at a restaurant by the river. We sat outside as inside there seemed to be a jolly formal Chinese party going on. Every now and then throughout the evening they brought out the chief participants to be photographed. They stood quite near to us, so we had a good view, as they took the photos of the various people, always only two at a time. They then held a canopy over them and made presentations. We never found out what it was all about.

Next day I went to change some money, or rather travellers cheques, in a funny little bank. I was ushered upstairs where two young men sat at a desk, one a Malay, the other Chinese. On handing over my passport and cheques, they noticed at once that I had been born in Malacca. This caused great excitement, with both of them exclaiming that I could have an ID card. 'You must get one. You are one of us.' They then showed me theirs. Later on I learnt that I would probably have landed up with no passport. Things are kept very under control there so forfeiting my passport, had I rashly done so, would have meant my sole document would have been the ID card, which would not have got me far.

I was in the bank for over half an hour. They asked me what my father had done. When I told them that he had been manager of a rubber estate, they asked where? I told them it was called Kemandore, between Malacca and Kuala Lumpur. 'Oh,' they said, 'we know it well. It is one of the largest estates, but it is now owned by us Malays.' I answered that I thought that was quite right, as it was their country. We had a great, very friendly farewell, and I was asked to come back again.

Many of the shops have beautiful batik materials in the most glorious colours. I bought some in a lovely shocking pink, which later on I made into a dress.

I then thought that I would go to the bus station to ask about buses to Kuala Lumpur – known everywhere as KL. On my way I passed many temples, one being a very large building, with a paved area on to the street. Unfortunately it was raining, so the colours were all rather muted. It had two large gorgeously grotesque Dogs of Fo, the male with the ball under its paw, the female with a pup. These dogs are always represented this way. They were on pedestals and in front of them were large bronze boxes ornately worked, standing on sculpted legs. In these boxes were piles of sand, into which the worshippers stuck their lighted joss sticks, not one at a time but in handfuls. The scent was very evocative as the smouldering remains threw off the heavy scent. Blue-clad Chinese came up continually to offer their prayers and sticks. Prayer and friendship seem to be the mixture of life for them.

The roof also was fascinating, the usual lovely lines swaying down, covered with dragons and many other things of sacred reverence. The inside was a vast area, many people milling round and also crowded with the paraphernalia of all Chinese temples, so alive, so lived in by people, yet so sacred.

Almost next door was a domed mosque surrounded by palm trees. A little further up from that an was Indian temple with its sacred cows and many strange gods. All these places were equally full of people, even on this and every ordinary working day. The façade of the Indian one was so different – a great slightly v-shaped dome with a straight top. On this there were rows of figures and animals, again all representing part of their religion.

After that came the modern world – the only skyscraper in the town – now it is probable that they have many. All the six floors of this building were a store such as Harrods, filled to the brim with western clothes, cosmetics and the usual conglomeration of stuff found in any semi-good European city. I did buy some postcards, reproductions of scenes of Malayan country life and work, originally done in batik and reproduced as these lovely cards. One that I bought was of a Malay woman emptying the latex from the rubber tree into her can – a memory of my father.

The bus station told me that there was a bus to Kuala Lumpur at eight o'clock the next morning. We could not book a seat, so would have to be there early and hope. We then met for lunch, going to a small Malay restaurant-cum-cafe, where there were only locals; lovely. We had a delicious meal of rice, very cheap, very filling. The décor was unadorned, except for the white paint on the walls, small clean plastic-topped tables and very friendly company.

Next day, as I have said, we were moving to Kuala Lumpur, the capital of the Federal area, and again leaving early, so eventually it was early to bed.

The journey was as usual fascinating, watching the ever glorious scenery and watching our equally fascinating fellow travellers. We were now passing wooden houses on stilts, then fields of pineapple and banana trees, then for the first time the paddy fields where the men and women wore blue clothes and the typical conical straw hats with large brims. They stood with their bare feet, at least to mid-calf, in the water, which was shared by water bullocks, who looked like tiny-legged prehistoric animals, their legs of course foreshortened by being hidden under the water. We had brought rolls, bananas and a pineapple with us for lunch, and the inevitable cartons of fruit juices, which we never tired of.

We arrived in big bustling Kuala Lumpur, modern to a certain degree. No city, it seems, is ever completely European, thank goodness. The bus station seemed to be a large building under a motorway. We could not get a taxi, had no hotel booked and were very hot indeed. Luckily we had both brought little trolleys with wheels – no cases with wheels in those days – and these luckily saved our lives. We trolleyed our cases up to a small portion of the road that did not seem to be a motorway and eventually managed to hail a taxi.

We had heard that the YWCA here was very good. After many gesticulations and repeating 'YWCA, Davidson Road' with sort of international/continental vowels we managed to make him understand.

He wended his way through massive traffic, past huge low buildings, over a flyover and then to some lovely gardens. With great pride he delivered us, like rather valuable parcels, at the door of a large colonial-type house. It was situated slightly outside the city and was, as you will have gathered, surrounded by a lovely garden and parks. The parks were full of people hammering up flags, streamers, slogans and much else. It seems we had arrived the day before what they call the Sea Games were to start. This apparently is the same as our Olympic Games. In fact it is the SEA Games (South East Asia Games), an enormous event, this year being held in KL. People from all over the East were taking part, so KL was full to brimming.

As we arrived at the YW, a Chinese woman was coming down the steps. She asked if she could help us. We must have looked very hot, tired and bedraggled. We enquired if she had a room, just for one night. Looking very doubtful she said that there wasn't a room in the whole of KL, because of the Games. We must have looked very downcast because, turning, she said to follow her into the house, explaining that Miss Chinn, who ran this huge hostel, was away until evening but that as far as she was concerned, if we did not mind sharing with other people, in that way she could put us up, but *only* for one night.

It was rather interesting. I was put in a room with a young Chinese girl. Ruth was in another house in the grounds, sharing the room with a Malay girl. My room was tiny with two very narrow beds and, a small dressing table. Then outside the door was a large washing and ironing area, several showers all in a row with lavatories at the end. So far I had not met my Chinese occupant. She was a student at the University.

Having settled in, we then took a taxi into KL proper. It was almost impossible to walk there as the huge flyover had incessant traffic belting up and down it, and no pavement.

We made our way to the famous railway station, with its domes and turrets, a long sprawling building which incorporated its hotel. It looked like a very impressive mosque. It is such a famous place we thought we would go into the hotel and have an old-fashioned tea. The atmosphere was marvellous. You could almost hear a palm-court band playing and see the English Raj tea dancing on the small dance floor, but instead all was quiet, with even an English ladylike hush. The Malay waiters in their white overalls slid up to us, presenting us with the menu. We ordered tea and waited. Several of the other tables were occupied, mainly with what looked like Indians discreetly discussing business. The great roof fans gave a pleasant coolness to the air, a lovely feeling of cool movement. The whole place could have come straight out of a Somerset Maugham novel.

After tea we went upstairs, ostensibly to go to the ladies' room, but in reality to explore the rest of the hotel. There was no one to stop us. We found it rather sad, seedy and forlorn, the great days of its grandeur were past, I'm afraid.

Across the road was another similar long domed building, which turned out to be the civic buildings. What a marvellous skyline both buildings made with the palm trees mingling amid these ornate roof lines against the brilliant deep blue hot sky.

We crossed the road – fraught with many hazards – to investigate an enormous modern mosque that we could see half-hidden behind palm trees and flowering shrubs. Going up some steps we arrived in a large green garden which had the most elegant entrancing mosque at the further end. It was quite modern, one of the most beautiful things I had seen during the whole of my Far East travels. It was enormous, a huge white edifice surrounded by quietly dripping water and flowers. Always you get this Arab preoccupation with water in contrast to their deserts.

We arrived at another flight of white marble steps where we had to remove our shoes, the marble under our feet burning our soles. We were also lent silk shawls to cover our heads and arms. Round the mosque itself were long cool verandas of white marble and endless strips of cool water surrounded by many coloured flowers. The building itself had intricately worked latticed sides, which practically concealed the interior. We were not permitted to enter, but could catch a glimpse of magentas, yellows and blues of the men's clothes as they bowed in prayer. Only a hissing sibilance broke the hush. The interior was dark, except for the light coming through the latticed apertures, which gave it a reverent unreal feel. Behind it all we could hear the muffled drone of the city traffic pounding by. We sat for a while in this fairy tale garden, listening only to the birds singing and the eternal tinkling of water.

As we went out, we saw worshippers washing in the great basins before entering the mosque to pray. We looked back and saw again the beautifully clear-cut lines of the building, the tall narrow pillars and beautifully curving roof. This mosque is known as Masiid Negra, the National Mosque. It cost ten million dollars to complete and is the most modern mosque in South-East Asia. The minaret is 245 feet high and shaped like an eighteen-pointed star representing the thirteen states of Malaysia and the five pillars of Islam. The surrounding forty-eight smaller domes are similar to that of the Great Mosque in Mecca. It is the second largest in the world. It was so complete and calm, yet enervating, it left me speechless. What an experience and worth coming to KL for, that alone.

That evening we thought we would eat at the YWCA. It was a delicious meal of fruit, rice and meat. After the meal, as it was getting late, Ruth said that she would go to bed, hopefully before her roommate arrived. I felt quite bright, so made my way to the common room. The TV was on, but one of the four charming Malay girls who were sitting there turned it off and all but one came over to talk to me.

They were in their late teens and early twenties, I should think. We talked for an hour or two about what they did and where they came from. They all had good jobs. It was quite the thing to live in a place like this for, although they were emancipated so far, they still would not have thought of getting a flat and living on their own. They wanted to know all about England. One had already been there and loved it. She was now saving up to go again. Another was going to try and go the following year. Their chief interest was Prince Charles. They asked if I had met him, so when I said 'Yes' I was an honoured guest for life. They thought he was marvellous, having seen him at a distance when he had made an official visit to KL. They also were fascinated by the rest of the Royal Family, having watched the Queen when she visited Malaysia not long before. One girl said she thought it was because they had had British rule for so long that they felt they belonged to the Royals, an interesting statement from such youngsters.

One of the girls was very amusing. She was dying to go to Scotland and buy a kilt! When I returned to England I saw a postcard with a photo of Prince Charles, and sent it off to them.

As we chatted, the door opened and in came a plump Chinese lady. One of the girls whispered to me, 'This is Miss Chinn who runs the place. She is a marvellous cook and we all like her tremendously.' They introduced me to her, telling me I was very lucky to be in this particular house as Miss Chinn did all the cooking for it. She sat down beside me – the girls moved off to bed, it was getting late – and we then had a most interesting talk. She told me how oppressed the Chinese were in Malaysia, in spite of their seeming freedom. They had no passports, only an ID card, and that they were curbed in anything they tried to do. They had to speak Tamil and other languages fluently, otherwise they would lose their jobs – everything to try and get them out of Malaysia. A very short-sighted policy, as the capacity for work in a Chinese is immense; hence they held many of the best jobs, owing to their hard work. What the country would be like left to the charming indolent Malays, I cannot imagine.

She was a charming woman, aged about forty I would think. She said it was so good to have someone older to talk to because, although she chatted and was friendly with the youngsters in her care, she could not 'let her hair down'.

She said it was a fascinating job, all the people who came and went were so different. At one time she had had great trouble with the 'hippies', as she had let them put their vans in the garden, telling them they could use the bathrooms and provide themselves with water – all for no cost. But she had had so much stolen and been taken advantage of; they even took the garden seats. She had to stop allowing them access. She said it was a pity because the real true hippie types she had found were most interesting and honest, but that one could not differentiate between them on arrival.

She asked me if I were going to have lunch here tomorrow before we left, to get the train for Penang. When I said I was, she said, 'I will make you a special Malay meal before you go.'

At last I went off to find my room. My companion had not arrived yet, so I crept into bed and slept, only waking enough to see a young Chinese girl arrive and climb eventually into her bed. Early in the morning I saw her working hard at her studies. I greeted her and got a quick shy smile, then she buried herself in her books again. Later she became quite chatty. I think it must have been at the prospect of losing her elderly roommate. I learnt that she was a translator and worked very hard but did not get a very large wage so could not afford breakfast, but she did go and make herself a cup of the eternal worldwide Nescafé, on a ring outside our room.

Ruth and I went off to the museum, a beautiful building set in large flower decked grounds. On the way there we saw a horde of racing cyclists practising for their event in the SEA Games. I managed to take a photo of them for my nephew, who was at that time doing very well in cycle competitions. The SEA Games were starting that day. Next day I read in the newspaper that the cyclists I had seen had done very well indeed; they were from Thailand and had won the gold medal.

The museum was intriguing, very well laid out in light airy rooms. These places of course were very well air-conditioned. It had fascinating old costumes from the old court life; the history of rubber planting and tin mining, with working models; and a most interesting geological section – one of my great interests. I was able to write down the main geological sections and features of places we were going to and where we had already stayed. The building is based on old Malay-style architecture and has two large murals on the front depicting historical episodes and a section of Malaysian crafts. Traditional Malay designs were adapted to the pre-cast concrete entrance screens, the carved panels in the central hall ceiling and the giant wrought iron grilles at one end.

Ruth, who had been looking at the plants outside, joined me and we went and had coffee in a small open-air café. A young boy joined us telling us that his brother ran the café, which was doing very well as it was so central. He was helping there until he got a job. He had arrived back from England, where he had been studying at a university – they all set great store by this, really working hard. He had done engineering, a popular study for these people. We found this all over the East. He told us that it would be a useful study to have done to get a job. He had loved England, but was very happy to be home. He was a most intelligent boy; we had a long talk with him on many subjects.

Ruth then went again to the Botanical Gardens, while I went back to have a last look at the beautiful mosque. As I went barefoot up the steps a turbaned man told me I could not go further as today was the Hari Raya Haji, their most sacred day. It is a time when everyone who can goes to Mecca; every man has to try and go at least once in a lifetime. I was allowed to stay in the lower garden, which is about 160 acres and known as Lake Gardens. It is amazing how many green parks and open places they have in this hot modern frenetic city.

It was fascinating seeing all these hundreds of men of every race – Malays, Arabs, Indians, and so on – of the Muslim faith making for the mosque, every shape and size from young boys to very old men. I am told that once they have been to Mecca they are entitled to wear a white *songkok* (small white crocheted, I think, cap) and are addressed as *Haji*. It was enthralling watching their faces, men with long white beards and marvellous faces, devout business men, shopkeepers, the lowliest to the highest, it seemed. I found a small café just inside the main gate, and so ensconced myself at a table outside to watch this religious throng. It is interesting; their religion seems just part and parcel of their everyday life and seems to give them great satisfaction.

I was so carried away I did not realise it was nearly time for Miss Chinn's special lunch. Also we were catching a train about two o'clock. I had to run down the flyover with its murderous motors, join the many at a corner road who were trying to get taxis. I was lucky and got one almost at once, doing my usual barter with him and off we went. But instead of going straight to the YW he went to an old part of the city. I said 'Davidson Road' very firmly, but he just nodded and smiled; still we went around the city. I was getting a little worried, which he must have noticed, because he said, 'Traffic too heavy other way, we go this way.' Eventually we got back to the right road. I don't really know why we did this circuitous route. However, he did not try to charge me any more and gave me a warm farewell.

I got into lunch just in time. It was a delicious satay with the usual peanut sauce, coconut rice, and then a most unusual pudding. I don't know what its ingredients were, but it really was good. When I finished it, Miss Chinn handed me hers to eat. 'For a treat,' she said, 'I made you this special lunch.'

We then got a taxi to the station, buying our tickets for Penang and paying a little more for the air-conditioned coach. There were only two of these coaches on the train, which was immensely long, and immensely hot. It goes right from Singapore to Bangkok – an express.

Again it was a very intriguing journey, through miles and miles of jungle, sitting comfortably in this so-called Super Express (*Ekspres Mesra*) which went slowly enough for us to see the scenery as it passed. I don't know what their non-express trains can be like? It was very clean and comfortable. A man in front of us kept leaning over the back of his seat and lending us newspapers, luckily in English.

We stopped at many stations, small and large, such as Ipoh – which was large – and passed many country scenes such as Chinese graveyards, terraced circular places with odd shaped walls and small rooms, presumably the graves. Apparently they are always built on a hillside, because of robbery, floods, and other destructors. The higher up the hill the better; it shows the family is well off. Many of the small fields had bullocks standing dreaming in the sun, their wet feet keeping them cool. There were very few animals about apart from these, but masses of coconut, papaya, durian and banana trees; no doubt also many I did not recognise.

The mosquitoes were busy. We were glad we were taking our anti-malaria tablets (Piriton) and had been thankful in many of our cheap hotels to have our malaria coils smouldering on the windowsill all night. They burn very slowly so last quite a few nights.

It was beginning to grow dark with the most splendid sun set. They are startling and sudden as if the whole world is on fire, which brings a sort of breathless hush. As an Irishman once said, 'It is the lonely part of the day.'

The train was running late and we did not reach Butterworth until midnight. Butterworth is the industrial town on the mainland where you get the ferry to Penang Island. We had rung our Chinese friends in Butterworth, and told them the arrival time of our train. They kindly said that they would meet us, and had also booked us into a hotel on Penang Island. We had asked them to get us a cheap one – and hoped they would.

The train, as I said, did not reach Butterworth until midnight, but mercifully and kindly they had waited for us. We had met the wife, Joyce, when we were in Hong Kong years before and also when she had come to see her cousin Mimi Hui get her diploma from the College of Art and Dress Design in Bristol. She was now married to a charming man, Alex Wong, and had a delightful small girl of three and a half, Tania.

Like all Chinese, they worked very hard and long hours, but our train was so late it had meant their hanging about waiting for us. When we eventually arrived she gave us a lovely greeting, introducing us to a Chinese man who was the boss of the large firm where they both worked in the export side. Her boss had waited with her as he had offered to drive us to our hotel in Penang. The Wongs lived in Butterworth.

It was lovely on the ferry after the hot airless train journey. The night was still hot but beautiful, clear stars massing the sky. Beyond, the land we were heading for across the water looked like an extension of the sky, with its pinpricks of lights – the mysterious unknown.

The journey did not take long. As we were coming up to the hotel, our new Chinese friend told us that a room had been booked for us. It was a single room, he said, but it had two beds, and that we had to go into the hotel singly as that way we would only have to pay for one person. We were very unhappy about this arrangement but, as they had done so much for us, thought we would comply.

I went to the desk and booked myself in, while Ruth went to the restaurant, just off the reception area. She later joined me in our room, and we only paid for one person. We were told this was often done, but discreetly. I was left with all our luggage and to get someone to help me carry it to our room!

At the reception desk a girl asked my name. When I gave it, the manager came over and said, 'Are you related to the famous Captain Lindsay?' I had to confess that as far as I knew I was not. However, he was still very friendly and ushered me to the lift. We had a huge room, very comfortable with the usual shower and loo. We also found we shared it with several cockroaches, but that seemed the norm in these parts of the world, even in large smart hotels such as this. It was called the Continental, luckily situated in the centre of Penang town, in the Jalan Penang area.

Joyce rang us in the morning to say that Alex was working that day, Saturday, even although it was the special holiday of Hari Raya Haji, which fell mainly on the Sunday, but that they would meet us for breakfast at eight and in the evening would take us to the Orient later on for dinner.

This holiday festival falls on the 20th November. This year, by decree of Yang Dipertvan Aqung, and with the consent of the Rulers, Hari Raya Haji was to be on this day, and that Monday was to be a public holiday for those states which have Sunday as a weekend holiday, and the Sultan of Selangor would offer prayers. Otherwise there were many parties and rejoicings.

The Indian festival on the same day was the Festival of Light – Deepavali. This in other places is held on 11th December or when the moon is full; they do not trust in calendars. If it is cloudy and the moon cannot be seen, they have it on the next day, or rather the next moon-seeing day. This is the most important festival in their calendar:

> 'Long, long ago, there lived the evil one, Narakasura, who enjoyed torturing everyone on earth. The people were so sorrowful that they lived in darkness. And they suffered so much that Lord Krishna, the King of Heaven, took pity on them and decided to fight the demon.
> What a battle it was. Finally, Lord Krishna won! No longer did the people live in fear, because Narakasura was destroyed. The day of victory was proclaimed a day of rejoicing by Lord Krishna. And it was named Deepavali.
> Since then people have lit up their homes and celebrated the victory of good over evil.
> This Sunday, Pestabudaya NST invites you to join in the light festivities. Watch the Thiangarajan Dancers perform classical numbers. Listen to the mysterious strains of the sitar intermingled with modern songs and comedy sketches.'[2]

Penang is situated in the Indian Ocean and seems like a small sleepy version of Hong Kong, but older than Hong Kong, 1771. It also has a Peak with its cable car that runs from the waterfront to the hills. Penang means betel nut, and its town, where we stayed, is George Town.

A lot of the inhabitants are a mixture of Chinese and Malay, and they, we were told, were the most interesting people about. It is like so many of these towns, badly paved streets of shack-like shops, noise, bustle and dirt, but above all sunshine, colour, happiness everywhere and myriad

---

[2] Festival of Light, Penang.

temples of all cultures. In Queen Street there is a mosque, an Indian temple and also a Chinese one, not small insignificant ones but spreading their faith to the pavements in front of them.

For the promised breakfast, Joyce, Alex and Tania took us for a Chinese breakfast at a Chinese restaurant. It consisted of beef soup cooked in tea, with long thin snake-like noodles and innards of animals, washed down, as they say, with green tea. We then dropped Alex off at the EO Hotel, one of the most famous hotels in the East. He had to meet some overseas buyers.

We went to the Botanical Gardens, full of huge trees with great branches swathed with leaves, and full of monkeys, who leapt at one from a great height. We were particularly vulnerable as Tania had bought a bag of peanuts to feed them with.

We then went to a Hindu temple – the Waterfall Temple. The Hindu in charge of it had left Penang when the Japanese took it over, and went into the English Army, which took him to India. He did not return to Penang until the 1950s. He showed us round: the great cooking pots, the inner sanctuary with its gold and silver screens, and so much else which was studded with diamonds.

We then went to a Thai temple, the first we had seen, a low white building with a beautiful switchback Chinese-type roof, lovely sombre painted pictures on its façade, all set in a glorious garden massed with flowers and shrubs, and many golden and painted idols interspersed with animals; serpents and giants seemed to predominate here. The scent was intoxicating. Inside the walls are lined from floor to ceiling with golden plaques, each bearing a name, and many Buddhas, including an enormous gold-washed reclining Buddha dated 1018; his enormous haunting eyes seemed to follow one around. Everywhere were people praying, lighting joss sticks and putting them into huge bronze sand-filled containers in front of shrines. It was full of colour, sunlight and a reverence seldom felt those days in Britain. There were also exquisite blue and white Chinese jars which had the remains and photos of the dead. We put on our shoes and left. Hats were obligatory for women in these temples.

Opposite to this Thai temple was a Burmese one, which unfortunately we did not have time to see properly. It too had painted animals and the like on its façade. Its roofs were a mixture of triangle shapes and a dome, which had a shaped narrow spire rather as the temples in Thailand.

We then went to have lunch in a large half-open building called Drive In. It was not a café as such; it had little stalls all around with every kind of food, including Kentucky Fried! We had Chinese noodles, meat and fish in soup, then iced coffee. To be truthful, we felt so overfed with our large breakfast we could hardly manage to eat anything, but courtesy made us. We had tea as usual. At Chinese meals you have a large teapot, which you pour from all the time. When empty you turn the lid upside down and immediately someone comes and brings a fresh pot.

In the evening Alex joined us again, taking us to the Rajah Room Restaurant in Jalan Penang, a Malaysian restaurant; delicious, one of my favourite foods. The pillars had mah-jong decorations on them. It was large and noisy; the orientals, especially the Chinese, have rather high piercing voices. The drink was delicious on such a very hot night – melon juice.

They then took us by car for a trip round Penang, showing us the city by night. It was odd seeing places in the dark, lit only by gaudy glaring lamps. We also went into the expensive suburbs, where the Thai Embassy is, explaining about many of the millionaires. The road was called Millionaire Road – large houses set in the most beautiful gardens. One very grand one belonged to the Sultan of Kedrah, who prefers it to his palace. We ended up on an embankment overlooking the sea. It was shaded with palm trees from the bright lights. Then, as a goodnight present, they bought us from a stall sheaves of flowers and a huge basket of fruit, papaya, mango, pineapple, durian (of the dreadful smell), small bananas and much else. We arrived back at our hotel exhausted, but happy. The next day the holiday for the Wongs was over, so we bade them goodnight, thanking them profusely for all their great kindness.

Next day we had to go to the immigration office, situated by the famous clock tower, to get our Malaysian passes extended; otherwise we would be in serious trouble. This took a while amid the milling hundreds of many nationalities who don't or won't queue. We also saw a man who took passport photos; we needed them for a visa into Thailand. He took us up to a balcony, put a small cracked mirror up in case we wanted to tidy ourselves, and then quickly snapped us, saying that they would be ready in ten minutes. As usual mine looked as if I were on the point of death.

Having got our extension forms and passport photos, we indulged in a taxi to the Thai Embassy, which we now knew was rather inaccessible and well out of town. As we bartered with the driver, he told us that we had better keep him to drive us back as there was no pubic transport – this we discovered was true.

When we arrived we found the Embassy closed – oh these long drawn out holidays. Full of sympathy, our driver brought us back. We would have to go back again in two days. We were dropped off at the Chinese Oriental Emporium, the nearest thing to our big multi-storeyed shops. It was fascinating to wander around the food department, the Chinese and Malay clothes, ornaments, and stationery, where I bought, again, some very well reproduced pictures of batik work, made into postcards. They were done by a Malay artist, most striking, country scenes in vivid colours – yellows, oranges and greens. I also bought some peanut butter for my breakfast rolls. We were still illegally making our coffee and having breakfast in our bedrooms. We had by now a huge boxful of plug fittings to carry around; every plug we tried seemed to be a different shape!

It was now getting on, so we took a trishaw to an Indian restaurant which we had heard was cheap and good, called the Darwood. It was a stark place, a large, white-tiled room, but oh, such delicious food. We had *chicken kapitan*, a speciality, and *dhal*, which I love, then a long cool drink of mango juice, freshly squeezed.

It was raining when we emerged, lovely cool damp air. I went off to look at a Muslim temple, the Kapitan Kling Mosque in Pitt Street. It is one of the largest in Malaysia, built on the Indian Moorish form, its minaret standing separately from the main building. It was all cream and yellow, with its lovely onion-shaped domes. I went into the garden and wandered round. I could see the men at their prayers, quite oblivious of their interested spectator. Again I was struck by the beautiful plain shapes and lattice work.

I later walked up the same road to a Chinese temple, quite a large one, called Kuan Inting, the oldest in Penang – a hundred and fifty-five years. Its roof tops are carved to represent waves and fire-eating dragons. The courtyard, which was open to the busy street, had two beautifully worked bronze containers, which came up to about my waist. They were filled, as usual, with sand and hundreds of burning joss sticks. There were also the two Dogs of Fo, also as usual made of deep green and yellow ceramic material. These temple dogs are always in a pair, the female has her one foot on her puppy, while the male has a foot on a ball. I find them fascinating. When I was about nine years old I saw a small green one in a junk shop in London, which I bought for peanuts. It has been my constant companion ever since. They guard the entrances to the Chinese temples.

The roof was a subtle shiny green, of the usual shape, sporting many dragons and other animals over it. The building was a dirty red and inside the clutter of all objects that one has come to expect, dusty and seemingly uncared for, although the caretaker was making a family meal in one corner. At the back was a huge Buddha watching all with a happy benign look; at least he was never alone, always prayed to. Outside were several beggars praying for alms. You find very little of this in the East.

I then went to the Museum, an English-style building, filled with glories of their culture: fascinating costumes, carved furniture, including a Chinese bridal chamber, also a marvellous collection of birds and beasts.

Later in the afternoon (supposedly our last) Joyce rang up and said she wanted to take us to the coast for our last meal. She arrived with Tania. All Asian children seem to stay up half the night! We bundled into her car, in which she had a cassette of *The Sound of Music* playing. We went through beautiful lush jungly-type country, for about three-quarters of an hour, eventually arriving at a huge modern hotel called the Casuarina (after the trees). We went through a wide archway in the centre, where you could walk down to the beach. There were tables and chairs. We settled down and were brought large green soft-skinned coconuts, the tops sliced off and straws stuck into them, so that you could drink the milk – delicious.

The beach was an unending stretch of white sand with many casuarina trees giving a pleasant shade from the ever-burning tropical sun. The sea was a shimmering deep greeny-blue. I found some beautiful shells and bits of granite. A Swedish woman and her husband stopped and spoke. She said that she was collecting shells as well, and would I like a large round mother-of-pearl one as she had several.

Later on we moved down to the hotel next door, called the Rasa Sayane. It was built like a Chinese complex covered with bougainvillaea; the clashing colours were thrilling on the winged red roofs. It is so strange – the red and orange flowers on the same stem. Again we sat on the beach, to watch the sunset. People came from far and wide to see this spectacle.

Joyce went off to order a special meal that they did in their restaurant, while we got our cameras ready. How sudden is this closing down of night. I stood on the beach and took about ten photos of it, each enchanting moment not to be missed. It really was magnificent, splattering all over the sky, above the calm sea, doubled in the reflecting water. Suddenly it flared to a deep orange and red fire. Almost immediately it became black.

We then went to the hotel's outside restaurant, lit by soft candle-like lights. We had Joyce's favourite meal, a Chinese dish called steamboat. They brought what looked like a large cake ring, putting the central hollow circle over the gas burner, which was on the middle of the table. All the tables have this equipment. They then fill the cake tin ring with boiling water and, when bubbling hard, you yourself drop in the chunks of raw meat, fish and noodles – or whatever. You watch it cook, then when ready you help yourselves, fishing the ingredients out on to your plate with chop sticks. We were now becoming quite adept at using these.

The next day we both had food poisoning, so much for our special meal. Mercifully we were not seeing our friends again, so they never knew how badly their *treat* had affected us. I was ill for three days, and pretty grotty after that for a while. It took us three tries before getting our visas due to holidays. This and getting our Thai visas delayed our departure from Penang. However, all was well in the end.

Just before we left we thought we must see the large temple complex just outside George Town in a leafy suburb. We managed to find a bus going to it. There were one hundred steps to climb. The steps had an awning over them and on each side were small stalls which sold anything which was cheap and cheerful!

This temple is called Kok Loksi and with its monastery covers about thirty acres. Eventually we reached the top, coming into brilliant sunshine, where there was a courtyard surrounded by Chinese buildings of every shape and size, dusty and gaudy, the animals and Buddhas keeping a watchful eye on us as we moved around. There were many more steps and temples as you moved upwards. We came to a stall selling cooling drinks, fairly smelly, but if you took a bottled one it was almost guaranteed to be safe.

At the top were the main temples plus a huge pagoda. I did not venture up there; my food-poisoned legs had not got their strength back yet. All the buildings were covered with masses of brilliant bougainvillaea, while at the back, against the shimmering blue sky, the trees etched themselves round the buildings. The trees everywhere were prolific: rambutans, casuarinas, papaya, mango, and much else. Their fragrance was intoxicating. This temple was one of the only ones in the East, combining structurally both Burmese and Thai elements in its design.

We then went back into the town, visiting a big fruit market with its masses of many coloured fruits, coconuts and brilliant green vegetables. Behind this was a Muslim temple, looking rather decayed and dirty, facing a dirty river. It is strange; there seems to be nothing between a splendidly kept mosque or temple and a scruffy one.

Feeling much better, we went out to a small restaurant for dinner. It was mainly Malay food. As is the delightfully civilised custom in those parts, they handed us pink face cloths, soaked in rosewater, to wipe our faces and hands. We ordered a simple rice-based meal and a cool rambutan pudding.

We were now going to go to the idyllic islands called Langkawi. They were off the coast of Malaysia, north of Penang. We ordered a taxi for 6.30 from the hotel, crossed to Butterworth by ferry and made for the railway station. There we caught the Butterworth/Alor Star train.

The country we passed through was lovely: paddy fields with their somnolent bullocks standing calf-deep in the water, women in beautiful coloured dresses doing ditto – they were in fact planting. Then we passed many rubber plantations, such as my father had managed. Also we passed masses of heavily forested country which looked completely impenetrable.

Alor Star had no porters or taxis. A kind man in the station saw our plight, managed to find a taxi and barter a good price for us. We had to get to Kuala Perlis for the ferry to the Langkawi Islands. When we finally arrived the boat was full of locals of all sorts and kinds. It had an awning type roof over it.

What beautiful people the Malays are, the girls and women with their delicately formed faces and beautiful coloured clothes, however poor. The men, small in stature, again have beautifully built slight bodies, very graceful in movement, as are the women, and handsome faces which are always smiling. One of these men was sitting over from us on our ferry, elderly, with a tallish black hat and a noteworthy silk jacket in deep pink and magenta. This was quite the norm for both sexes.

Kuala Perlis was very small. Looking over and around us we saw that the wooden houses all stood on stilts in the water. One could watch the people going about their household chores, laughing and talking, everything seemed to be open. There was a continuous trafficking of small boats, rowing between houses and the land, filled mainly with plump elderly Malay ladies in their lovely colours and parasols, trying to keep the penetrating sun off their heads – in contrast to the boatmen, in old hats, working their vessels with only one long oar, standing and pushing their gaudy loads. It was sad to watch, although you would probably find that they were quite happy with their lot – a characteristic of their race.

The journey was fascinating. The Langkawis are almost all solid white granite, with masses of conifer trees covering them. The sea was a deep bluey-green, quite calm. Just before we got to our destination we passed through a narrow channel. It is said about the channel to Langkawi, 'The sea is a secret labyrinth.' The ferry enters this narrow channel framed by the towering rock walls rising perpendicular from the sea. In places the cliffs are solid masses of white marble and others serrated quartzite and granite, which seem to darken the sky, enclosing your views as you slip silently through.

We reached the main island, Lanka Puala, in the late afternoon. Ruth found a taxi – marvellous. We knew there was a Government rest house, and asked the driver to take us there. We had not stayed in one of these famous places, but knew that they were cheap and reliable.

This one was actually partly on the beach, looking over the sea and facing west. What incredible sunsets we saw standing later by the moonlit water's edge; you felt you were in paradise. A few palm trees decked the edge of the sand, and the only other thing in sight was a delectable small pink and cream mosque, also surrounded by palm trees.

Our room was basic: two single beds, a table and hooks. At the back of this rest house was an uninspiring canteen but you could eat cheaply, Malay food, with plenty of nonalcoholic drinks. The beds were moderately comfortable but, as I said, the view was heaven!

There we met a young couple from Hong Kong. They were English but worked in Hong Kong, now taking a short holiday before Christmas. He was called Richard Taylor and his girlfriend Debbie Talbot, who we subsequently found lived in Taiwan, where she looked after her brother's son. Before that she had lived in New York. He was originally from Leeds; they had met in Taiwan. He worked for the famous company, Jardine Mathieson. They were a charming friendly couple aged, one would guess, in their late twenties.

Next day we walked to the mosque, which was shut, although its muezzin had been doing its duty, calling the faithful to prayer. Again, how relaxing, calm and peaceful. We then went into the little town. It was completely uninteresting apart from a signpost at the harbour, with several signs, saying: Rangoon, Hong Kong, Ceylon and Spain. Someone had a sense of humour; no boat in sight was larger than a ferry.

In the early evening we thought we would go 'posh'. There was an expensive hotel, with no local colour – sad – called the Langkawi Club Hotel, where we sat in the flowered garden and drank gin and tonic. I only hope that the whole island is not like that now. It looked ever so Torquay.

We were wandering back down the drive, when we just missed a large snake who was rustling back to the undergrowth; not a thing to relish. As we collected ourselves, we met the young couple again, who asked if we would share a fishing boat with them next day, to go round the other islands. The fishermen make some extra cash ferrying visitors around. We agreed and said we would meet them the next morning at eight o'clock.

We set off for the biggest island of Palau Tuba. It was hot and tranquil. Two Malay boatmen were in charge as we skimmed through the deep green water towards a marble quarry. As we went I was saying to the young couple how sorry I was not to have my geological hammer with me. I had left it in our rest house. As I spoke I must have done the movement with my arm, indicating hammering. A few minutes later one of the boatmen (who did not speak any of our languages) came up to me and handed me a hammer. I was delighted and thanked him profusely. Later on I managed to hammer off some beautiful pieces of pure white marble. As we arrived at the quarry we pulled up on a small pebbly beach, overhung with branches of trees and bushes. One tree had incredible fruits hanging from its boughs, about the size of a mango, pure green. At the foot of the fruit were two flattish leaves and hanging like string unusual mauve flowers, with stems upwards, covered with fluff. They smelt deliciously fragrant. I never found out what they were.

We now moved on to the next island, Palau Dayang Bunting; again it was just a tiny coral and shell beach. We were led by our boatman further up the little beach, which had masses of coral and shell fragments. This led to a tiny track. He beckoned us to follow; by now he was armed with a machete, most lethal looking. Jungle was around us. It was incredibly hot. Suddenly, seemingly coming right up to us, with an almighty crash – some animal moving either in fear or protecting itself. We could not see what it was, but we all looked petrified. Ruth turned tail back to the beach; it was safer there. The boatman's hand was held high holding the knife but nothing more happened, so we proceeded, following him through the jungle in single file.

At last we reached our destination, the 'Pregnant Maiden's Pool', a huge pale green pure water pool surrounded by jungle. The legend was that a couple who had been childless for nineteen years drank some of the water and then, later on, had a child. The other legend about the pool was that a Princess from the Province of Kedah drowned herself there, when not allowed to marry the man of her choice. There was also supposed to be a white crocodile who guards the lake.

In 1942, during the Japanese occupation, some soldiers were picnicking by the lake. The guard told them not to swim because of this white crocodile. In spite of the warning, one soldier dived in; he disappeared immediately. Then a few minutes later he was seen in the middle of the lake, but dead, in a crocodile's mouth. Another soldier shot at the animal, but no bullet penetrated its body. They were so upset that on returning they set fire to the guest house in revenge. No one will bathe there now, said our guide, with a smile. The lake looked so harmless, glinting in the hot sun.

Our guide dived into the water (in spite of the warnings!) fully clothed except for his hat. He kept his head underwater as he swam; it looked so odd. Debbie and Richard also swam, while I sat on the bank admiring the beauty of the place. When the guide came out, dripping with water, he went and sat on a boulder, looking like a pixie, stripping a piece of bamboo stalk with his knife. We all sat and talked, at the same time watching the birds, streaks of brilliant blues, oranges. One, larger than a kingfisher, had a large black beak and a white front.

We returned to our gaily painted boat, with no more mishaps, arriving back about 3.30 p.m., going straightaway to have some drinks – we were parched – and a light lunch of rice and fish.

We said our farewells to Debbie and Richard. She had given us her address in Taiwan, as we were going to go there. It would be fun to see her again. They both said that they were now hooked on geology and would be taking home their collection of rocks. They had hired a motorbike and went off to see the rest of our island as the next day they had to leave.

When we got back to our room we found a water buffalo tied to a tree near our window, rather like a huge dog on its lead.

We went again to the Langkawi Country Club – nowhere else to eat. Again we took the lovely walk in the dark silence, this time keeping well to the paths to avoid snakes. Although dark, there was a moon – a tropical island one dreams of. We again sat outside for our meal. The table mats were paper decorated with a painted map of the island. I asked the waitress, a most beautiful girl, dressed in a long sarong, if I could take one of the mats as a souvenir. She said, 'Of course, but I will get you a fresh one.' With that she went, returning in a few minutes, with about a dozen for me. On leaving we also had a chat with the manager of the hotel. He was most interesting about Langkawi. Then finally the girl at the reception desk started to talk and begged us to come back and talk to her again. What a very friendly warm people they were, as in fact is the same all over Malaysia. We went back to pack, as next day we were off to Thailand – what a romantic name.

Next morning we set off by ferry to Kuala Perlis. From there we went by train to Kangor, where we thought we would spend the night before going on to Thailand. As usual at Kuala Perlis there was chaotic orderliness and from its midst while we were docking a small Malay boy – he looked about ten years old – shouted to us, 'Carry your bags, miss.' We said yes and with that he leaped on to the part of the boat that was fairly near the quay. He leant over passengers to speak to us, 'Pass me your two bags.' We shouted back that he could not possibly carry two heavy bags, especially as he was going to manhandle them over the iron bars and other obstacles. He agreed and said,

'Don't move them, I'll get them in a moment.' He then squeezed through several small gaps and arrived at our feet. Telling us to get off and he would follow with the said bags, still doubtful we obeyed, watching this small determined being somehow or other carry or drag them on to the quay. This money probably meant either eating or not.

We were waiting to get a taxi, then trying to barter for a 'share' one – a familiar form of transport in the East – for we wanted to get to Kangor. We were not having much success when our diminutive porter came up to me and said that he had managed to get a taxi for us, for a quarter of the money the present one was asking. We very gratefully tipped him and gave him a bit extra. It was still cheap. He grinned all over his face. He should get somewhere in life with his drive, charm and authority.

Our taxi was full, but we sat in state in the back while body after body crammed in beside the driver. They kept looking round at us and giggling. We arrived at our hotel. Richard had said he had noticed it when passing through Kangor.

We deposited our luggage by the door and looked around. The hotel was in a small side street surrounded by rotting vegetation. We looked at each other in horror. However, Ruth said that she would go into the hotel and ask about rooms if I waited with the luggage. Rather mercifully they were full up but, in the kind ways of the Malays, the owner said he would try and get us a 'share' taxi to the border as there were no other hotels in Kangor. He said that we could sit in the lounge until it arrived and brought us a drink. He also told us that he would advise us to go, as quickly as we could, once the taxi came as the only border crossing left open into Thailand would be shut at six o'clock, owing to military troubles, and that they did not know when it would open again. We sat in a dark sordid room – luckily the chairs were comfortable – and watched the Chinese and Malays coming in and out, always a fascinating occupation.

In about one and a half hours the manager came to us again, all grins. He said he had managed to get us a taxi. He said so many people were trying to cross the border that it had taken him a while to procure one. There was a young Malay girl in the back. Obviously very shy, she turned her back to us, looking out of the window. We were just about to start when another woman arrived and got into the front seat. Off we went, but shortly the taxi stopped again, to let a thin elderly woman get in, again into the front; luckily she was thin, as by this time there was hardly any room for the driver.

It was about a two hour drive to get to the border post. The time was getting dangerously near to six o'clock, the deadline for closing the frontier. We were going through dense jungle country. Every so often we were stopped by soldiers in uniform, interrogated, searched, then waved on. We passed many of these military groups watching the road leading to the border. The journey was rather a frightening nightmare as the difficulties were quite serious.

The time was about 5.45 p.m. when we screeched into the borderline area, with our driver telling us to hurry and that he would take us on, in Thailand, to the first town. We were pounced on by five young boys, who said, 'Hurry, no time to waste.' They grabbed our bags, shouting 'Follow.' We did, but over railway tracks, tiny paths and all around the border post. We eventually arrived, realising we had been truly had by these young scoundrels. We went through the customs. But of course our youngsters had our luggage. They were standing beside our taxi, with the man demanding his fare before we even started, and the boys all shouting at us. Everyone else had shut up for the day – or more. We were alone in their hands.

Then the driver started yelling at us, saying he would not now come on with us and that he wanted double the money because of the waiting. He was egged on by the boys. There was nothing to do but pay. At last they all went, leaving us to walk quite a way, where we eventually found another taxi. This was the only time we were cheated by anyone.

Thailand, 22nd November 1977

Thailand at last, also a place that I had always wanted to go to. We set off through the equally lovely countryside. It was interesting. There were clearings every so often, where they had built two or three small beautiful wooden houses on stilts, rather like Austrian houses, apart from the stilts. Round them the naked children played, an occasional hen was heard, a few goats seen and of course the inevitable water buffalo.

It took us about an hour to reach Hatyai, the first town, where we thought we would stay for the night, changing our currency and having a break, after the scramble to get into Thailand. We asked our driver to take us to the station, as we had seen in our guidebook that there was a hotel which was cheap there.

We arrived at the station, which was large and clean. Disembarking from the taxi we could not see the hotel, so we went to the tourist office that was also in the station, where we were informed that the hotel was above them. We went up to a palatial foyer and booked in. On asking about its restaurant they informed us that it was the station buffet. The hotel – Hotel Hyatte – was a very modern building, as I said, built above the station. The station food was delicious. Thai food for me is one of the most delicious, as is Malaysian food.

After our meal we thought that we would have a look at the small town, as we were leaving by train the next day about one o'clock for Hua Hin, hundreds of miles north. It was a fascinating, tinselly town. Everything was open and alive; brilliant lights, strange captivating music, chattering and bartering. It got dark at about six o'clock everywhere, so one saw much by electric light and, like Greece and many places at that time, naked light bulbs swung precariously above one's head as one hopefully looked for bargains on their rickety tables.

Our new currency was the baht, which we were trying to get used to. We did buy some fruit and biscuits, cartons of mango and papaya juice, useful for drinking on buses and trains which were all stifling hot.

The next morning Ruth took a quick trip by bus to Songkhla, a place she was particularly keen to see – a small town by the sea. I went again to the town, to see it in daylight.

Opposite the back of our hotel was the one main road, not very broad, but bordered on the other side by gardens, the long hedges being cut into the shape of incongruous elongated twisting dragons. What works of art! By day the streets looked duller, not so garish; the sun showed up the eternal dust. But there was a friendly atmosphere in the streets and more shops than I had realised, including the immense markets curving into dark alleys covered with dark awnings. This small town is unbelievably the largest commercial centre in the south of Thailand.

In the market I saw many young Buddhist monks, with their saffron robes, shaven heads and small bags, which contained their shaving equipment and any food given to them. They live only on food given to them by the public, who in return feel that they have won honours points towards heaven. One very young monk lagged behind the rest and with tentative, surreptitious fingers stroked a small toy train and its carriages. His face was a picture as he longingly looked at it. Then, tearing himself away, he hurriedly joined the others. All young boys have to become monks for a while. Also they have to go into the army for a period.

At one stall I met a young man who spoke English. He had a fruit stall and obviously wanted to air his ability, asking me where I came from, then all the usual questions. He seemed very happy with his job, although I gathered he did not make much money.

In the afternoon we collected our luggage, as we were catching the Singapore to Bangkok Super-Express train. What thousands of miles it travels. We had already bought our tickets, treating ourselves to an air-conditioned coach, in all costing about £5. The train was to leave at 1 p.m., reaching our destination, Hua Hin, about 3 a.m. We had booked a hotel beforehand, as we were arriving at such an ungodly hour, where they said that they would meet our train. It was one of the very few times we had booked ahead.

As it was only 12 noon we went to the buffet for lunch, had a good meal and watched for the arrival of the train, which was to come into the actual platform where the buffet was. We boarded it, after finding the one and only air-conditioned coach; extraordinary, as the train was extremely long. We found two seats together just into the coach, which meant we would have a slight (although hot) breeze form the door as well as the windows.

A Chinese man, sitting in the seat in front of us, kept passing us local Chinese newspapers to read. As we did not know Chinese we flicked over the pages, from the back to the front, in the approved Chinese way.

In the coach behind us we could see – and hear – a crowd of Thai boys and girls, who were returning from competing in the SEA Games in Kuala Lumpur. Looking at them they were all dressed in their scarlet and white blazers and shorts, the Olympic uniform. They were in an unconditioned coach, so had hung their blazers on hangers, which swung with the rhythm of the train. The whole place looked rather like a Chinese laundry.

Up and down the train, all day long, went Thai boys with large tin buckets filled with ice and bottles of Coke, Fanta and suchlike which, stuck in the ice, kept beautifully cool. They banged the pail with a metal spoon as they came so that anyone wanting to buy a drink was ready for them. There were also buckets filled with a hot rice, meat and fish mixture, in small packets of greaseproof paper, half enclosing the mixture, which was quite delicious and very cheap. We sampled it for our evening meal. It was excellent.

We stopped at one large town only during our long journey. I don't know where it was, as one could not read their script. We stayed there for about half an hour, different vendors coming through the train, selling things like shadow puppets, a thing I have always wanted. I asked the man the price, which was more than I could afford. Stupidly, it was not until the train was moving again I realised that in fact they were very cheap. I had been forgetting I was not now using Malayan currency. I could have kicked myself.

The country around this town was strangely unlike the rest of it, tall sharply pointed jagged rocks, dark against the deep cloudless blue sky, rather eerie. Many Buddhist monasteries broke up the landscape, one group on top of a sloping mountain and surrounded by dark trees. Our train was so long our coach was not even near the platform. It grew dark with a marvellous sunset, deep startling oranges, pinks and fiery reds, then suddenly black.

A young Thai girl on the seat by the side of mine but across the corridor started to talk to me in very good English. She had been to America and taken a degree in philosophy, married a fellow student who was also Thai and who was just finishing his degree there. She had come home for a year where he was to join her; later they both hoped to work in America or England. She came from Hat Yai but was on her way to stay for a fortnight with her married sister in Chang Mai (Rose of the North), the old capital of Thailand. It was a place I would love to have seen but money and time precluded it. It is much more unspoilt than southern Thailand, this old capital with its ancient temples and customs, really just a large rural town with beautiful mountainous country surrounding it.

This girl on the train said that she found it difficult now, in Thailand, to decide what was best for the Thais, the village people. She said they are all so happy, although poor, and what right had the likes of her to disturb their content, trying to modernise them – a thing I often ponder on myself when travelling, comparing our unsmiling faces with the calm, smiling, happy non-striving natives, be they Thai, Malays, Chinese or any other structure of contented society. Why try to civilise them, so-called? So often in talking to them their wisdom and philosophy are so much better than ours; money is for needful things, not for greed.

When it was about 2.45 a.m. I woke Ruth, saying, 'Do you realise we cannot see when we reach our station, in this deep dark, and anyway we cannot read their script. Also our coach never comes into the platform.' I looked around our coach, finding one of the train officials fast asleep in one of the front seats. I went down and shook him awake, saying, 'Hua Hin, Hua Hin,' in rather a frantic voice. He shook himself awake, saying 'Hua Hin,' and pointing to his watch, showing we would be there in five minutes. I went back to my seat, where we lugged our two heavy suitcases into the corridor. Luckily a tall Malay man who was sitting near us leapt to his feet and carried our cases the length of the coach, to where my small official was standing hanging out of the door window, with a huge torch, which he was swinging backwards and forwards to get the driver to stop. What a palaver. The train ground to a noisy halt, where we had to climb down the steps of the train on to the line. We were, as expected, well out from the platform. Our kind Malay handed down our bags, while out of the darkness came two porters to lead us to the safety of the station itself, then with bows left us. Mercifully, as we were being accosted by a group of ragged men and boys who were trying to grab our bags, a man came up to us, shooed off the mob, saying to us, 'I am from the hotel. The car is outside.' He took our bags and led us to a minibus.

It was a moonless night and windy; we had no idea what the place was like. The hotel door was well lit and welcomingly wide open. After signing in, we were taken to our room. We were staggered. It looked like a ballroom, sparsely furnished, with plain wooden furniture. Outside the darkened windows – shutters closed because of mosquitoes, open them at your peril – we sensed a veranda. We went straight to bed, desperately tired, but commenting on the strange swishing sort of noise. It was very windy. We could hear the trees swaying constantly.

In the morning when I opened the shutters the hot sun poured in. There was the huge veranda with cane table and chairs and an armchair plus standard lamps adorned with art nouveau lampshades. It looked as if Somerset Maugham had just vacated the place. Beyond, through the trees, I could see the sea; hence the swishing sound heard last night and the odd siren sound of the fishing boats off to work. The wind had dropped, leaving the sea with the soft, comforting lap of waves contented to relax. After breakfast I went across the garden, filled with magenta and orange coloured bougainvillaea, all its clashing colours giving life to the scene.

We had evidently arrived at the station in the literal teeth of a storm. The garden has, as at Hat Yai, hedges cut into the shape of dragons and other animals. The hotel itself was a huge old colonial-type building, white, with two storeys. Outside its gates was a sandy track down to the beach; on either side of it were small stalls of souvenirs, sweets, fruit and of course the usual inevitable Coke and Fanta. The beach itself, with its white sand, had also a scattering of odd stalls which had tatty tables and chairs; the tables, with their lino covers, reminiscent of England's poorer seaside spots, but it was the beach that caught one's eye. The storm had wreaked havoc on it; the white sand was thick with the bodies of fish, watersnakes, rubbish, plastic and otherwise, mingled with branches of trees, flowers torn from the garden, and, as always, paper. The most sinister were the snakes. Although not large they were big enough to have done damage if alive. I kept clear of them just in case, but one could hardly walk on the beach because of all this junk. The sea itself was now calm and beautiful, greeny-blue in colour with small waves quietly slapping the beach. Growing in the sandy soil were beautiful casuarina trees, a feature of this part of the world, their strangely fretted leaves making an uneven lattice work against the deep blue sky.

Later on I walked into the town, passing a compound on my right with its high walls. I ventured through the open gate and saw a most beautiful temple complex; such exotic colouring, such peace after the busy street outside. The swaying shaped roofs were orange and bright green and gold. Gold was everywhere glistening in the sun. Everywhere were saffron coloured robed priests or monks. They were hoeing the earth very diligently. No one lifted a head as I passed by, so I took some photos.

I then went into the market, where I again found that one or two of the young men spoke English. I bought some bananas for our next journey. What a fascinating place it was: piles of brilliantly coloured fruits, many again I did not recognise, then many piles of very fresh green vegetables, much brought into the town by farmers in the outlying villages. One of the stall holders asked me all about London. He had not been there, but had obviously read about it. As I left I congratulated him on his ability to converse so well in another language. He blushed deeply and bowed.

We had our evening meal in the courtyard of our rambling hotel. One of the things on the menu was *plakaplong frittergrilly*. I thought I must try it and how glad I was: red mullet, Thai sauce, which has cucumber, spring onions and much else in it. It was quite delicious. On our way to the restaurant we passed through the foyer, where the manager was working at the reception desk. Ruth, who was very keen to know why they never gave us coconuts with the milk in them, taxed him with this. He answered that there was no demand for them, but quickly added that he would send into the town for some and that we would have them in about twenty minutes. As he had said, in twenty minutes they ceremoniously brought two large coconuts out to our table. The tops had been sliced and straws put in the milk all ready for us. The other diners seemed to think that we were mad.

The public rooms of our hotel were enormous white areas, with full length windows which were kept wide open. The ones on the south side faced an elegant sweep of drive, bordered by shrubs and a riot of coloured flowers; the ones on the north side looked sedately on to a vast balcony, which ran the length of the building. There you could sit in the cane chairs and chaise longues, broken up with tall stands of green plants.

Everywhere inside had dark highly polished wood, most of it carved where possible. The shallow-treaded staircases were the same and everywhere the staff were at the ready to help one, dressed in their immaculate white jackets, trousers and shoes.

Our next stop was Bangkok, a place I have always wanted to visit. Against all our friends' advice, we booked seats on an air-conditioned express bus to Bangkok. The reason for their advising the train was because the Thais were murderous drivers, the roads bad and pedestrians worse, as we soon found out.

The air-conditioning, we discovered, was a small circular fan, rather battered, which hung from the ceiling of the coach, and which was off rather more than on! We had been early for the coach, so had gone for a drink in a flower bestrewn little open café. It turned out to be run by a little old man and his wife. He had been a Bangkok official and had retired here, running the café for an interest. He was very proud of speaking several languages, so in his best English he persuaded us to try a juice called *mangase* (I think). It has a slightly fragrant turnip taste, sharing also the colour and texture of the aforesaid turnip.

We found things much more expensive than in Malaysia. Everyone we met was so friendly and kind, always smiling and willing to help us.

We had started our hair-raising journey. It was a matter of he who goes fastest, loudest and was the pushiest got there. The whole two and a half hour journey was fraught. It was best to look ahead. If you looked out of your side window you frequently saw the road littered with dead, dying or injured bodies, results of accidents just before you arrived. No one seemed to be bothering either in or outside the coach.

A Thai man who sat next to me said in good English, 'Did you see that last accident?'

I said, 'No, I had not dared to look' to which he replied fervently, 'I only wish I had not either. It was ghastly, one of the worst I have ever seen in my life.'

When one had a peaceful stretch of road, one could admire the fascinating scenery: coconut trees, paddy fields with their inevitable water buffaloes, betel and mango trees, salt flats with small windmills, and darting in and out of trees the most exotic birds, emerald green heads and tails, with soft brown bodies; also many that looked like swallows but best of all what looked like small white cranes.

One town we passed through, called Petehburi, had masses of temples. One was huge, sitting on top of a hill, spreading its tentacles over the high incline. We arrived, by the mercy of God rather than the driver, in Bangkok in the rain and the rush hour in a dismal huge bus station. The light was failing as it was nearly sunset. The milling hundreds looked like millions of agitated ants battling their way home. I have never seen such acres of closely packed people before, even in Hong Kong, and that is certainly saying something. All were pushing and chattering on to already full buses. Many in fact were hanging on the outsides of the buses. The traffic noise was intense, while the pollution fumes filled the air. For the first time I suggested that we escaped from this mad town and went on.

With difficulty we got a taxi and asked him to take us to the YWCA. He did not speak English, so we also gave him the name of the street where it was situated. We started off on another hazardous journey. Bangkok is enormous, the traffic a slow nose-to-tail. In the whole of the city there seems to be only one set of traffic lights, and each street seems to be about three miles long. Looking at one's street map it all looks quite compact! Walking it later on I learnt, to my cost, that this was true.

We came out of the garish lights into a more residential area. I was sitting next to the driver, with Ruth crushed into the back with our cases. The driver gave me a beaming smile every now and then, as if to say 'all is well'. Three-quarters of an hour later we were still going, except that our driver stopped frequently to ask anyone handy where the YMCA was. Each time I waved my bit of paper at them and shouted, 'YWCA?' without luck. Eventually we arrived at yet another long road, the usual type, with a narrow *klong* (canal) running down the centre of it. Believe it or not, exhausted and baffled, we had arrived. I had actually written and booked in here, as Bangkok is such a busy city, but I might as well have saved myself the bother; the letter had not arrived.

We were met at the reception desk by a rather glamorous plump Thai lady in a most exotic caftan, who informed us that sadly she was full up, but directed us about two hundred yards down the road to the YMCA. Our luggage was too heavy by now to carry it that far and our taxi had gone. Luckily a young Thai girl said she would carry the cases to the pavement and get us a taxi. She stood on the edge of the road of thudding traffic, hailing taxi after taxi, which stopped but on hearing about the short distance refused to take us. However, one who had already said no came back for us. He had relented and returned in sympathy for our plight. Oh how marvellous!

The YMCA was a huge building, with many rooms. In that part of the world the YMCAs are like cheap hotels; they put up both sexes and even families. This stood in its own grounds. The reception desk and restaurant were very large and cheerful. Our room was plain and clean, with a bathroom and air-conditioning. We later found that its silencer had ceased to work, so every four minutes there was a terrific banging and clashing, making sleep impossible. Ruth managed through sheer tiredness to sleep.

I found it impossible, so went and sat on the loo seat for half the night. We eventually solved it by shutting it off and opening the window so as not to suffocate. The mosquito net over the window had a hole large enough for any self-respecting insect to come in, so we put an anti-mosquito coil on the windowsill, leaving it smoking all night.

The restaurant meals were interesting and delicious; as so many nationalities were there they had a wide choice of very well cooked foods – Malay, Thai, Chinese and Indonesian. The service was done by Chinese boys who looked like students learning their craft. It was also, mercifully, very cheap.

As we were there for only three days, and the city was so vast, we thought we would indulge in a couple of organised tours, which one could book at the reception desk. The ones we chose were the 'Temple Tour' and the 'Rose Garden Tour'. We booked them, being told to be at the desk by 8.00 a.m. next morning, where the coach would pick us up.

The coach turned out to be a rickety minibus manned by a young driver and another young student who was our guide. Later on we found that he was still at school; it was one of the ways they could make some pocket money. He was charming, speaking fairly good English, obviously delighted to show off his city. We were unfortunately right over the other side of the city, away from the temples, so it wasted much time just getting there.

The temples – what breathtaking edifices, soaring in all their colours and shapes, glistening, into the almost dark-blue sky. The first one we visited was the Wat (temple) Traimit, to see the solid gold Buddha, which is ten feet tall and weighs five and a half tons. It had had an interesting life; years before it had been brought to the compound of Wat Traimit from an abandoned monastery in downtown Bangkok, in fact on 25th May, 1953. The image had crashed to the ground when the hook of the crane holding it broke under the strain. During the night a thunderstorm raged over Bangkok and torrents of rain fell on the cracked plaster of this giant Buddha image, to its detriment.

Following the rains, the abbot of Wat Traimit undertook to clean the image, which was not only cracked but also covered with mud and dirt. While cleaning it the abbot saw glittering metal through one of the cracks. He called the other monks, the plaster was removed and underneath it was found that the Buddha's image was of solid gold.

It was one of the two images left in the abandoned Wat Phraya Krai, when the monastery area was taken over as part of a project to expand Bangkok's port facilities, and when this larger one was moved to Wat Traimit. When it arrived there was no building large enough to house it, so it was put into temporary shelter in a quiet corner of the monastery compound. Later it was put into Wat Traimit itself. There is still a mystery about the origin of this golden Buddha, but it was probably cast during the Sunhothai period, AD 1238–1378. It was thought that the image was covered with plaster to conceal its true value from invading and looting armies.

With Buddhists, you must never touch their hands. Also the Thais grow the nails on their little finger very long. They, certainly the dancers, also have long caps (like the thimble we wear on a finger when sewing to save pricking oneself) on the end of their fingers, which makes them about an inch longer, and pointed. You can buy these from street vendors outside temple complexes.

We were then taken by our minibus to the north-western part of the city, where there is another large complex of temples, and also the palace and the museum. The road and pavements are wide and spacious. It has an air of opulence and quiet. Here also are the universities and at night the great open-air markets are held under big lamps.

We went into one of the largest monasteries called Wat Po, with its fabulous temples, enormous, ornate and glowing with gold, greens, blues and reds, beautifully shaped roofs curving and narrowing up at the tops. These roofs towered up three tiers; everywhere were saffron or brilliantly yellow-robed monks, seemingly just wandering about in a cloud of incense, which perfumed the brilliantly sunlit air and made designs against the almost intolerably hot sky. Many of the spirals of the burial edifices also made an interesting design against the horizon.

This one is known as the Monastery of the Reclining Buddha, which has four large and forty-one small *chedis* (pagodas); *chedis* is a bell-shaped structure, now a general Buddhist symbol, like the Christian cross. It has the largest collection of Buddha's images in Thailand, and also famous panels of bas-relief depicting scenes from the Ramayama stone inscriptions. The *bot* (main chapel) is located in a courtyard surrounded by double rows of galleries containing three hundred and ninety-four sitting Buddha images, a low wall with eight gates, each one guarded by bronze lions surrounding the building. The boundary stones (*bot*s are surrounded by eight symbolic boundary stones) are housed in small pavilions crowned with spires. In the northern *vitharn* (repository for sacred objects) the Buddha is represented seated in the western manner. The four large *chedi* represent the first four kings of the Chakri Dynasty. The *vitharn* of the great Reclining Buddha is in the western courtyard, the image representing the Buddha as he was attaining Nirvana. It is 160 feet long and 39 feet high, made of cement-covered brick coated with gold leaf. The soles of the feet are inlaid with mother-of-pearl with one hundred and eight signs, marks and qualities by which a true Buddha is recognised.

The term temple is incorrect for describing Wat buildings, as no 'god' is worshipped here.

The last temple that we went to was Wat Paduavanarma, where our young guide would not let us buy postcards (they sold cards and the long silver finger nails, like the dancing girls wear, that I have already mentioned) as they were much more expensive than in the tourist shops! Later we found this to be untrue.

Having seen several temples, he then took us to a craft shop for our postcards and anything else we wanted, then later on he dropped us back at the Siam – pronounced by them Seeam – Intercontinental (Siam means gold). This is a huge shopping precinct which has very expensive goods in the shops. It also had a huge Hong Kong and Shanghai Bank on the top floor, the Bank that my father had always used, so needing money we took the escalator up to it. What a sumptuous place, shaded by white blinds, and deep comfortable chairs scattered around. It was odd for me to be there. I had seen the name of it for so many years on my father's cheques and bank letters.

Having had a lunch of delicious Thai rice, we went over to the very expensive Siam Intercontinental Hotel to have a non-paying exotic wash and tidy up. We always did this. It got one into these extravagantly decorated hotels (they had the best ladies' rooms), then we walked out to resume our sightseeing. The shape of the roof of this one was so gracious; it swooped down, like a huge umbrella, making the building look one-storeyed. Its gardens were superb, right in the middle of this teeming town, masses of ornamental shrubs and massed beds of glorious flowers.

We then came down to earth, catching a tram which took us back to the YMCA. These trams are an experience, very long with doors at the centre and at each end. The young conductor hopped in and out of the different doors to collect his fares, the bus being too full for him to work his way down it, and no fares must be lost. Because of the traffic it took us forever to reach our destination.

It was now 1st December 1977 and this was the day that our tour took us on the Floating Market and the Rose Garden trip, plus the Largest Pagoda. Our coach took us thirty-eight kilometres out of Bangkok. At one time we passed a signpost which had River Kwai on it, an awesome thought. Eventually we arrived at a large *klong* where we disembarked and boarded small narrow long boats. This place was called Katchaburi in the district of Damhern Saduak. We were whisked, at great speed, down the *klong*, passing open wooden houses built on stilts deep in the water. The people were so used to sightseers that they took no notice of us. The women were doing their usual chores, it seems the same all over the world, the children playing and laughing on the open balconies. There was also dense jungle growth with overhanging branches, which often caught one's head. The speed of the boat sprayed us as we went, cooling but also surprisingly wetting.

We eventually turned yet another corner and there was the most colourful sight you can imagine, crowds of narrow boats stacked up with fruits and vegetables, brilliant fresh greens, yellows, reds and purples. The women themselves also added to this confusion of colour. Most were wearing denim blue Chinese-type jackets, black trousers and huge basket-like straw hats as if a round basket had been put on to the head upside down, but underneath this hat they wore a straw cap close to the head, probably joined to the other one, but which kept them firmly on their heads.

The water was muddy and overhung with branches. We got off our boat at a tourist building. It looked like a huge high raft, with railings round it and a lavish roof. Here they sold all the usual tourist stuff – blouses, shell souvenirs, hats like the boat people and much else. You could also buy pineapples, lemons and papaya, the juice squeezed ready for you to drink – very welcome.

As I drank it I leant over the iron balcony to watch the boat people, who seemed only to be buying and selling among themselves, ignoring us snap-happy tourists. Thai life has been associated with the *klongs* for hundreds of years. There had not been many roads; therefore the rivers and man-made canals were the source of commerce.

The old capital of Thailand, Ayuttaya, had fifty-five kilometres of waterways, the most important river being the Chao Phraya. It is made up of four smaller rivers with the delightful names of Ping, Wang, Yom and Nan. They join together at Naknon Sawan, two hundred kilometres north of Bangkok, and become the Chao Phraya. In the old days this river had much traffic and cruise ships. It also irrigated the countryside with its rice fields.

A small girl kept asking me my name, an impossible one even for the English. She gave me a pencil and paper to write it down, as she wanted me to write to her. She spoke fairly good English and was deliciously friendly.

Our next visit was the pagoda one. This was the largest and oldest *chedi* in Thailand, with its huge golden sitting Buddha. People were paying a small sum of money and writing their names on a tile, which was then stacked at the foot of a temple. I learnt that this meant you got 'good prayers' and it helped them to pay for the new roof of this main temple. I paid for a tile, wrote my name on it and hoped for the good prayers. It is amusing to think that one's signature is sitting on top of one of Thailand's most famous temple roofs.

After this we went on to lighter entertainment – the Rose Garden. This is a very large area devoted really to letting hurried visitors see the crafts and entertainment of Thailand. It is at Nakorn Pathon, and well worth going to. First of all we had lunch sitting amid a profusion of roses of every colour and scent. We were very hungry by now and had a most delicious Thai meal.

We were then taken to a large barn-like hall, open at the front – lovely and cool. A huge stage took up the entire width of the back of the building. We sat on chairs at such a rake one hoped that one would not slide down on to the stage. We were to watch the Thai Village Culture Show. They gave a very good performance of classical and folk dancing from various regions, the girls and men in their brilliant Thai silks of shocking pink, bitter lemon, vivid blues, deep bluey-greens and much gold and silver work. They were also wearing the long false nails that I have mentioned, which looked as if they were made of gold. They come to a point about two inches from the finger ends, used as a great part of the dance movements.

There was also Thai boxing (quite different from ours) and sword fighting, which is six hundred years old. Then there was cock-fighting, mercifully a very short item. Then the show finished with a full traditional Thai wedding ceremony and the Buatnaag, the procession and ceremony of ordination into the Buddhist monkhood.

After the ceremony you wander round different stalls scattered among the rose beds: parasol-making, pottery, silk – so much to take in. You can then finish up by having a cobra hung round your neck, a thing I did not partake in!

It is interesting that, of all the South-East Asian countries, only Thailand has always been independent. This surely must affect its culture.

The following day we met a friend of a friend of Ruth's at the Siam Intercontinental. They had not met before; however, we managed to find each other in the lounge. She knew friends of his.

He said that he would take us to the British Club for lunch, but on the way he looked hard at us, saying, 'I have changed my mind. I will take you to the Sporting Club.' We gave a silent grin to each other; we were obviously more *with it* than he had expected. This turned out to be a huge white rambling Raj-type building, right in the centre of Bangkok, and even more unbelievably it was surrounded by its own racecourse, two golf courses, tennis courts and much else and in a city which seemed to have no open spaces. It took your breath away. A tall stone wall enclosed the entire estate. The flower beds, lush green lawns, trees and birds made the place idyllic. Passing these high walls, when on the pavement, one never dreams what lies behind them; rather like Buckingham Palace.

The dining room was beautiful, white walls with dark wood surrounds. Down the centre of the room was a long table with a gleaming starched, damask cloth and shining silver, where one helped oneself to a most splendid cold meal. The choice was endless. The Thai waiters, in their dapper spotless white jackets, moved completely noiselessly about the room.

Our host turned out to be an Englishman of about forty, married to a Thai girl. He and his family lived in Bangkok. He loved the place, saying he would not live anywhere else in the world. He had travelled a great deal, so knew what he was talking about. He spoke, most interestingly, about the city, and said he was sorry not to be able to entertain us at his home, but that he was off to Singapore first thing in the morning, taking his family on holiday, and for his wife to buy new clothes; also, he added, for the general entertainment there.

It was such a pleasant, friendly meal. After lunch he dropped us off at the famous Jim Thompson shop, and sped off home to pack.

Jim Thompson in that part of the world is a byword. He had traded in Thai silks for years, making them known throughout the world, then one day when he was still quite young he went into the jungle and has never been heard of since. That was many years ago; it is an eternal mystery.

His shop is lovely – rather like Liberty's in London – with its light walls, many beautiful dark wood staircases, part of the ceiling and the pillars. It stands in a bustling street of expensive shops. The interior is filled with silks or cottons in the most glorious colours, a veritable rainbow, nothing harsh or ugly. He also sold some beautiful, but most expensive, clothes and scarves. I treated myself to a small miraculously coloured silk scarf. One can also see his house, which is in a separate part of the town; we did not go as time was running out for us. It is a magnificent Thai-style house, I understand, showing his marvellous collection of objets d'art and antiques.

Bangkok has the most fascinating skyline of skyscrapers, with their intriguing modern designs – gold, green and red swooping tiled temple roofs, spiral pagodas of the burial roofs – all against a deep blue sky and pricked out by the dense green leaves of the tall trees, which seem to grow in every possible piece of earth that they can find. This of course was the expensive area of the city.

Through not getting our visas in Penang on time we just missed two colourful ceremonies. One was the launching of thousands of *krathongs* – banana-leaf boats – with their flowers and candles, a sign of religious merit-making.

The other was the King's fiftieth birthday, which was on the day we left. They started decorating the city about 8.30 p.m., then by next morning everything seemed to be covered with flowers, flags and swags. We had to get our flight to Hong Kong about 8 a.m., so unfortunately we only saw what could be seen from our taxi window. Oh, those splendid decorations – a festooned city.

As we got on to the Thai (Cathay Pacific) plane each woman was given a beautiful orchid, the sign of Thailand. Then in the pocket of every seat was a folder with a copy of old Thai paintings all over it. Inside was notepaper, also headed with these Thai paintings, envelopes, picture postcards and a map. The seats were all covered in lovely coloured Thai material, while the air hostesses wore Thai silk close-fitting blouses and skirts, the typical Thai dress. How dainty, elegant and beautiful they all looked, although I found the Thai women less attractive looking, too heavy in the face, compared to the truly beautiful Malay women.

Hong Kong, 28th November 1977

We were again coming into Hong Kong, or rather Kowloon, where the Kai Tak airport is. I had been to Hong Kong about three years before, but to me it was still a hazardous landing. Descending with speed, the plane flies between high skyscrapers, this screaming jumbo jet cleaves through the incredibly restricted area to land on a narrow strip of reclaimed ground. As you were actually landing all you could see out of the cabin windows on both sides of the plane was water rushing by. I have always had a phobia about water and here I seemed to be in a nightmare. The plane stopped just before it reached the open sea, although I understand that before now it has not been able to make it in time! Dicey, but with a merciful God we made it.

Our hosts had come to meet us, but had to wait two hours, as we made our very slow way through the Customs. We had, after all, flown straight from the Golden Triangle. The examination of most of the passengers was thorough and time-consuming. When they got to us they mercifully passed us through at once. They seem to sense opium dealers.

Our friends drove us back to their high-rise flat on the Peak. We came through the underwater tunnel which joins Kowloon to Hong Kong island, or rather Victoria Island, past the Governor's house, up the steep hill, until we eventually arrived at their block in Po Shan Doh. It stood in a pretty road bordered by shrubs and flowers.

The view from my bedroom was a dream, looking out to the sky and down over the rooftops to this incredible harbour; the intermingling of the centuries with its junks, sampans, hydrofoils, steamers, Mississippi-type ferries, yachts and much else, while cutting through the air, as I mentioned before, were the screaming jets low over the whole scene. This harbour is never quiet; hundreds of these craft are perpetually moving. How they do not collide I cannot imagine. I failed to say above that in fact the best view of all was from my private loo seat. What a spot to see this, the most beautiful and busy harbour in the world!

It was lovely to be back and Don and Liz gave us such a welcome. He was now head of Hong Kong TV, a very important post. The flat was large and imposing, with a huge communal room, again overlooking the harbour, and bedrooms, kitchen and the rest off it. I remember one morning I woke early. I could not get to sleep again so, putting on my dressing gown, I moved a chair by the window and watched the world. How well worth while it was the lack of sleep. It was still dark, the lights of the city picking out certain features. It was quiet all around us, but in the distance you could just discern a hum of life. Hong Kong never sleeps. Gradually the dawn broke; what a sight over the rooftops and spreading over the water.

It was November, the Chinese thought it very cold; going about in padded dressing gowns is de rigeur there. In fact it was about 75°F. It was a Sunday morning, so no commuters were out, the hour was about 6.30 a.m. Then gradually one saw single or several Chinese figures climbing the steep pavements doing their slow Chinese exercises – *tai chi*. This is done while slowly walking and moving the arms, legs and body in rhythmic movements. The old people practise this to keep themselves fit. It is now being taken up in this country by many people. The time had flown and I felt I knew quite a lot more about the early hours of the country.

We took many journeys to the islands. There are hundreds of them, the biggest being Lantau (of which I have already written), where the large new airport is being built. It was quite unspoiled in those days, and we used to finish our visit by having a drink and cake at an untidy café situated nearly on the beach. This was run by a young Australian and called Ned Kelly's Bar. Kelly and his Asian wife lived and worked there. This was at Silvermine Bay, where the ferries came in, and the casuarina trees grew on the beach. These hundreds of beautiful islands were washed by the jade green restless sea. Their names were like music – Lantau, Cheung Chow, which has a bun festival once a year, buns being hung on huge tripods. It also has a big Taoist temple called Paktai. Then there is Peng Chau, a very small island, dealing in cottage industries. Quite near to Hong Kong is Lamong Island, most beautiful and quiet. Here many commuters live, travelling by ferry – the famous Star Ferry – every day to work. All their beaches are very white, composed of decomposing granite from the cliffs, and mingling with the dainty white shells with their delicate brown designs. They are so beautifully marked you feel someone with a fine paint brush must have designed and painted on them these dainty pictures and then returned them to the beaches.

The open, yet secret, living of millions of the small Chinese workers, their lives seem punctuated by the clacking of mah-jong counters, angular music and laughter, their singsong high voices endlessly talking. Walking past the small open-fronted shops, they seem to be content and happy, working nonstop to make a living whatever time of day or evening you pass them.

At Wanchai the Susie Wong area has long overbusy streets, jammed with people, traffic, noise and voices. Every shop, restaurant and any building, in fact, can be festooned with flags and banners, scarlet very often, with huge Chinese writing in white, these double happiness banners are on many cafés, where someone is celebrating a birthday, wedding or anything else they can think of. On top of that, the old-fashioned trams clank their monotonous way up and down the streets, people filling them to the brim. Even in winter they sit on the open tops of them. This part is also the area of nightclubs. Getting back to where we lived, we passed the intersecting, intercrossing high rise life of teeming HK, where the assorted intelligences of the straying Europeans live in the waning shadow of the British Raj, amahs quietly smoothing their paths of life, while behind their dignified not-losing-face faces lies the imponderable, which is Hong Kong itself.

At the TV studios a I met a young woman called Mary Price. She was working there as a producer; a talented girl. She was married, but her husband Hal was on a fascinating journey which was subsequently shown on a BBC *World About Us* programme.

This was an enterprise by Kuno Knöbi and Arno Denning, who, having done a great deal of research, were convinced that in prehistoric times junks had sailed from Hong Kong to South America. It was thought that the currents of the Pacific would mean that any unmanned ship would be driven from Asia to America. The junk being the oldest type of sailing vessel in the world, they thought that they would construct one by researching pictures of prehistoric junks from rock carving and other drawings. Many had tried this before and failed.

With many trials in the Hong Kong shipyard and many experiments, the Tai Ki (meaning 'cosmos') was launched, with a crew including Hal Price, who was to be their photographer. Sadly they only got as far as two thousand nautical miles off the coast of North America, when the craft started to sink. Mercifully there was a ship fairly near them. They were transferred to this and taken to America dejected and deeply disappointed. For a while Mary did not know if he were dead or alive. He was alive and well. They started the voyage on the 6th June, 1974 and were rescued on 9th October, 1974. The part of the journey they did had been filmed by then and was later shown, as I have said, on the BBC's *World About Us*. Later on in England I renewed my friendship with the Prices, staying with them from time to time, so Hal was able to show me many unpublished photos of the voyage – fascinating.

The Chinese food was a delight, so different from any anglicised Chinese fare. We were taken to various restaurants, mainly Cantonese. I still shied off eating snake. This Cantonese food is considered by specialists to be the best. It retains its own natural flavours, especially with the sea food, and is also known for its fragrance, colouring and taste. Chinese food has no dairy products in it, so is very good for one.

One of the great meals, especially at lunch time, is dim sum. It is a succession of various kinds of food, added to which they bring a huge pot of tea, which is drunk copiously all through the meal, so much so that the pot is quickly finished, but equally quickly you turn the teapot lid upside down on the pot. Immediately a waitress rushes up, removes the pot and replaces it with another full one. This is done several times during the meal. When asked why, they answer that it is what keeps them so fit compared to us! The tea is often green tea, very weak and hot.

Another feature of the Chinese is that they employ *feng shui* men. This is a very old custom. They advise anyone building anything from a temple to a house or office where they should place the building, which way it should face, where the rooms should go and even which way your bed, or anything else, should face. If you do as they say you will have no strife, and good luck will be yours.

I heard of an Englishman in Hong Kong who failed to do this. Every day in his office he had trouble one way or another. In desperation and urged on by the Chinese staff, he called in the *feng shui* man, who changed certain things around. From then on all was harmony. Even high-up European officials say that it works and find their advice good.

The flat where we were staying had a Filipino woman called Jovita, who did all the housework. Many of these women come to Hong Kong to get a job, so that their families can eat. The Philippines are desperately poor and jobs difficult to get. This is a sad plight, for this woman, aged about 40, was married with five children, yet she had had to sign on to go to Hong Kong for three years, during which time she could not go home. Again due to money shortages she spent almost nothing on herself, sending most of it back to her husband to buy food for himself and the children. He could not get a job.

Ruth and I took the train on the Canton Railway through the New Territories so that we could see the border into China proper. The huge train left Kowloon travelling at great speed. We had a map so could see how far we were at any time.

The countryside was a joy – great paddy fields with the large straw-hatted groups of Hakka women of every age, stooping and standing, often calf-deep in the water planting the rice. Their hats were different from the general Chinese hat. The crown fitted the head, then the straw brim came down, making a very large brim, but what was different was that the edge of the brim had a black fringe, sewn all round it. I don't know if it kept away the mosquitoes. With them were bullocks dreaming away oblivious to their wet feet and legs. Everything was a bright green fresh colour.

We also passed Lion Rock, a wind-carved rock looking like a lion, and Amah Rock, which could have been a nurse and baby. It is said to be a woman waiting for her fisherman husband, who never came back. We also passed through many small rural villages. Then we stopped and saw by our map that we could go on one more stop before the great express train crossed the border into China. It was impossible in those days to enter it without dire consequences.

We sat waiting to go on when suddenly a young train attendant came screaming up to us. They always use a high-pitched scream if annoyed and he was more than annoyed. We did not know what he was saying and no one else spoke English, so in the end he grabbed our purses and jackets, dragging us by our arms to the door of the coach, then more or less threw us off. We learnt later on that in fact you have to get out at Sheung-Shui, the stop before the last. I know not why; we got a bus to the border.

In fact the border was rather dreary. Everywhere there were notices saying, 'No photos'. A railing ran across the viewpoint, where all we saw was uninhabited country of no distinction, with a meandering river. By sheltering each other's arms we both managed to get a photo. The only other thing there was a stall full of the little red books of Chairman Mao – in Chinese; we refrained from buying!

We got a bus again, which took us to a small town which we wanted to see. It was on our train route back, but a little nearer Hong Kong than we had been at Lok Machau. It was intriguing. Many shops had open fronts, everything very basic, none of the *old days* glamour. We were hungry, so went into a dairy-like café. Of course no one could speak English, so we mimed that we were hungry and wanted to eat. They all laughed, pointing to a small table on the pavement, and shortly out came a delicious rice dish – very cheap. The town was rather dreary, so we went to the station and caught the next express back to HK.

We went several other times to the New Territories with the Kerrs – one time to a beautiful bay called Shak-O; wide white empty beaches, but a very rough grey sea and, to cap it all, rain absolutely tipping down. We went and had a drink in a café before returning home. On other visits we had brilliant sunshine, at Tai Po, with its lovely little harbour where several junks were moored, and where men were carrying pail after pail of water from a pump to their boats.

Most junk people never come off their boats on to the land in all their lives. You can see them on board, hanging out their washing, cooking, watering their many pots of plants, and even (I saw this in the harbour at HK) a man tying a piece of string round his dog's neck and lowering it into the water, where it swam around for quite a while, its owner hanging over the rail with the string attached to his wrist, ready to haul it up again.

Don and Liz also took us to several restaurants. One of the best, the Java Rijsttafel, was run by a Shanghai friend of theirs called Maria. It was a Korean restaurant and oh what delicious food! She also kept showing us photos of her son's pictures. Their daughter now, she said, had also started painting pictures, like her brother. They were very good artists.

We also explored the streets near the harbour. Fascinating. Some had very steep-stepped pavements, with stalls on either side, glaring under their neon lights. One was called Ladder Street. Its stalls held buttons, hundreds of different colours, sizes and patterns. Another had lace of every description. Then yet another was piled with the most gorgeous coloured ribbons, the like I have never seen before. Everything was very cheap and tempting. Other streets like this one sold other types of goods. The entrances to them were so narrow you could have missed seeing them altogether. They were off streets with rather crude exotic names like Hollywood Road and another Caine Road.

Nearby to this spot was a temple called Man Ho, which was only built in 1848. You could smell it well before you got there, with its joss sticks hazing the air all around, the smell so strong it almost intoxicated one. Man and Ho were two military men who were well known for their high intellectual abilities.

We also went to Cat Street. This is a famous street for its junk shops, antique shops and odd pieces from old China. It is always filled with hopeful tourists and therefore fairly pricey. The name Cat came from the pidgin English term 'catchee', which means 'to buy'. We were taken there by a great friend of my sister Rosemary.

When Rosemary worked in Japan for three years for the famous Jardine Mathieson she made great friends of a man and his wife, who also worked for this august firm. In the Far East they say 'First Jardine Mathieson, then God'. So when Rosemary heard that I was going to Hong Kong she wrote to these friends, who were now there, as he had been made head of the Hong Kong area for Jardine Mathieson.

Audrey, the wife, asked us to lunch in their most beautiful flat, high up the Peak. She had lived all her life in that part of the world, so knew and loved it very much. They had the furniture that I would love to have brought back if I had had the money – dark wood with large carved swirls, otherwise quite plain. It is what one always notices in Chinese paintings. They had had to decide what to collect in Hong Kong, as it had so very many treasures, and had decided on chop-stick holders. How incredibly fascinating they were. Audrey had had a very long sideboard made in the above pattern, then asked the creator of it to put a long wide panel of glass on the top. In this they kept these lovely chop-stick holders. They were mainly, if not all, Chinese and in every kind of shape and colour you could imagine. They also had beautiful single pieces of ornamental Chinese statues and much else.

We had our lunch on a long Chinese scrolled table, served by an old amah who had been with them for many years. Looking out of the window, so high up were we, that you looked at the deep blue sky with occasional little fleecy clouds, then on going to the window you looked down on trees, their branches slightly moving in the warm breeze, then between the branches far below the pale blue sea with its, as ever, crowd of crafts. It seemed almost as if one were looking at an immense picture painted in water colours.

I too had friends in Hong Kong. Mimi Hui, the Chinese student whom I knew in Bristol, had given me an introduction to her 'favourite bluther' and his wife, who lived in smart Stanley Bay. No Chinese ever entertain in their house, but luckily Sandy Hui (her brother) asked me there to dinner one night. I was delighted; Ruth could not come.

I got a taxi right along the coast of Hong Kong (or, as it is really called, Victoria Island) to Stanley Bay. Their flat was delightful, very Chinese and colourful, but with great taste. His wife Maggie was Australian. Before she married she had been a model in her home town, Sydney. I became great friends of theirs. They also had two delightful children called Sonnet and Koan. They were all at the meal, which also included Mimi's godmother, an unusually tall slim Japanese woman. Sandy himself worked for Glaxo, in the colour section of the firm, and had to travel all over the world. There was also a cousin of Mimi and Sandy, Joyce Wong.

We had a lovely evening. The food was done as the Chinese do it, in large fascinatingly coloured dishes from which we all helped ourselves with our chop sticks – Sandy helping me, as I would never have had enough to eat otherwise. There was much laughter and talk. I was also being shot by a mischievous young Koan, who had been given a mock pistol for his birthday.

Maggie had been so fed up trying to find nice clothes for the children that she had started to design and make them for her two. It had been such a success that shops had asked her to supply them, and so 'Darling Child' clothes came into being.

While in Hong Kong we were also taught the Chinese calendar, which operates on a twelve-year system. The Lord Buddha was supposed to have invited the animals of the world to visit him to New Year's Day. They were told that they would be rewarded if they came. As it was, only twelve came: the Rat, Ox, Tiger, Rabbit, Dragon, Snake, Horse, Sheep, Monkey, Cock, Dog and Pig. If you want to know which you belong to you do not go about it as we do, with our astrological sign. With theirs it is the year in which you were born that counts so, because I was born in 1916, I am a Dragon – delightful!

We had now decided to go to Macau for a few days, but before we went I visited a fascinating street performance of a Chinese opera. It was being held in a tiny square, in a densely populated part of the city, where the houses were poor, ill painted and badly kept, through lack of money on the part of the people who rented the rooms. They were hanging out of their balconies, hundreds of them, laughing, shouting and enjoying every minute of this strange performance. The theatre proscenium had been erected at the end of this minute square. It looked truly penny plain and twopence coloured, but the people wanted the old ways, knowing every note and word of these stylised performances, with their discordant musical shouts and speech. The strange musical formations of sound are quite unlike anything we have heard in this country – except perhaps at the Edinburgh Festival, who engaged the first-class Peking Opera to perform one year. The completely covering mask-like make-up alters the face until it is quite unlike any human face one has seen, and their symbolic jerky gestures are so odd, so foreign to us and yet quite captivating. Mary Price was with me, explaining as much as she could about the reason for much of the performance, which goes on for hours. We stayed, I think, about 1½ hours and were engrossed.

She said to me (who had run a make-up department for the BBC) that should I want to I could come back the next day, but much earlier, and peep behind the proscenium curtains. I could then watch them doing their elaborate long drawn-out make-ups. I did not go, as I felt it was rather a rude intrusion. Later on, I wished that I had done so.

Mary then took me to their flat, where on one wall was hung about twenty or more small masks, each one showing the type of make-up used during the operas. It has been a marvellous insight into what was really a folk version of their operas.

The culture of China is – and was – highly developed. I love the way the poets used to drink wine while composing poetry; it has been a favoured pastime of the Chinese literati for centuries.

Macau, 6th December 1977

We set off for Macau, buying our ticket at the harbour, near the Star Ferry. We thought that we would treat ourselves to the jetfoil, as it did the thirty-three miles to Macau in an hour, both the Hydrofoil and ordinary ferry taking much longer. I always find it an odd feeling, this skimming over the water, low to one's horizon. Perspective is a funny thing. This old Portuguese colony by the Pearl River Estuary is fascinating, run by the Chinese already, although it is technically still Portuguese.

Our boat was full of Chinese women coming over for an hour or two's gambling at the huge modern hotel/casino, the Lisboa, which dominated the harbour. It is a garish, expensive place. The women come over frequently, then rush back to cook for their men. The Chinese are inveterate gamblers, betting on everything and anything. It is said that 'The three Kings of the Orient take second place here to the four Kings in a pack of cards'. It seems to be a compulsion to every Chinese person.

We went into the Lisboa one day during our visit. What a sight. Inside it was dark, except for the hundreds of glaring neon lights hanging over one's head rather like spacemen's eyes. Everywhere were juke boxes and every one in use. The noise was intense as the money was fed into the machines – and occasionally accompanied by high squeals of delight. Further in were the gaming rooms, where the men (mainly) were frenetically gambling. The whole place had a desperate, unhappy air.

We stayed in the world famous hotel, the Bella Vista. Not many people go there now; it was a most nostalgic place with its shades of former glory. It used to be frequented by Somerset Maugham and his toadying satellites.

We had a huge bedroom overlooking the estuary, with its yellow water. It was most comfortable, smothered in faded English-type chintzes. The dining room was enormous, staffed by aged Chinese waiters, who crept silently about, handing you menus or food, whichever required, bowing obsequiously as they served you. It was teatime, the trio was playing quiet, discreet music; one could have been in the Pump Room at Bath. It also reminded me very much of the Grand lost-in-time Station

Hotel in Kuala Lumpur. These famous hotels seem to have been lost in time, all over the world, and are always worth visiting.

Outside the main entrance was a wide granite staircase, lined by weary potted plants, but at the top of them you walked over the most delicately painted, very old, Portuguese tiles. At the side of the building I saw, for the first time ever, Banyan trees, so associated with Kipling and the Far East (India). They have a fascination all of their own, their roots and branches mingling with each other in fond embraces.

The hotel stood above the roadway, which was a major road although rather narrow. It followed the edge of the water, with its waist-high curving sea wall. What was fascinating was that China proper – forbidden, untouchable mystery – was only a short span across the estuary. One could see the houses with their smoking chimneys and the people peacefully going about their lives. In the evening it had a much more sinister look, as each day many Chinese try to swim across to freedom. More often than not, they get caught by the ever vigilant patrol boats that speed up and down this patch of water, night and day, and woe betide anyone who is caught. There are also sharks in the water, which shows what they dare to escape the régime.

Following this sea wall we found many delightful old houses, in various states of disrepair, all with flowers and trees surrounding them. One of the houses to see is the Sun Yat Sen Memorial House. The old one was burnt down. The new one looks very pleasant, surrounded by a garden where there is a statue of the man himself. He had been a doctor in Macau, although his birthplace, Zhongan Centre, is across the border. Macau was really the gateway for Christianity to become known in China and Japan.

There are many cobbled streets, the cobbles outside the town hall painted blue and white. Around this old part the architecture is purely South Eastern-European, quite delightful.

We thought that we would go to their most famous ruined building, the Basilica of St Paul. It was destroyed in a terrible typhoon in 1835, leaving only the beautiful façade intact. It is situated on a hill, which is a splendid setting for it. It was built by Christian, Chinese and Japanese refugees from Nagasaki's persecution. The best time to see it, in fact, is as the sunset comes through the empty windows, an eerie sight, as if there were life in the high non-existent rooms. What magnificent sunsets they have there.

The Portuguese are well known for their poets and probably the best known one worldwide is Luis de Camoëns, still to be had in our Penguin paperbacks, and his best known epic poem is the *Os Lusiades*. He lived in Macau for quite a while, and probably wrote this poem here.

We then went to see a large temple called Kun Iam Tong. This is a fifteenth century Buddhist temple. At the front it has a famous stone table, which was used in the signing of the first treaty between America and China in 1844 and signed by Viceroy Yi and Caleb Cushing.

The temple has a very ornate entrance to its great hall. In the hall stand three very impressive Buddhas, who represent the Past, the Present and the Future. They stare at one with very penetrating eyes. In the next hall is the Buddha of Longevity, quiet and peaceful. The halls go on and on with their Buddhas and goddesses, all flickering in the candlelight and the hundreds of joss sticks which smoulder to the praise of their gods and the betterment, we hope, of their donors.

Perhaps the most impressive sight are the pavilions, each complete within itself. Down the sides are stone benches, like tables, flowers throwing colour everywhere in their tidy beds, everything surrounded by hedges and delicate trees with pale golden leaves, where the birds twitter and rustle the leaves contentedly in the dense sunlight, which is so pleasurable. Further up the slope are stone cranes, lions and peacocks, in seeming contemplation of us, the intruders. Near there, too, is the Sweetheart tree, with its gnarled trunk, under which lovers pray that they will know happiness – a worldwide habit.

As you climb the temple complex, you can look over a wall into the old Catholic Cemetery, where the huge sarcophagi and plain grave stones mingle with the many monuments. Cemeteries are fascinating, each country having its own way of carving the stones which honour their dead. For example, in Turkey the men have a stone column, on the top of which is either a turban or, after the reign of Kemal Atatürk and as decreed by him, a fez. Then, for a bit of excitement, if you find a man's tomb with a fez or turban lying at the bottom of the column it means the man was executed. Sadly, I never found one! The women have a broader stone carved with garlands of flowers. The churchyard was like most others, filled with flowers and peace.

One day we went to get a bus so as to see round the town. We were contemplating which one to take when a Chinese boy asked if he could help us. We explained what we wanted. With that the bus came and stopped where we were. He took us up to the bus, then hopped on as well, paying for our tickets as he entered. He was a charming lad, in his last years at school. He knew the history of his town very well and was a delightful guide. He told us that his name was Jimmy Tam, giving us his address so that we could write to him. He took us, by bus and on foot, all over Macau, showing us the places of interest – a great help. Eventually he took us to the Macau 'People's Republic of China's' border, a heavy stone archway leading into China proper, but not open to tourists. He pointed to a large table filled with books and with a lovely smile and twinkling eyes turned to us, saying that he could proceed. He then thanked us for a lovely day, waved and disappeared through the grim archway. What was so refreshing was that he had never asked for money or in fact for anything, and had paid our fares whenever we had gone on a bus.

Another time when we were walking around I found a small quarry beside a red-walled temple. This was a joy to me as I indulge in geology in my spare time. To my delight I found a granite section then, even better, it had small bright green particles in it. I had never seen this before. I was not surprised to find granite as the geology professor at Bristol University had told me that Hong Kong itself was built on disintegrating granite. The result is that, as one hears, in a typhoon one of the high tower flats just slides down the Peak and becomes a mound of rubble; very nasty. He said granite was to be found all around large areas. I hammered off quite a few small pieces of this rock. I wanted to take home some that had the green crystals.

We then proceeded to a public park. It was high above the town, with a glorious view through the trees to the sparkling water far beneath us. The skyline of the town was rather like an unfinished jigsaw puzzle, the roofs with their different styles making a jagged pattern.

The park itself was mainly concrete; grass in hot countries is difficult to grow well. It had some flower beds with straggly flowers, unkempt looking, but the trees were a pleasure and underneath them all were benches, many in use. Under one of them was a youngish man sitting in front of a sort of card table. He was writing. Opposite to him sat an old man who was obviously dictating a letter very hesitatingly to him. One still sees these letter writers all over Hong Kong, Macau and many other places, as many of the older people are still illiterate.

As we were leaving we passed an old Chinese woman who still had bound feet. It is now, of course, strictly illegal.

I wanted to take a photo of her from her back view, so as not to embarrass her, but sadly by the time I got my camera out of my capacious bag she was too far off. What a terrible fashion it was. One could see how painful it was for her to walk with these malformed feet.

As we were leaving the park I saw, in an uncultivated corner, a pile of rocks. I went over and, finding an interesting one, started with my hammer to break a piece off to bring home.

As I worked a Chinese man came running over, asking if he could help me.

I said, 'No,' explaining what I was doing.

With that he started laughing loudly, saying, 'Oh, I thought a snake was attacking you and that you were in danger.'

We parted friends, both of us still laughing, but how kind of him.

On the last day we thought that we would go and see the two islands off the west coast of Macau. We understood that there was a small one, Taipa, which you reached by a causeway, then beyond that island one called Colonana. For this one they had built a bridge to join up the islands.

We managed to get a bus, which took us to within a mile of the causeway. Having paid our fare we asked the driver what time the return buses went. Horror on horror, he told us that this was not a regular run and that he had no idea when – if ever! – we would get one back. By this time we had gone quite a long way on our journey; we would hope for the best. He gave us a fond farewell as we got out; a bit ominous, we thought.

We walked over to Taipa. The sand was black, the island lovely, but beginning to be spoiled by light industry. We soon came to the bridge leading to the larger island of Colonana. In contrast, it has beautiful white sandy beaches, lovely little, very green, embowered villages. The whole island is very much filled, still, with the memories of the famous St Francis Xavier, who had come from Macau to work there. He was one of the founders of the Jesuits in the sixteenth century. This island, I believe, is being made into a popular tourist resort, which seems sad.

We had crossed this second island, found a stall under a tree selling soft drinks and light food. The place was crowded, obviously a popular spot. It was crowded with schoolchildren who were obviously out for the day and enjoying themselves; their laughter and smiling faces were everywhere.

We noticed that one lot had arrived by coach. Our hearts rose. Perhaps the driver would have some empty seats and be willing to take us back. We approached him tentatively and put our case to him. He smiled, saying that he had two spare seats and that he would be happy to take us back. We had mentioned that we would pay him our fare. However, he brushed that aside. He said he did not want any payment; the pleasure was his.

Soon we saw the girls moving to the coach, so when they were on we joined them. Ruth had a seat at the back while I had one on the front row to myself.

We started. The bus was fairly silent, then the girls began to chatter. Then I felt small fingers tickling my neck; I turned round and smiled. With that they started talking to me in very good English, asking questions and telling me about themselves. After a while they started singing beautiful old Portuguese songs. The whole coach joined in. It was lovely.

As we neared the town of Macau they asked if I would come back and see their school. I was very tired by now, and I knew that Ruth was as well, so I thanked them so much for asking us, explaining that we could not accept their offer as we had to go somewhere else. Their faces fell, but as we got off the coach they waved, shouted and cheered us.

We got back to the Bella Vista dead beat, climbed wearily up the steps to the entrance and spent a quiet, happy evening over a delicious Chinese meal.

The next morning we were off back to Hong Kong. We had planned to go fairly shortly to Taiwan, which has the most fabulous museum, and we had to go at once and get our flights booked, and of course a visa.

Hong Kong, 9th December 1977

We had left Macau with sadness on the 9th December, 1977. We had found the people kind, but this had been true in every country we had visited. After all, people are just people, whatever their culture or creed.

We were walking over to the customs shed in Hong Kong harbour when Ruth turned to me, saying that she certainly was not coming through the customs with me, as I was carrying a hammer and rocks in my bag. All around us were communist-type countries, making the Customs men very strict. Having delivered this speech, she moved well back in the queue.

I was one of the first to go in. A tall youngish Chinese man asked me to open my bag. As I did so, his face lit up. He took out the hammer and some of my precious rocks. Then looking at me he said, 'Geologist?'

I nodded.

With that he pointed to himself saying, 'Me too, and what else have you found?'

He took all my finds out, laid them on the counter, leant his elbows beside them and with great delight asked me to tell him where in Macau he could find them. I told him exactly. With that he carefully wrapped up each piece again, returned them to my case. With a grin, a thank you and a hearty handshake he said that he would go over on his next day off and find some of the rocks for himself.

Next day we thought that we would go to a tourist office and buy our air tickets for Taiwan. Of course we also needed a visa to go there. We had to go to Kowloon for both items, so getting the Star Ferry across we searched for the tourist building. All went well. We were ready to leave in about two days.

The next day I did not feel very well, so went and lay down. I very quickly got worse and worse, so much so that Ruth went to Kowloon and cancelled our flights. I realised that I had what was being called in England Asian flu. The young son of our friends was already down with it. Later, as you know, it spread all over Europe and Britain, a particularly bad virus. I stayed in bed feeling very ill, dozing most of the time. I knew what time of day it was, mainly by hearing the midday gun. It is like Edinburgh, my home town, where it is fired every day. The custom over here was that it gave the Taipans (heads of the major Chinese coast trading companies) of Jardine Mathieson an official send-off. It used to be a twenty-one gun salute, which annoyed the locals, so was later cut to one shot at noon every day. Every day someone seemed to be being seen off.

I was in bed for several days, then got up for a short time each day, feeling very weak. Time was gradually running out for us. We did want to get to Taiwan. About a week later, still feeling fairly groggy, I went to Kowloon and re-booked the tickets now for 14th December. My head was still fairly fuzzy. The queue for the tickets was long. However, I eventually got them and quickly shoved my passport and all my documents into my purse.

I arrived back at Po Shan Doh and lay down for a while as everyone else was still out. After a short snooze I got up, cleared all the documents out of my purse, then shock! I could not find the air tickets. What should I do?

With that the telephone rang. A voice said, 'Is that Miss Grisell Lindsay?'

I said it was, whereupon the man said that he had been in the queue behind me in the ticket office, and heard me give my name and address. Then after I had gone he had moved to the counter and had found my tickets there. He said that if I could come to Nathan Road (a very well known street in Kowloon) he would give them to me.

The flat was still empty. I was very worried, hoping that it was all above board, and wondering why he had not handed them back to the office. However there did not seem any answer to the problem, so I got the minibus down to the Star Ferry yet again. On arrival at Kowloon, I verified the name and address that he had given me: Mr Ahmed, the Basement of the Hyatt Hotel, Kowloon. It was very usual in that part of the world to have shops and offices in the basement of large hotels. I set off on foot, as I knew that it was not very far away, then on reaching the Hotel took the stairs to the basement. Here it was very gloomy and rather dusty, even not too clean. I found the bell with Mr Ahmed on it and with pounding heart rang the bell. He answered it himself, bowed to me then with a smile handed me my tickets from his inner pocket. He smiled again, saying how glad he was to be of help and shut the door.

I was so relieved, having heard so much of their underworld, and still feeling very weak with the tail end of flu. I went to a café, treating myself to a very strong black coffee. When I arrived back an hour or two later the flat was still empty. No one knew of my adventure. When finally I told them that evening they just fell about laughing, saying how lucky I had been.

The next morning we set off to Taiwan – at last.

Taiwan, 18th December 1977

We arrived at Kai Tak airport well on time as we were to fly on China Airlines.

When we were queuing to put our bags through the ticket desk, a very nice middle-aged Indian man came up to us, saying that his daughter, who lived in Taipei with her husband, had just had her first baby and that his wife was travelling there on our plane. He explained that the reason why he was bothering us was that his wife's luggage was well overweight due to all the baby clothes, small blankets and much else she was taking to her daughter for the child, as Taiwan was still a poor country. After some hesitation and conferring we agreed to do this. All we had to do was to take some of her cases with ours through the baggage control.

We got on to the plane with the Indian woman sitting next to me. We did not talk much as she knew very little English.

Soon after take off the air steward brought us all a huge dossier that we had to fill in if we were aliens – non-Chinese – and which we had to hand back completed before arriving at Taipei airport. These forms were four foolscap-size sheets, asking such questions as, 'What was your grandmother and grandfather's surnames, or maiden name as far as grandmother was concerned, and age?' I knew few of the answers so just wrote anything; but the poor Indian woman was completely baffled, asking me to help her. I tried by asking her the questions, but in a mystified voice she asked, 'Why do they want to know even about my grandparents?' I said that I was bewildered as she was, and had just filled in a fictitious family tree! One way and another I filled in her form as well as my own – a couple of fairy stories.

The journey was much longer than it should have been, as the plane was not allowed to fly over some warring country – probably China. It was a very ill-equipped plane, no food, in fact no comforts at all, except very basic lavatories.

Not long before we reached Taiwan we went into a terrific storm, thunder and lightning flashing past our windows. The air steward announced that everyone must put on their seat belts as there was a very bad storm in progress. He then seated himself and belted up. The whole of the plane – Chinese – ignored his request, which to give them their due they may not have understood as he had given it in English and Cantonese, but none of the other several Chinese languages in current use. I find it incredible that these languages in China cannot be understood, even if you know one of them. One Chinese family I know could not all speak to each other. One spoke Mandarin and Cantonese, another Cantonese and something else, or some no Cantonese or Mandarin. What a confusion! Hence it was possible my plane-load were in the same box. However, they seemed to have no worries, coming and going to the lavatories, shouting and talking happily to each other while standing in the aisles.

As I said, I was in a front seat, with the distraught steward on a flap-down seat nearby. The plane was rocketing about like a cork. It seemed chaotic inside and outside the plane. He leant towards me saying he did not know what more to do, that we were in a very dangerous situation. I was very frightened myself and felt like saying, 'So am I,' but refrained. I hate flying at any time and now it was really alarming. After what seemed like weeks we landed at the Chiang Kai Shek airport, passed through Customs, who gave us a great grin, saying, 'Welcome, welcome to Taiwan,' and so on to find our bus.

We caught the airport bus which took us the twenty-five miles in to Taipei. Taiwan was known as Formosa in the sixteenth century, the Portuguese having called it that as it was so beautiful; it means 'beautiful island'. Before that it had become a Protectorate of the Chinese empire in the time of Genghis Khan, who founded the Yuan dynasty. In the nineteenth century it was ceded to Japan, who kept it until the end of the Second World War, when it was again returned to China. In 1949 Chiang Kai Shek withdrew there with 500,000 troops; the communist régime had taken over China. He became the head of the Chinese Nationalists in Taiwan.

It was evening when we arrived, having travelled through what seemed many, many miles of not very exciting streets. They had a seedy air in spite of their huge boulevards, bright with many lights, noise and as usual great red-coloured posters, also as usual hundreds of people and cars. We discovered later on that each street seemed to be about three miles long, and that each one looked fairly identical to the others, except for the very occasional grander building. Looking at our rather sketchy street map, it had seemed nothing was too far from our hotel, but how wrong we were.

In the daylight one saw that those wide streets had many car lanes, and that the heavy moving traffic was interspersed with motor bikes. There were shops, restaurants, hotels, high blocks of flats and offices, many painted in gaudy overdone colours. Then to try and smarten the place they had planted palm trees every so often on the edge of the pavements.

Our hotel was large, functional and basic, but the service was excellent. The main thing was that it was cheap. We were by now having to watch what we spent so as to make our money last out the trip. The reception desk was large and well manned. We asked one of the English-speaking attendants to write out the name of our hotel in Chinese so that, should we get lost, we could show it to a taxi driver, for almost no one spoke English. Japanese was their second language due to the invasion of their country by the Japanese earlier on.

Our first port of call was to go to the world-famous National Palace Museum. We had been told always to take a taxi to it, as it was situated in a difficult area to find by bus, so we asked the hotel to order us one.

We set off and, not surprisingly, went for miles out of the town, or rather city, twisting and turning all the time, eventually reaching a leafy hilly suburb with ornate family mansions dotted about the forested hills. Then came the marvellous sight. High on top of a hill stood a magnificent Chinese temple, in fact the museum, also surrounded, at a slight distance, by trees.

This museum had been the brainchild of Chiang Kai Shek, as was the beautiful Memorial Hall in the centre of Taipei. His two great sayings were, 'To live is to seek a better life for all mankind' and 'The meaning of life lies in the creation of a life beyond life'. An interesting insight into the man... This museum, opened in November 1965, was for the people of Taiwan and stands in the suburb of Wai Shuang Hsi, in the Yangming Shau (Glass Mountain Park). It is considered the finest museum in the world; hence our wanting to come to Taiwan to see it.

All around us were elderly people in the national blue denim jeans and jackets, doing their *tai chi* exercises in the warm sun. In 1948 the Taiwanese had smuggled out 3,000 cases of treasures from China, which was being overrun by Communists, keeping it all hidden until this building was ready.

We climbed up the long zigzag white marble staircase, with its balustrades of ornate carvings and occasional Dogs of Fo, leaving the small statue of Confucius at the bottom, with one of his famous sayings in our minds, 'A gentleman takes as much trouble to discover what is right as lesser men take to discover what is wrong.'

The air was warm, the sunlight caught the glinting gold of the roofs, and the birds sang. We looked up, as we climbed, to the sweeping gold and green roofs of the museum and its scarlet and many-coloured walls and pillars. Then, rather to our surprise, at the top of the stairs was a large statue of Chiang Kai Shek himself, as if welcoming us to his masterpiece. It was overpowering, the aesthetic beauty of this marvellous building, and, although the statue was beautifully conceived, it somehow seemed rather like seeing an advertisement in a church!

We entered the building. What spacious halls and galleries, painted white so as to show up its exquisite contents. Each room had a three-tiered container, like our vegetable baskets. On each of the three shelves were sheets of a type of (I think) rice paper, printed with the descriptions of each object in that particular room – top one in Chinese, second one in German and third one in English. You could keep these when you left, happily; there was no payment for them.

The museum has about a quarter of a million treasures. They can only show about three thousand at a time, thereby allowing the beauty of the objects to be given full value. One also finds one is not overwhelmed by quantity. The objects are changed every few months. What is not being shown, I am told, is stored in a large tunnel deep in the hill behind, which is covered with trees. It has been scientifically done, with its modern ventilation and burglar-proof devices.

Many of the exhibits were collected in Imperial times, so are irreplaceable. They include painted scrolls of great delicacy and beautiful painted porcelain and china of every shape and colour. Although much of the china is a mustard yellow with deep leaf greens, there is the famous white with sapphire blue designs decorating it. Then there are the well known red lacquer objects, often decorated with gold, and jade – which is a particular feature in China, with its great significance to the people. Very, very expensive, it has to be imported and then carved by master carvers. Many pieces are of endless value – even shops and street stalls sell so-called jade. Everyone wants to own a piece, real or not. Jadeite and nephrite are equally valued by the connoisseurs.

On the top floor they have made the whole gallery into a mandarin's study – fascinating – showing the beautiful dark rose wood furniture and the fascinating objects that he would have used to help him in his work and study: a round globe of the world and oh, so many treasures.

The building itself is a copy of the classical Peking style. What money must have gone into this creation. We spent the day there and knew we must come back the next day; it was too fascinating to miss. It had been one of the main reasons why we had come to this country. It was interesting that it was opened on the anniversary of the great founder of the Republic of China, Dr Sun Yat Sen, whom I mentioned when writing of our visit to Macau.

There is only one proviso I have about the thinking of the designers and that is: I wonder if they should not have had Chiang Kai Shek and Confucius' statues the same size and standing side by side? There is a temple in Taipei dedicated to the great sage Confucius, who was born in 551 BC. He had a vast influence in China and, for that matter, in many other cultured parts of the world, and still has.

We debated as to whether we should take a taxi back to town but decided against it as taxis were very expensive there. We thought the bus journey should not be too difficult to accomplish – little did we know!

The buses did a vast circular route, so we decided to get off whenever we saw a familiar building or road. We boarded the bus we had been told to get into Taipei, paying as we got on. The fare covered however far you wanted to go.

Eventually we reached the shopping area and sat with our noses glued to the window so as not to miss any familiar sights. The roads passed by, the shops passed by, nothing looked at all familiar. The time went by, the lights in the town were lit, it was getting late. After about an hour and a half we decided that we must now be on the second circuit of the town, so decided that shortly we would get off anyway. This we did, the conductress giving us what used to be called an old-fashioned look. The place was crowded with people coming home from work. We were buffeted as they hurried past. Still everywhere was strange, shop after shop looking like nowhere.

We decided to stop at a café and have our evening meal. It was now about eight o'clock. We found what looked like a good Korean one; luckily it was good. Eventually, having regained some strength and hope (we still wanted to save any taxi money), we tackled the streets again.

Very slowly walking down what looked like the most likely main street, with joy we saw, in the distance, down a less well lit turning, our hotel, its lights showing it up, even though it was right at the other end of the road. We had asked many people where it was, showing the hotel card written in Chinese, but all had looked blankly back at us. We must have looked villainous.

Two days later (we had been back to the museum again) we now thought we should see a bit more of Taiwan. We had booked a tour that took one to the aboriginal village of Sun Moon Lake, in the amazing Taroko marble gorge. The coach, or rather minibus, arrived for us with an erudite young student as guide. There were only the two of us, which was good, as he told us all about Taiwan. During the journey he also told us, with much pride, how very well Taiwan had done since its troubles. He said that they were now self-supporting and also said how they had all worked for little money to put their country on its feet, and that now it was not necessary to import goods. All was done by themselves, and how they prayed that China would never take them over again. He then laughed and said, 'The people we are going to see have eyes like yours, not slit like ours.'

It was a fascinating drive, going through the dark craggy mountains and passing a chair lift up to the snowy summit, luckily not our way. There was much dank vegetation, it all looked rather grim, but the day was dark and wet with the odd clap of thunder and lightning. As we alighted from our minibus a young man – with eyes like ours! – rushed forward, took our photos, then rushed away again.

We walked to the entrance, where there was a delightful coloured statue of an aboriginal chief. We then paid our entrance fee and, walking on the damp brown earth, were ushered into a huge shed, three of its sides open to the inclement weather. The fourth was blocked in and had across the front of it a long platform very brightly lit, no shades over the bulbs to stop the glare in one's eyes. On this platform were several small densely saturated brown people, who were performing one of their national dances. Luckily our chairs were on a well sloped ramp, so we were able to see, for the shed was already packed with tourists of all nationalities. It was the usual tourist offering, but gave one a glimpse of what the people's culture was. This was a tribe called the Ani people. We watched them boxing, dancing with swords, as one sees in Scotland, then singing and much else, amid shouting and laughter.

There was also a temple there which consisted of three mythical animals, the dragon, phoenix and the lion dog.

The latter, we found, seemed to proliferate in all these temple areas.

Immediately our time was up our young guide swiftly took us back to our bus, only being held up by the quick reappearance of the enterprising photographer, who rushed up to us. Then, with a beam, he held up in each hand a white plate; in the centre of each was a round grimacing face – our photos, how awful. I am afraid we disappointed him. We declined gracefully to buy them and subsided in fits of laughter into our bus. The day had been well worth it, although it was sad the weather had been so bad.

On returning to Taipei we went in search of a book shop that people in Hong Kong told us sold English hardback books for a quarter of the usual price. We had been given orders from friends to buy certain books that they wanted. The shop was in one of the long streets near our hotel; we were now more or less used to finding our way around. What a splendid place it was, so tempting, but we ourselves had no more room to carry things home. Luckily for us, we could not find any of the books our friends wanted.

There was one more major thing that we wanted to do. That was to go slightly outside Taipei, to where the great river meanders through a delightful part of the country, or so we were told.

We got off the bus as instructed by the hotel, and started wandering around – a beautiful part, with fields, trees, farming and of course the river. Then, turning a corner we looked over to a slope and saw what appeared to be a huge new brightly painted temple. It was in fact the Grand Hotel, modelled on the Imperial Palace in Peking, quite unlike any other building we had seen, spreading over its hilltop for twenty acres. This was the grandest and most expensive hotel in Taiwan, I understand.

It was too tempting to pass. We walked up to the ornate scarlet and gold gates, carved with curls, dragons and flowers, up the drive and into the palatial entrance hall, to be confronted by the most enormous Chinese yellow, deep piled wall to wall carpet, miles of it, it seemed. The deep pile made one feel one was walking on cushions. The pillars were high, square and scarlet with capitals of multicoloured designs. Surrounding it all was a most staggeringly beautiful balcony, carved and polished. The wide staircase that led up to it was also carpeted in the exotic yellow of the hall, its banisters carved marble, then above it all the ceiling of carved wood, with long hanging lantern lights giving a soft glow. Much use is made of Taiwanese marble and handmade furniture from their lovely exotic trees.

There were several enormous restaurants, one serving only Chinese food. Several others all served the national dishes of many countries and there was one coffee/snack bar, which we thought we must try, even if very expensive. But first we grandly walked up the low treaded staircase, found a ladies' room and indulged. It is amazing what the rich are given free in these rooms.

Feeling refreshed, we descended to the coffee bar. After seating ourselves on most comfortable stools, we chose the cheapest thing we could find on the menu. Even then, it cost us the price of our evening meal!

That evening we had a very light snack at a very cheap and cheerful place, which was crowded with youngsters. Again it was very noisy but had much laughter.

Next day we took the airport bus to catch our plane for Hong Kong. We were getting used to dangerous Kai Tak airport, so did not dread it. As we were queuing at the entrance to passport control, the attendants were frisking many of the Chinese and Taiwanese before letting them pass through. The woman who was just ahead of me (she looked like a young mid-aged housewife) seemed to be known to the staff because, as she stepped in front of them, with a swift movement one of them found a handful of notes on her – or rather inside her. She was immediately removed. We too had to be passed by them, but were allowed to proceed at once to the passport control.

Later on I saw the above woman on our plane. Her face was red with weeping. I expect they had kept her money and allowed her to return to Hong Kong. One wonders what the background to the whole sorry saga was.

Several years later, we were having dinner one evening with our friends Joan and Eric Dehn, their daughter and her husband Bob Baxter. It came up in conversation that Bob was going to Taiwan to help them with the objects in the Taipei Museum, a very prestigious job. In fact, several years after that, he worked on their new museum, which I think was just outside Taipei. He had already mounted several excellent exhibitions at the British Museum.

Hong Kong, 22nd December 1977

It was good to be back in Hong Kong and to stay yet again with our very kind, long-suffering friends. It was our last visit there before returning to England. It was also interesting as it was to be the first time that we had been in the Orient for Christmas.

At breakfast one day our host, Donald Kerr, asked me if I would come over to the TV studios in Kowloon later that morning, as he wanted me to talk to the make-up girls. He said that they were using very out-of-date make-up and putting it on far too thickly. He also said that all the producers were complaining about the results. I told him that I really could not go and tell the girls what to do; they would only be angry at an English make-up supervisor telling them how to do their job. The make-up staff were Australians. However, Don told me that the girls had heard that I was here and had especially asked if I would go and help.

I duly caught the ferry over to Kowloon, then a taxi to the studios. The girl to whom I spoke was charming, telling me that they had had no tuition since colour TV had started. She said she really had no idea what colours or textures to use. I asked her to get hold of the next person whom she had to make up and that that would give us plenty of time to try out what I suggested. She went off to collect the newsreader who would appear shortly, and we set to work.

I scrapped all the old dark, heavy grease sticks – a legacy from theatre days when lighting was bad. I explained also that one did not need nearly so much make-up now one had colour. In fact, I used my own light make-up on the speaker. Luckily it worked well and I left her with a long list of cosmetics to buy, telling her to throw away all her stock.

It was interesting as, when I was there, Anthony Laurence came into the make-up room. He is the famous author and overseas correspondent for that part of the world – a charming, highly intelligent man. The result was that I then showed the make-up girl what a man required when in front of the camera – very little or nothing.

Don and Liz gave a party when we were there as one of the top staff was leaving the studios. They ordered a sumptuous Thai meal, which was brought to the flat by a group of young Chinese waiters, who laid it out on trestle tables which they had also brought with them. There were about fifteen guests, mainly young Chinese and mainly girls, most being producers, directors and other studio staff, a most glamorous collection of people. As I was talking to Liz one of these young women came over saying to me that I would not know her but that she knew me. How true. It turned out that she had been one of the overseas students at a lecture I had given to the Bristol University Drama Department. I had been talking to this group about make-up for stage and TV. She told me that they had listened avidly (what a mercy!) and that now when producing she could gauge how much time the make-up girls needed. I asked her name so as to tell her head professor, Georg Brandt, of my encounter. When I returned home I contacted him and told him how very well she was doing. He was thrilled to hear of her and said that he remembered her as she had been a very bright student.

That afternoon we went out shopping, first to the Ocean Terminal, a gigantic area filled with small shops, many with very expensive and oh such tempting goods. In fact, all we did there in the end was to sit in a café eating luscious cakes and drinking beautiful strong black coffee. In this complex there was also a small, but popular, Marks and Spencers. We then went to the Communist Store, a huge multi-floored shop, selling the magic of the East at very low cost. Everyone living in Hong Kong shops there – bed linen, soft silk materials, clothes – in fact anything you can think of. How lucky they are to have such a store. They also had exquisite jewellery, very Chinese-looking and again cheap, so beautiful.

I went on later to an Arts and Crafts of China shop, which was selling off lovely little chops. Chops in China are, for example, a two inch long squared piece of marble, or some other stone. Then on the top is carved, say, a dragon. On the square bottom they carve your name in Chinese. I had to keep repeating my name slowly until they got the sound. Then and only then they engraved it on to the base of the stone. You are also given a red paste to dip it into, in order to stamp (or chop) your letter. You will always see a chop mark on a Chinese picture as they sign it in this way. One time my young Chinese friend, who was studying in Bristol, said, 'Oh, I must go to Newport and get a chop on my passport.'

The day before all the Christmas decorations went up Don took us to the yacht club for lunch, a very ritzy place, but beautifully situated by the water. When you go somewhere like that you lose all sense of what country you are in, sadly.

It is quite close to Typhoon Corner. Hong Kong has the most terrible typhoons. Everyone has to shutter their houses, and not go out. It has even been known, more than once, for a huge skyscraper block of flats on the Peak to collapse and crumble down in a heap at the bottom of the hill. However, junks have no fears like that, but whenever they hear the typhoon warning they all rush to Typhoon Corner, a sheltered bay, which can accommodate many of their boats. The warning is given over the radio. Luckily we never encountered one of these storms.

About two days before Christmas we woke up, looked out of the window and, as if by magic, all the very tall blocks of flats were completely outlined by coloured bulbs – an amazing sight, especially at night. The trees had Christmas decorations of every imaginable colour, shape and light. Carols were playing nonstop over the traffic noise, and every shop was the same.

On Christmas Eve we went with the Kerrs to Kowloon for a meal; as always, delicious. We took our time, enjoying the Christmas carefree atmosphere, then decided to go and look over the harbour to the Victoria Island (Hong Kong island) lights. We were up on a headland, standing in the becalmed warm air. The view was moving in its splendour. Everything was lit up with every coloured bulb imaginable. All around us was the happy sound of laughter and talking.

We went down to get the ferry back home, following the crowds. We squeezed on to the boat. It must have had about double the normal amount of passengers. We were all jammed up against each other. I had young Andrew, aged about ten years, squashed against me. The craft started its very uncertain journey across the water.

A small voice from somewhere in my tummy region said, 'Oh, I am so scared.'

'Oh, so am I,' I said in reply.

The journey was slow owing to the weight of the passengers. However, at long last we made it, everyone happily tumbling off.

Andrew, the small voice, was a marvellous sailor. At weekends many a Chinese millionaire yachtsman used to ring him up and ask him to come and crew for them – a thing not often done for youngsters his age. Usually, on his way home from a day like that, he would ring his mother, saying that he was off for a special meal at McDonald's, his favourite eating place.

When we got home on Christmas Eve I went into the kitchen for a drink. There was Jovita, head pressed against the window, listening to the carols far beneath. Down her face were streams of tears. It broke one's heart; she was so far from home and family.

Christmas Day was not celebrated much by our hosts. However, we enjoyed ourselves and started preparing for our return journey home. I wonder if I will ever return to this incredible city of intersecting, intercrossing high-rise life of teeming Hong Kong, where the assorted intelligences of the straying Europeans live in the gradually waning shadow of an expiring empire, where behind their dignified not-lose-face faces lies the imponderable which is Hong Kong itself. How lucky I was to see it in the reign of the taipans and the remnants of its glory – for everyone there, rich and poor, it was good, although there are always in every country the far too poor.

This is a coda to our fascinating, wonderful, sometimes worrying, but always worthwhile journey in the East.

We arrived at Kai Tak airport for the last time, surrounded by all our Chinese friends, our hosts and the odd English friend. The Chinese friends piled our arms with 'double happiness' presents. It never seems to be single or even triple happiness, but how heart-warming. They all talked at the same time, with laughter bubbling amid the sorrow at our departure.

Mimi's old mother had come as well, as Mimi was in England again. She hung on to my arm, nearly being swamped into passport control's domain. She was giving me hundreds of messages to give to her distant and youngest daughter, all in Cantonese with tears.

We eventually arrived at our plane. We had managed to get cheap tickets home through some agency. The plane was large, but sparse. It seemed like hundreds of Chinese or other Asian women were on board with their tiny and not so tiny crying children. It was a pattern of what was to come. Still, we survived.

One of the places where we had to refuel was Baghdad at about two o'clock in the morning. What an eerie airport it was. The lounge had almost no lights; we groped our way about it. There was nothing to drink or eat. I thought well at least I would buy a postcard to prove that I had been there, but in vain I looked for a counter with such things. In the end I asked a man who was loafing about the building. He wore the airport uniform. He just understood what I said. I had asked the price as he showed me a choice of three cards. He boredly said the equivalent of about four pounds. I shook my head. He wandered away.

We had stopped in India before this. It was not much better – again almost no lights – and when we had to be frisked before re-entering the plane, a middle-aged, sari-robed lady sort of felt the material of my dress and that was all. She evidently thought it unseemly to get nearer to me.

We arrived at England's Heathrow airport, where friends of Ruth's were to meet us and drive us to Bristol. What bliss. We got to customs, where three men and one girl were on duty. I said to Ruth that I would prefer to go through where a man was on duty, rather than the girl, as we had rather a lot of extra baggage, nothing valuable, but in those days the customs did not let much into the country.

As luck would have it, the girl became free. Imperiously she beckoned me up to her counter, then asked me what I had brought home that was new. I thought hard and told her some material and some other things. Then, oh then, I dried up. She looked hard at me. Ruth stepped into the breach, saying, 'Don't forget your "double happiness" presents, the embroidered slippers.' I nodded, the girl gave me a pained look and passed me through. Obviously she thought I looked too dim to do anything serious in the way of smuggling!

When we got through all this Ruth rang up her friends to say that we had arrived. They said that they would come at once. We settled with a cup of coffee on some comfortable seats and read our books. Time went by, but no friends. An hour or so later than they were expected they arrived, plus a small son and larger daughter. Apparently their car (in fact Ruth's car) had broken down, but now all was well.

For a year or two after that if the little boy, Tom, heard my name mentioned he always said, 'Oh, that is the lady who lives at Heathrow.'

Last stop, my flat. Ruth was being dropped off later at her house. Bristol was cold, rainy and grey, but it was good to be back home and near to so many friends.